Animal Traps
and Trapping

Model showing the use of half-barrel mole traps in a mole run

Animal Traps and Trapping

by JAMES BATEMAN
BSc, MIBiol, AMA

DAVID & CHARLES : NEWTON ABBOT

STACKPOLE BOOKS : HARRISBURG

This edition first published in 1971 in Great Britain by
David & Charles (Holdings) Limited Newton Abbot Devon
and in the United States in 1971 by Stackpole Books Harrisburg Pa

ISBN 0 7153 5340 3 *(Great Britain)*
ISBN 0 8117 0103 4 *(United States)*

Library of Congress Number 70-144110

© James Bateman 1971, 1973

Set in 10 on 12pt Times Roman
Printed in U.S.A.

Contents

		PAGE
LIST OF ILLUSTRATIONS		6
INTRODUCTION		11
1	An Historical Study of Trap Development	24
2	Modern Manufacture of Traps	62
3	The Traps of Nature	71
4	Man-made Insect Traps	89
5	Fish Traps	107
6	Bird Traps	121
7	Mammal Traps: 1	153
8	Mammal Traps: 2	205
9	Baits	237
10	The Ethics of Trapping	248
11	Trap Legislation	254
ACKNOWLEDGEMENTS		268
BIBLIOGRAPHY		270
INDEX		274

List of Illustrations

PLATES

Model showing half-barrel mole traps in use
(*In collection of the Welsh Folk Museum, St Fagan's*)
frontispiece

PAGE

Orb web of *Speira marorea* (*Photo: the late Frances Pitt*)   33

Bug trap from Poona, India   33

Row of putchers at low water   34

Putts in use on the River Severn   34

Young's Suffolk eel trap   34

Decoy bird cage trap from north-west Zambia (*Horniman Museum Collection*)   51

Sparrow net trap (*S. Young & Sons Ltd*)   51

Dove decoy in goshawk trap (*Photo: Philip Glasier*)   52

Hawk releasing dove from trap (*Photo: Philip Glasier*)   52

Havahart No 2 box trap   85

Monmouthshire mole trap (*In collection of the Welsh Folk Museum, St Fagan's*)   85

Eskimo squirrel snares (*Horniman Museum Collection*)   86

Guillotine-type mole trap (*Photo: from trap loaned by MAFF, Aberystwyth*)   86

String of Burmese snares for jungle use (*Horniman Museum Collection*)   86

Duffus mole trap   103

Wooden full-barrel mole trap   103

Single-hole guillotine mouse trap (*Cranbrook Collection*)   104

6

PAGE

Three-hole spring-loop mouse trap (*John Judkyn Memorial Collection*) 104

Man trap of the type used in World War I (*Imperial War Museum Collection*) 137

Eighteenth-century man trap warning notice 137

Rabbit gin in set position 138

Fox gin (*In collection of the Welsh Folk Museum, St Fagan's*) 138

Bear trap (*Grantham Museum Collection*) 138

Fenn trap set in tunnel (*Photo: Forestry Commission*) 155

Juby trap 156

Everitt rat trap 156

Squirrel taken in Imbra trap (*Photo: Forestry Commission*) 156

Fuller trap 189

Lloyd trap 189

Sawyer trap 189

Victorian cage live trap for mice (*Cranbrook Collection*) 190

Arouze-type wire cage mouse trap (*John Judkyn Memorial Collection*) 190

Pottery mouse trap from Djerba, Tunisia (*Horniman Museum Collection*) 190

Legg multicatch squirrel trap 207

Young's 'whole family' rat trap 207

Clausius tunnel traps (*Photo: Forestry Commission*) 207

Cage trap used in Wales for badgers (*In collection of the Welsh Folk Museum, St Fagan's*) 208

German self-setting mouse trap (*Photo from trap loaned by B. E. Chaplin*) 208

Giraffe wheel trap from the Nile region of North Africa (*Horniman Museum Collection*) 208

LINE DRAWINGS IN THE TEXT

FIGURE | PAGE

1 Cave murals at Pileta, Malaga, Spain 29

2 Details from rock paintings in Val Camonica, Italy 31

FIGURE		PAGE
3	Treadle trap found at Auquharney, Aberdeen-shire	32
4	Detail from the Clonmacnois stone	38
5	German steel trap	44
6	Italian cage mouse traps	45
7	Two deadfall mouse traps	46
8	Facsimile of the Mérode mouse trap	47
9	Mascall's sixteenth-century iron trap	50
10	Seventeenth-century Austrian jump trap	53
11	Newhouse wolf trap	66
12	Pullinger's repeating mouse trap	67
13	Verbail chain loop trap	70
14	Venus' fly trap	73
15	Half of an orb web, showing construction	82
16	Pit of the ant-lion	87
17	Insect box trap	92
18	Hiestand's insect trap	93
19	Williams' Rothamsted light trap	94
20	Robinson light trap	96
21	Hungerford underwater light trap	97
22	Greenslade's experiment with pitfall traps for insects	100
23	Malaise trap	101
24	Radiant-energy trap	105
25	Formalin fly trap	105
26	Inkwell and Leakey pots	109
27	Eel traps as used on the Adriatic coast	116
28	Box trap for fish	119
29	English brick deadfall trap	123
30	Log-cage deadfall trap	124
31	Potter trap	129
32	Chardonneret trap	130
33	Hand-controlled box trap for birds	131
34	Single version of clap-net trap	133
35	Eclipse sparrow trap	134
36	Ministry of Agriculture's Mark I rook, jack-daw and carrion crow trap	136

FIGURE		PAGE
37	MAAF Mark II rook, jackdaw and carrion crow trap	139
38	MAAF Mark III rook, jackdaw and carrion crow trap	140
39	MAAF feral pigeon trap	141
40	Collecting-box for aviary-type bird traps	142
41	Heligoland trap	143
42	Skokholm dunlin trap	144
43	Plan of decoy pipe	150
44	Siberian hoop-fence noose traps	151
45	Arctic fox trap	158
46	'Figure 4' trap with stone deadfall	162
47	Pole deadfall trap	163
48	Trail-set deadfall trap	165
49	Deadfall mouse trap	167
50	'Mortis' mouse trap	167
51	Box deadfall trap	168
52	Board flap trap	169
53	Antelope foot trap	173
54	Aldrich bear trap	174
55	Carolina hanging snare	175
56	Bait-set snare	176
57	Pole snare	176
58	Cluster snares	177
59	Portable snare	179
60	Double-box snare	180
61	Tongs-type and scissor-type mole traps	183
62	Folding breakback mouse trap	186
63	Examples of beaver traps	193
64	Jump trap	193
65	Horizontal coil-spring steel trap	194
66	Trail-set for steel traps	199
67	Idstone trap	201
68	'Terrier' signal trap	202
69	Imbra trap	210
70	Trap for pocket gophers	214
71	Conibear trap	215

FIGURE   PAGE

72 Longworth small mammal box trap   221
73 Bamboo mongoose trap   223
74 Section of a plastic tube trap   224
75 Havahart 'Ketch-All' automatic mouse trap   231
76 Young's automatic mouse trap   232
77 Rat and lizard trap   233
78 Spiked-block trap   234
79 'Wolf's Garden'   234
80 Antelope crush trap   235

Introduction

THE subject of traps may seem an improbable one on which to base a book, especially when the objects themselves are apt to be regarded as miscellaneous hunks of metal and can often be found in a muddled heap at the back of a hardware store. Yet they hold a fascination for men which has persisted from earliest times, for they were amongst the first tools manufactured by man and used by him to improve his standard of living.

It was the ability to use his hands to fashion tools that put man several leaps ahead of his nearest animal rivals. He, and he alone, had the combination of mental development and manual dexterity which enabled him to learn from experience, find solutions to problems and invent mechanical devices to make his lot on earth a more pleasurable experience.

Early human needs were basic, and were primarily directed towards ensuring protection from danger and finding enough to eat. The only other requirement, that of perpetuating the species, is unlikely to have posed any greater problem for the caveman than it does for the modern city dweller; in all probability, inhibitions would have been fewer.

Keeping well fed and out of danger were full-time jobs, and as these could be made easier only by the development of tools and weapons, the early men must have expended considerable ingenuity and energy on inventing them. How they arrived at the methods they used in the beginning will probably never be properly understood, but at some time their attention must have been drawn to the tactics of more lowly creatures. If these could devise traps to capture animals and secure food, why should not men with their superior intelligence and nimble fingers do as well or even better? The construction of a net or cage trap may well have been inspired by a humble web-spinning spider. Its relative, the trap-door spider, could have pro-

vided a blueprint for the pitfall trap, while insectivorous plants like
the butterworts and pitcher plants could easily have suggested the
use of a lure. These hints apart, there were even more obvious
lessons to be learnt when our ancestors came across large animals
brought down and rendered incapable in naturally occurring pits
and swamps. Inevitably men would have been stimulated into digging
artificial pits, more especially after they had perfected the art of
making trowels of wood, stone and bone.

It is extremely likely that the first designs for traps have been
handed down from generation to generation, or, from time to time
have been re-invented. This would explain why some in use today
among the primitive peoples of the forest and icecap have such a
strong resemblance to the ones used by their forbears of many
thousands of years ago. By good fortune, the modern backwoodsman
may be able to trade the products of his simple husbandry for manufactured traps, but he will still rely for the most part upon the traps
he can devise and make himself.

An unusual feature of man's determination for self-perpetuation
brings the story full circle. Modern army units in many countries,
including both Britain and the United States, are now being trained
to make use of natural materials such as timber and rocks for
fashioning traps. The reader may well ponder upon the necessity for
this in the face of so many sophisticated weapons for attack and
defence, as well as modern food-preserving processes which ensure
the freshness of food for longer and longer periods. In fact, it is the
knowledge that such technological achievements of our civilisation
could all be rendered useless by a nuclear catastrophe that prompts
us to train personnel in the simple art of living off the land—the so-
called survival training.

Types of Trap
Since the greater part of this story is concerned with traps for particular types of animals, it may be useful first to consider them
collectively as mechanical objects which can be listed in groups
according to their method of construction or action.

Few materials have not at some time or another been found suitable for trap construction, and many men today, as well as countless
small boys, still employ anything that comes easily to hand. Some of
these home-made traps function extremely well despite their often
crude construction and, of course, they enjoy the merit of being in-

expensive. Except for steel traps, which cannot be made easily without the resources and skills belonging to a blacksmith's shop, most types of traps can be made by anyone with a mechanical turn of mind and sufficient manual dexterity. The example set by North American Indians in making deadfall traps and snares from logs, rawhide and horsehair was quickly copied by white settlers and passed down through generations of descendants, so that for many small boys in this part of the world learning to make traps and putting out a trapline is a normal part of the process of growing up. Furthermore there is the incentive of reward, because a few muskrat or mink skins will bring in money enough to compensate for rising early in the morning and running out a few traps.

Youngsters in Britain, unhappily, do not enjoy similar opportunities. The restrictions on using traps and the difficulty of finding open country where a line of traps could be run out are only equalled by the scarcity of fur-bearers necessary to make the effort worthwhile. Nor is trapping a lore taught to British Boy Scouts as it is to their American cousins, though the writer has come across many British boys who have found great enjoyment in inventing traps, usually because they were of country stock, the sons of farmers and gamekeepers.

Pitfall Traps

The first general group of traps are those known as pitfall traps. There is no particular reason why, among modern traps, these should come first, except that historically they were probably the first ones used by the early hunters—men living in crude tree shelters or convenient caves.

We shall see later how pitfall traps have been used to catch most kinds of animals, except perhaps those living permanently in water. Often the pit part of the trap would be nothing more than a hole dug in the ground, but even cavemen soon learned tricks of camouflage which enabled them to introduce an element of surprise into their tactics.

Elaborate pitfall traps have been made by lining the pit with split logs, so preventing the earthen walls from caving in and making it more difficult for burrowing animals to escape. Thus such traps can often catch animals alive, even though they may sometimes suffer injury from their fall, but this was seldom the object of early man who is more likely to have driven stakes into the pit floor, leaving pointed ends uppermost so that a victim would become impaled and killed. An alternative to spiked staves has been to fill the pit with a sufficient depth of water to drown any animal that fell into it.

More recently there have been elaborations of pitfall traps in which a pivoted lid is fixed in the upper part of the pit. The lid is usually baited so that an overgreedy animal, like a fox, would jump on top of the lid to secure the bait, and immediately be tumbled into the bottom as the lid tilted.

Pitfall traps can, therefore, be used either baited or unbaited, the choice depending upon the kinds of animals which a trap has been designed to take.

Spring Traps

This is such a large category of traps that some people might prefer to subdivide it and include steel traps in a separate group. The steel trap, better known as a gin trap in Britain, has been used extensively and almost exclusively in some areas of trapping and, in consequence, has acquired an esteem sufficient to suggest uniqueness. While acknowledging its pre-eminence in the world of traps, it is none the less still dependent upon the tension of a spring in order to be effective.

Two kinds of springs have been incorporated in traps—flat springs and coiled or helical springs. Traditionally, the flat spring has been used for steel traps, although in more recent years coil springs have been built into some of the varieties known as jump traps. The first flat springs were used long before man had acquired the skill of winning metals from their ores; he simply made use of the natural elasticity of certain woods. Quite good springs could be made from hazel or spruce, but the saplings of most other trees have an elasticity which persists until the wood matures and hardens. Suitably bent, switches of young timber have a recoil which can be highly effective when under the control of a trigger release mechanism. Frequently such a spring is used in combination with a snare, so that an animal running into the noose activates a trigger, whereupon the released spring jerks the quarry into the air and keeps it free from molestation by scavengers. The same principle has been incorporated in a box trap so that a hidden noose is tightened by releasing the tension of a springy piece of wood to which it is attached.

Before steel coil springs were developed, twisted horsehair or plant fibres were used in combination with a clapper. An instance of this use is seen in the old type of wooden-framed bow saw, where the blade is tensioned by tightening a twisted cord spring with a wooden clapper pushed through the strands. An example of this kind of spring used in a trap is described later.

Metal coil springs are now commonly found in mouse and rat traps of the type sometimes known as snap or break-back traps, but they are also found in gopher and mole traps. In Britain, the outlawing of the steel or gin trap has encouraged inventors to produce humane traps for catching animals such as rabbits, stoats, weasels and squirrels. Most of these new traps approved by the British government depend upon the use of metallic coiled springs and are commonly referred to as *spring traps*.

Snares

The use of snares for trapping not only goes way back in history, but continues today with increasing popularity. Probably no other traps combine so well ease of manufacture, simplicity of operation and portability. To these attributes we can add silent action and considerable efficiency when in the hands of a skilled trapper; in other words, all the features that a good trap should possess.

Snares, of course, vary considerably and in later sections of this book many different kinds will be described and illustrated. They can be purchased in almost any hardware store in country districts, although the home-made article is likely to outnumber its commercial rival.

Snares have been made from all kinds of materials, including horsehair, rawhide, sealskin, dried animal sinews, plant fibres and, more recently, from various synthetic cords and wire, especially stranded brass wire. The simplest version is a plain noose with a slip-knot. More elaborate kinds have stops, swivels and brass eyelet holes to ensure greater certainty in taking the catch and to reduce the possible suffering of animals caught. We have already seen how snares can be spring loaded.

Foot Traps

Foot traps also have a long history, going back at least to the Upper Palaeolithic (Stone Age) period and perhaps even further. Important examples were the so-called treadle-traps used in lakeland areas to catch animals such as deer and antelopes when they entered the water to drink.

Foot traps are still in use in several parts of Africa for catching antelope and giraffes. They take various forms, but a popular version is the wheel trap, consisting of a circular rim of plaited grass or reeds having radiating spokes of sharply-pointed wood stopping short of the centre (illustration, p 208). Anchored to a stake in the ground and suitably camouflaged with grasses, these traps grip tightly the leg of any animal which pushes its foot through the centre. Also included in this section could be the steel or gin trap, because it, too, is usually intended to take an animal by its foot.

Cage Traps
Of all the traps mentioned so far, these are the only ones purposely designed to take animals alive, and for this reason can be considered truly humane.

Some of the traps in this group could also be called box traps, but it matters little which term is used for they all consist of an imprisoning chamber into which an animal is lured either by the presence of a bait, or to satisfy its own curiosity. The important feature of all of these traps is a door so triggered that the release pedal cannot be stimulated and the door closed until the animal is completely inside the trap. There is conclusive evidence of these traps having been in use as far back as the Middle Ages, and they come in a variety of sizes to deal with aquatic, terrestrial and aerial animals and to take creatures ranging from shrews to antelope and large cats.

If there is a sheltered area inside the cage and a supply of bedding and food is provided, trapped animals can survive for several days in these cages, so that it is not essential, as with some other types of trap, to make daily visits to a trapline of cage traps. The prisoners cannot escape and would-be predators cannot molest them.

Elaborate Trap Systems
There are a number of traps in use which cannot easily be included among the groups already listed. Most of them are large and were probably originally designed with the object of exploiting animal capture for commercial gain.

One example is the boom fishing trap, which can vary in design from one part of the world to another, but consists basically of restricting barriers, or booms, erected in bays or estuaries so that fish are channelled through the entrance to the trap.

Another example of a trap difficult to classify is the wildfowl decoy, the prototype of which was most probably designed in Holland during the fifteenth century. Its action is not unlike that of the boom fish trap, since it also makes use of channelling barriers, but on an artificially created decoy pond. One might also include under this heading an unconventional but quite effective type of insect trap which depends upon radiant heat as an attracting force.

Uses for Traps

Turning now to the purposes for which traps are used, it has already been suggested that trapping was originally a means for aiding human survival, both by removal of dangerous animals and as a method of securing food.

Traps are still being used for these purposes, especially by the more primitive peoples of the world. On the Indian sub-continent, in Africa and in South America, traps are set outside villages to protect the inhabitants from marauding carnivores—the tigers, lions and jaguars which can develop man-eating habits and terrorise the simple people who live on their hunting paths. In situations such as these, even when modern rifles are available to hunt down a quarry, traps can still provide some security by remote control when they are laid on animal tracks which pass close by human settlements.

Among primitive hunters, traps are more often used to provide meat than for self-protection, and here the term 'primitive' in no way denigrates peoples who practise such simple cultures. Their lives by our standards may be uncomplicated and primitive but they do possess both a deeper understanding of the natural world than we have and greater ability to live in close harmony with it. The bushmen of South-West Africa are well known for their use of poison-tipped arrows, but are probably less generally recognised as the expert trappers they undoubtedly are. They employ nooses, pitfalls, foot traps and cage traps to capture monkeys, antelope, ostriches, small birds and fish. All of these animals are used by them for food, although the dishes they prepare from them would not find a place in *Larousse Gastronomique*.

But trapping animals for food is not the prerogative of people in underdeveloped countries, it is also a serious business in many civilised territories. Fish trapping is a convenient and effective method of catching fish living close to the shore—a form of static inshore fishing—and fish which ascend or descend rivers, such as eels and salmon, are also caught in traps. Rabbit pie and jugged hare are favourite dishes in many parts of the world and only in recent years have chefs come to rely more on the tame animals than their wild cousins. Formerly, rabbits were almost invariably taken by trapping and rabbit trappers could enjoy a lucrative business by selling the carcasses for meat and the pelt for 'coney' fur; which brings us to the fur trade.

Men living in cold parts of the earth soon discovered the value of a second-hand skin for keeping their own bodies warm in winter. When trading developed as a social practice, fur skins became valuable commodities for barter, and there are indications that an organised fur trade existed as far back in time as the seventh century BC, since Aristeas, a writer of Ancient Greece, reported that Siberian hunters carried on a vigorous trade in fur with people from south-eastern Europe. Within another fifteen centuries, fur markets were an established feature in Europe, with trappers from northern Asia and Scandinavia meeting merchants from southern Europe and the Middle East at fairs held in the cities of Novgorod and Kholmogory, in what is now the USSR.

Among the early fur traders, certain skins were prized and more eagerly sought after than others, in much the same way as their modern counterparts have their preferences. The old favourites were ermine, mink, sable and blue fox. Ermine became a feature of the robes of dignitaries in western European countries and for this purpose has retained its importance to the present day.

In more recent times the fur trade has become especially associated with North America, where it had its beginnings at the end of the fifteenth century AD. At this time, explorers from Europe, visiting the shores of the American continent for the first time, exchanged goods from their own countries for skins collected by the North American Indians. John Cabot is reputed to have brought back nooses bartered from Indians as a gift for his sponsor, King Henry VII of England. Before the white man arrived in America with his horses, firearms and steel traps, the Indian had depended upon primitive but none the less highly effective hunting methods, with the noose high on his list of useful possessions. He hunted the grizzly bear, buffalo, elk, beaver and birds. The eagle was a particular prize, for it was from this bird that he took the feathers to adorn his headband and show his status as a warrior. A fuller story of the American fur trade will be found in the next chapter.

A review of traps used on a commercial basis would not be complete without again mentioning wildfowl decoys. These were used in the first instance entirely as a means of culling birds for the table. In the early days, the number of birds taken would likely as not be restricted to the personal needs of an estate owner, but the opportunity to build up a surplus would provide the obvious advantage of disposing of them for financial gain. In the same way, the personal needs of early fishermen would often be less than their catch and so fish trapping became an accepted commercial occupation.

In more recent years wildfowl decoys, which suffered a decline in numbers during the late nineteenth century, have been given a new lease of life and are now used in Britain for scientific research into aspects of bird migration.

Traps and Research

Research in general is today one of the most important objectives in the use of traps. Scientists concerned with research on animals often find difficulty in obtaining the live specimens required for a variety of investigations, including observations of wild animal behaviour under controlled conditions. It is not easy, for instance, to discover how animals which burrow under the ground feed, but this is possible if live animals can be watched in a laboratory. Such observations have shown, for example, that the golden moles of southern Africa use a special technique when feeding on earthworms. They orientate the worm's head to face their mouth and then devour it by a ribbon-feed process using the front claws as a take-up mechanism and the tongue and incisor teeth to propel the food into the throat. This continues until the whole worm has been swallowed. Animals for this kind of investigation can only be obtained in sufficient quantity by means of suitable live traps.

In the past, the study of animals has been dominated by their taxonomic relationships one to another, but zoologists today are generally more interested in their environmental behaviour. Animal dispersal and migration movements are often related to seasonal changes in climate and breeding cycles. Bird sexual organs begin to enlarge at the onset of a breeding season and, apart from the rise of secondary physical characteristics such as song and breeding plumage which accompany the change, there is often also the urge to fly off to new breeding grounds. Such movements are best investigated when individual animals can be marked and their subsequent wanderings followed, and here trapping them alive is an obvious prerequisite.

Knowledge of animal distribution and population statistics also depends upon using marked animals. Almost always animals which are trapped alive for scientific research will be subsequently released.

Complaints that live-trapping animals for research is inhumane can be countered by the experience of zoologists who find that small mammals and birds frequently become trap-prone and, having once tasted bait laid in traps, cannot keep away from them. This is verified by the results of experiments carried out a number of years ago and now recognised as false, because repeated visits to a trap by the same animal were mistaken for visits by different animals. Recent developments in animal-marking techniques have proved that animals will return to traps, even when these are left unbaited. When using Longworth traps in field experiments, the writer has opened their doors several times in a single day to discover the same smiling vole face peering out from the nest inside.

Scientists who use traps in research hail from many organisations, including universities, government departments, museums and field study groups such as the Field Studies Council in Britain and the Wildlife Management Institute in the United States. In Britain, the Nature Conservancy, and in the USA the Fish and Game Departments of Federal States, carry out regional surveys which involve live-trapping, while increasing interest in this type of work is being shown by professional bodies such as the Mammal Society of the British Isles and the American Society of Mammalogists. Interested readers will find many accounts of experimental investigations into trap usage in the journals of these societies. Ornithologists are also live-trapping birds for migrational surveys; indeed, the British Trust for Ornithology (BTO) has sponsored not only research into problems of migration and distribution, but also the development of trapping procedures, with emphasis on humane methods and compliance with Bird Protection Orders.

Pest and Predator Control
Once early man had gained mastery over his major enemies, he would have enjoyed a more settled and civilised life, but against this background he would have become increasingly aware of a number of minor irritations. Among these must have been pests such as the mice and rats which made inroads into his stores of food, fleas which were uninvited visitors to his bed and personal clothing, and moths

whose larvae ate away the skin coat which he had stored away for the summer in the back of his cave. Thus, quite soon, man would have become conscious of the problems of pest disinfestation and would set about devising suitable traps with which to combat these scourges of his existence.

Among the first of his new inventions would, no doubt, be mouse-traps, and if this book may seem to be preoccupied with traps for mice and other small mammals, it can at least be excused on the grounds that a larger number and greater diversity of traps have been invented to deal with these little creatures than any others.

Any living organism which competes with man for the necessities of life assumes the character of a pest. In certain instances this appears to be an inborn characteristic, but often it is a secondary development of some abnormality, as when multiplication of a species is at a rate greater than man is prepared to tolerate. Man has also a habit of creating trouble for himself by interfering with natural processes. Thus, if for one reason or another we remove a predator, its prey may then increase in numbers from lack of natural control and so achieve the status of a pest. Another common man-made situation leading to creation of a pest has been the introduction of foreign animals into a country. Finding no natural enemies in its new surroundings, the animal's rate of multiplication becomes prodigious and often uncontrollable, at least by individual men, and so calls for action by government departments. In Britain, the intro-duction of grey squirrels has created just such a situation, and mink and coypu escaping from captivity have produced local pockets which even the resources of the Ministry of Agriculture, Fisheries and Food have been insufficient to eradicate. The introduction of the rabbit into Australia has become a classic example of the dangers of such action and is still a cause of profound concern for the Australian government. Where control measures for pests become necessary traps find a use, and trapping systems are constantly being reviewed in an attempt to achieve still greater efficiency.

It is worthwhile at this point to distinguish between a pest and a predator, since these terms are sometimes confused. A pest is any living thing which comes into conflict with man as, for example, horticultural weeds, since they prevent man's crops from developing their full potential. Parasites may also be pests if the plants and animals they attack are important to man. In the context of trapping, however, pests are normally birds and mammals which attack stores of man's food, his crops, his domestic animals and the premises in which he lives and works.

A predator, on the other hand, is an animal which habitually hunts, captures and kills other animals. Predators usually kill in order to obtain food, but some animals develop a predatory habit which seems to have no logical incentive other than the lust to kill. The writer can think of no animal which naturally adopts this behaviour, but we know rogue elephants become imbued with an unaccustomed savagery following injury or after being outcast from a herd. At the other end of the scale, the domestic cat will frequently exercise an inborn instinct by killing birds, mice and shrews, but will not eat them because it is already well fed by its owner and is simply in need of exercise. It thus becomes obvious that predators in some situations can also be thought of as pests. Conversely, it is not imperative that a pest should also be a predator.

Finally, then, we come to the traps used for predator control, though it is not always easy to establish whether their victims are predators, pests, or both. When a gamekeeper is trapping stoats and weasels preying on his gamebirds he is exercising predator control, yet he would certainly describe the predators as pests. The difference may be the degree of nuisance caused and the scale of attack necessary to combat it. Pestilence will require large combating forces organised like a military campaign, whereas predator control is more likely to be a local affair administered by small groups of individuals. Even so, the traps used for predator control tend to arouse the interest of government departments, who also respond to public pressure by attempting to legislate against the use of inhumane methods.

The outlawing of the gin trap in Britain followed public revulsion at the cruelty it inflicted upon its hapless victims. Richard Jefferies writes of a gamekeeper's wife who had a number of rugs made from the skins of black and tabby cats, which had been caught accidently in traps set for vermin. But if accident caused the loss of some of man's domestic animals, it was no accident when landowners and gamekeepers in eighteenth-century Britain set even larger gins specifically to catch marauding poachers. For a long time before they, too, became illegal, man traps guarded many large estates against the human predator who, when caught, was described by the magistrates as a pest.

Nowadays pest and predator control can often be achieved without recourse to the use of traps, but many individuals and organisations will continue to believe that trapping is a more efficient and humane method of control than the use of pesticides, drugged darts and the rifle. Pesticides, it is true, are among the least specific of killers; the efficacy of drugged darts is difficult to assess and they may well produce harmful physical effects in a wild animal without killing it. And straightforward shooting may not be quite so straightforward in the hands of a poor shot.

Later in this book the ethics of trapping will be discussed, because whenever man engages in a practice which puts the lives of his fellow creatures in jeopardy he has a moral obligation to examine his motives carefully and to assess the methods he proposes to employ.

CHAPTER ONE

An Historical Study of Trap Development

Prehistoric Era

In the absence of archaeologically-derived proof from excavations directed towards discovery of the earliest forms of men, we have no evidence as to the period of man's history when he first devised traps on his own initiative. There are, however, indications from other directions that the trap was one of man's earliest instruments.

It seems more than likely that pits were dug by Palaeolithic men to bring down the larger animals roaming the earth at that time. The bones of giant beasts such as mammoths, woolly rhinoceroses and cave bears, found associated with remains of early man, showed that he had used them as tools, probably clubs. He had also split them with hand-axes for the marrow inside and to produce jagged edges useful in domestic life. Some of these animals he could have brought down with a *bolas*, a three-stoned sling device which he hurled so as to entangle the forelegs of his prey, but the quantity of bones found in some excavations indicate that he would have needed other methods as well. He no doubt utilised natural pits where the terrain provided these, but remains of large animals have been discovered in situations where such pits would not have occurred naturally, and one can hazard a guess that man might have dug these pits himself. As his mental processes developed, early man would add cunning to his industry and camouflage his pits with grass and foliage supported on reeds and branches. I. W. Cornwall in *Prehistoric Animals and their Hunters* has suggested that the pits would only need to have been deep enough to hold the animal by its legs; clubs and spears would be used to finish it off.

What were the animals that early man had to contend with like? The mammoth, woolly rhinoceros and cave bear were all creatures of

24

a world much colder than ours, for this was a period, perhaps some fifty thousand years ago and more, when much of Europe was enduring sub-Arctic conditions. The woolly mammoth, *Mammuthus primigenius*, had a number of geographical subspecies. The typical form ranged over much of northern Europe, Asia and North America as well, although three subspecies, *M. p. alaskensis*, *M. p. americanus* and *M. p. compressus*, were located only in the New World. Unlike the typical mammoth which had died out in Europe by the end of the ice age, the American forms survived for a considerable period after the ice had receded.

The typical woolly mammoth, despite its name, was not enormous, probably less than ten feet high at the withers. We know a great deal about this creature for many were preserved frozen in the flesh in permafrost soils of Alaska and Siberia for many thousands of years. We know also that they were mostly herbivores, for even the stomach contents were preserved. But in spite of their relatively small size and vegetarian feeding habits, they would, like their modern cousins the elephants, still have been big and frightening to primitive people.

There were a number of varieties of rhinoceroses with which people in different parts of the prehistoric world had to contend. The typical woolly rhinoceros with its long single horn and hairy coat was, like the mammoth, adapted for life in tundra and cold-steppe areas; but other two-horned varieties lived elsewhere in Europe in forest conditions and warm-temperate environments. The rhinoceroses had thick skins which could resist primitive spears, were powerfully built, and presented a truly formidable appearance when charging with their nasal horns thrust forwards. Only by using pits and concerted hunting methods could early man have overcome these animals, which had few other enemies.

The rhinoceroses were vegetarians like the mammoths, but early man had competition from fierce carnivores as well. The smaller ones, such as the wolves and hyenas, were often quite enough to terrorise simple men, but the bigger bears and sabre-tooth cats must have presented special problems, since they would be likely to invade caves in which man himself sheltered.

But the biggest of these prehistoric beasts did possess at least one characteristic which would assist the trapper. Providing he used a pitfall trap, their lumbering, often aggressive rampage through the forests or across the grasslands was far from cautious enough to prevent them from falling into well camouflaged holes.

A further development of a simple pitfall trap would be to place pointed staves in the bottom, so as to impale the creatures which stumbled into it. This could have occurred to early man as a result of abstract thought, but it is also possible that observation of the pit of the ant-lion larva, with the massive pointed mandibles of the larva projecting upwards from the base of the pit, might have supplied the inspiration.

The Palaeolithic or Stone Age, associated with the period when man first manufactured tools deliberately, is subdivided chronologically by archaeologists into eras related to particular industrial and cultural developments. Alternatively, these periods may be identified according to the type or race of men characteristically held responsible for the cultures. Thus the very early cultures, known as Chellian and Acheulian cultures, might have been developed by Heidelberg man before 40,000 BC. After this date, during the Mousterian period the Neanderthal race appeared. This was the period of the earth's history when ice crept southwards from the North Pole to cover a good deal of northern and central Europe, as far as southern Britain. Towards the end of the last of four ice ages, about 25,000 BC, there appeared a race of man, Cro-Magnon Man, more nearly identified with modern races and responsible for the so-called Magdalenian culture.

The pitfall trap in various stages of sophistication would have been used by men of the Chellian and Acheulian periods, and would no doubt have been retained even when different types of traps were developed. Indeed, primitive societies still use the pitfall trap, and even today giraffes are caught in them by tribes in Central Africa.

The early men, according to J. G. D. Clarke, probably considered herbivorous animals as converters of vegetation into useful domestic materials and, apart from flesh for food, their bones and sinews would be useful in making traps. Cornwall has also pointed out that the Mousterian industrialists could have used rawhide to manufacture fairly advanced noose traps. These might have incorporated a bent sapling as a spring, and sinew as a motivating tripline. There is no direct evidence for this, but traces of rawhide snares suggest the possibility of use in a more elaborate form. Before the end of the last ice age, large animals would have moved southwards annually to avoid the extreme cold and lack of vegetation during the winter. Man would have been able to survive on small mammals, such as hares, and birds. Bones of these creatures have been found associated with human remains and it is likely that they were trapped by man, using snares in the same manner as they are employed all over the world today. This use of snares was probably continued by the Magdalenian cave dwellers, since considerable quantities of bones from grouse and hares occur in deposits of this period. Clarke mentions the use of reindeer sinew in this connection.

Trapping in Primitive Art

From the Upper Palaeolithic period onwards, we have more certain information concerning the use of traps, for it was about this time that men started to produce graphical impressions of their surroundings, the activities of their fellows, and the habits of wild animals. The artwork was produced on the flat stonework facings of cliffs, and on the walls of caves in which families dwelt. The drawings and paintings, produced with pigments such as ochre, probably mixed with animal fat and oils, have endured remarkably well over a period of some 25,000 years. Once the ability to express himself graphically had been achieved, man continued to depict aspects of his daily life by this means, although the skills and art forms have varied considerably from one age to another. Not all artistic expression took the form of murals, for these early artists had also developed the skills of engraving, producing relief sculptures, and modelling in plastic media such as clay. Such three-dimensional handwork, known as 'mobiliary art', has been informative but it is from the murals that we have learned most about the traps which were used at that time.

The sensitive expression of animal form and function depicted by the Upper Stone Age artists is in curious contradistinction to the veiled features of traps seen in their murals. The creatures of this period, such as reindeer, giant ox, stag, mammoth, ibex, wildcat, bison, fox, horse, birds and occasionally fish, were all depicted with not only remarkable accuracy of anatomical detail but also in a manner which captured exactly the stances and movements we know to be typical of these creatures. Man himself was also portrayed, and the cartoons depict the methods he used in hunting and fishing.

With all this attention to detail in his artwork, why did early man avoid similar accuracy in illustrating the traps he used? The answer probably comes with an understanding of the superstitions, mystiques and taboos which played such an important part in his daily life. Though heathens by our reckoning, these men no doubt obeyed the call of higher and unknown, but fancifully imagined, spirits. Sun that could scorch their skins and parch their throats, rain that could flood their homes and wash away precious possessions, were forces to be reckoned with, and were controlled by whom? Little wonder then that they sought to keep secret the details of their own weapons for fear that magical deities might recognise them and render them ineffective.

Because murals often showed animals associated with unexpected structural representation—vague enclosing lines, a meshwork indicative of some form of net, or crude devices attached to feet and mouths—we have to use our imagination and construe that these were hints of traps. Sometimes the hint was exceedingly vague or especially subtle. Thus in a cave at Pileta, Malaga in Spain, there is a series of three scenes each hinting at a trap, with only representations of animal tracks inside. (Fig 1.)

When we pass into the Mesolithic, or Middle Stone Age period, the artwork indicates a new weapon developed by man, the bow. Many murals of this period show men, singly and in groups, engaged in hunting and chasing their prey, using arrows shot from bows. It has been suggested that development of the bow as an independent and portable weapon could have derived from earlier use of the kind of spring noose previously mentioned, which had not been completely abandoned after the Palaeolithic Age. And certainly Mesolithic hunters appear to have used hanging snares, a kind of running noose, in order to capture elk. These were giants among the herbivorous or plant-eating animals, and a noose designed for their capture would need to have been well anchored to a sturdy tree.

Towards the end of the Stone Age, in the Neolithic or so-called New Stone Age period, many new traps may well have been devised, and were probably often adapted for the capture of particular types of wildlife. The men of this time were largely hunters and gatherers of small game and could have used deadfall traps, cage traps and treadle traps for birds and mammals, while there is strong evidence to suggest that creels, sometimes associated with weirs, were used for catching fish. In the Nationalmuseet at Copenhagen, there can be seen osier creels which were used as traps by Stone Age men. Apparently, these were sometimes incorporated in heavy timber weirs.

During the later Neolithic era, man became, albeit gradually, a more settled creature and developed new skills which made him less dependent for his sustenance upon wild plants and animals. Once he

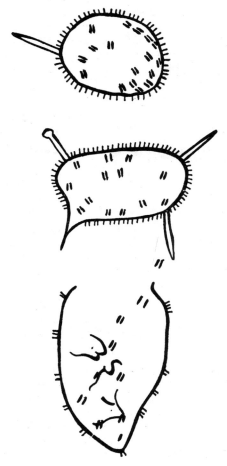

Fig 1   Three murals from a cave at Pileta, Malaga, Spain

had found a means of domesticating animals and cultivating plants, there was no longer the need to move house frequently. The first domestic animal is thought to have been the dog, probably originating from a wolf, and this would have been an essential stage in any attempt to domesticate other beasts. For without the aid of dogs obedient to man's will, it would have been an almost impossible task to tame wild oxen, horses and sheep.

Though a fixed abode associated with a more intensively indus-
trialised husbandry would necessarily involve considerable expendi-
ture of time and effort, it would also allow opportunity to store tools
and equipment, which in turn would have provided incentive for invention. Domesticated animals and cultivated plants would have
reduced the need to hunt and gather in the wild in order to satisfy
hunger, but there would still be the need to remove potential enemies
and pests, and so traps for these purposes would be devised.

The pattern of social evolution over some 1,500 years of this
period can be discerned from the artwork known from the civilisation
of Val Camonica in the North Italian Alps. In particular, on La
Grande Roche de Naquane, there are many artistic representations
of animals caught in traps and these fall into four main groups. The
first shows animals being caught in devices which have trapped their
feet, such as a sprung noose using a sapling for a spring. A second
group consists of examples of animals caught by their mouths. Here
details are often obscure, but it is usually apparent that the captive
prey is small and has been lured by some form of bait. Perhaps the
devices were akin to our relatively modern mouse traps. A third
group of trapping devices uses nets. Again details are not clear, but
the nets might have been fixed to entangle animals on game tracks, or
sprung to enclose animals tripping on a line. In either instance the
trapnet was not a killer in itself and hunters needed to finish off their
captives with lance and spear. The final group consists of enclosure
traps, built of wooden staves, and contrived to lure animals by
means of bait, sometimes live bait, such as a goat when carnivores
were being hunted. The enclosure served as a restrictive area within
which hunters would be able to direct spears for the kill. The Val
Camonica artwork carries over from the Stone Age into the Copper
and Bronze Ages and as far as the late Iron Age, the final stage
covering the period between 250 and 16 BC.

We have other evidence from Bronze Age archaeological sites, and
one such site in Northern Sweden has yielded material which suggests
the use of snares for catching waterfowl. We shall see later how this
method has been used during recent times in Siberia for capturing
the same prey.

J. Garth Taylor has described how Eskimoes in Northern Ungava
used baleen snares to catch diving birds. The line, carrying up to
sixty small snares, might be 20ft long and would be stretched beneath
the waters of a shallow lake. These were frequently used by the

Fig 2 From paintings on La Grande Roche de Naquane, Val Camonica, Italy, showing (*above right*) animal trapped by its mouth, (*lower left*) the use of nets and (*lower right*) enclosure traps

Eskimoes before they learned to hunt with guns, some three hundred years ago.

Early Types of Treadle Traps
But perhaps one of the most arresting stories associated with the discovery of early traps concerns those which are described as treadle traps. It has been suggested that these might have been developed in Mesolithic times, but certain evidence does not appear before the late Bronze Age. For a long time the existence of these constructions was known from archaeological excavations, rock art and monolith

engravings. Interpretations of their function were many, and not the least popular explanation was that they were musical instruments. Before detailing the history of the discoveries of these traps and the various explanations that were offered, a description of the kind of apparatus under discussion is necessary.

Typical of all the treadle traps discovered, but more complete than many, is the one which was found in the Moss of Auquharney, Aberdeenshire, in 1921 and subsequently presented to the Anthropological Museum of the University of Aberdeen by Mr William Yeats McDonald. A description of this trap was originally supplied by Professor R. W. Reid in a paper published in the *Proceedings of the Society of Antiquaries of Scotland* for 1922.

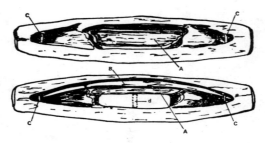

Fig 3   Treadle trap found in the Moss of Auquharney, Aberdeenshire

Reference to Fig 3 will give an idea of the general features of the trap. Known as a univalvular type, it differs from those found in other parts of Europe in having the movable parts duplicated and fitting into a main block containing a pair of openings instead of the single one depicted here. In the Auquharney specimen, the body measures 3ft 10¼in in length, 9¾in across the middle, 5⅝in at one end, 6⁵⁄₁₆in at the other end, with a maximum thickness of 4⅞in. The body here is made of alder wood. In other examples the body varies in length from just over 2ft to almost 5ft and the majority are of oak.

The loose or movable parts of the trap consist of a valve (A), in this case made of birch, a bow (B) and two pegs (C) made of willow. The valves are sometimes described as flaps or doors, and the bow has been referred to as the spring. The body, shaped by a tool serving like a hatchet, has a rectangular opening measuring 1ft 2¾in by 4in. One side and two ends of this cavity are described as having straight

Page 33 (*above*) An orb web of *Speira marorea;* (*below*) a bug trap from Poona, India

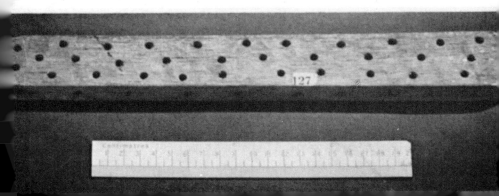

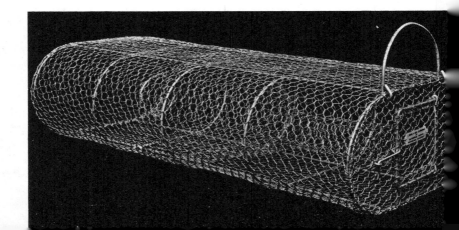

Page 34 (*top*) A row of putchers at low water showing method of removing captured fish; (*centre*) putts in position for fishing on the River Severn; (*below*) Young's Suffolk eel trap

bevelled edges and the other side as having a rounded bevelled edge, when viewed from the outer surface. This outer surface, as described by Prof Reid, had a blunt eminence on either side of the aperture, such that there were flat slopes to the centre and curved chamferings towards the ends.

The opposing surface is smooth and flat, but the central aperture, though of different shape in this view than when seen from the outer surface, has no bevelling. The aperture provides a platform, with sockets on either side, to hold the valvular door, or flap, in such a fashion that it cannot be pushed through the square opening of the aperture on the outer surface. At either end of the platform are grooves deepening towards the end of the trap body and designed to hold the bow in one or other of two positions, ie, a bent or flat state. The bow is secured by willow pegs inserted into either end of the body, but allows a to-and-fro movement of the bow as it assumes the bent or flat states.

The valve itself is described as decayed, but retaining sufficient shape to suggest a correspondence with that of the aperture. It has lugs on either side to serve as hinges in the sockets provided at the sides of the aperture. The lug-carrying edge is thick compared with that projecting into the aperture. When in position, the surface adjoining the rectangular opening of the main block aperture shows an oval depression, apparently burnt out. The bow, made of willow from which the bark had been peeled, had fashioned and pointed ends, but was in two pieces when discovered.

When set, the bow is in the bent position, held back by the valve which is in turn secured, presumably by a third peg (d) never discovered, lodged in the oval depression on one side and held by friction to the aperture surface on the other. With the trap placed in such a manner that the so-called outer surface is uppermost, an animal depressing the central securing peg with its foot would release the valve, and this in turn would be sprung by the bow taking up the straight position and so gripping the animal's foot. Even a large animal could not move far with its leg held by so heavy a trap as this.

In the bivalvular type found outside Britain, the body is a single unit but has a double-sized and double-fashioned aperture, two valves and two springs. The operation of setting and release is the same, the valves presumably being kept apart by a peg wedged between them. Often the valves appear as if originally fashioned from a single piece of wood through the centre of which a number of holes had been burned. When split down the centre, the cut edges of the two valves, between the semicircular depressions left from the holes, would function as teeth. These would grip an animal's limb as do the teeth of a steel or gin trap.

The documented history of the discovery of these traps goes back to the mid-nineteenth century. The first lead came from Ireland, where in 1859 at the town of Coolnaman in Co Derry 'an antique wooden implement' was discovered, an account of which was given in the *Ulster Journal of Archaeology*. As with all the other traps, this one was unearthed from a bog, where it was four feet below the surface in a bank of thick black turfs. Those associated with the find had no true conception as to its original use, one suggesting that it might have been a fish trap, another that it was a machine for making peats, a third thought it might be a cheese-press and a fourth that it was a pump. The appearance of the implement was almost identical with that of the Scottish one described, although the body, as was more usual, was of oak.

In 1873, 1874 and 1877 accounts appeared in the *Proceedings of the German Anthropological Society* of another three such traps found respectively at Tribsees, the Moor of Samow, near Gnoien (both in Mecklenburg), and Friedrichsbruch in what was then West Prussia. The first was reported to be a device for catching fish, in conjunction with a net, while the other two were described as otter traps. These were alike in being bivalvular, but were otherwise similar in construction to the one already described.

Also between 1875 and 1877, two similar traps were unearthed from a peat moor near Laibach, in Yugoslavia. The moor had formerly been a lake and the traps were found associated with Stone and early Bronze Age relics of lake pile-dwellings. Once more they were bivalvular, but details of the discovery did not emerge until after details of the German ones had been published.

Wales also provided evidence of the use of these devices when, in 1878, one was rescued from a mountain near the parish of Caio. Apparently it had been dug out some three years previously by a tenant farmer who was removing peat, but he had slung it aside as rubbish. In common with other British samples, this was univalvular in pattern, and at first was thought to be a kind of ancient Welsh harp.

The next discoveries were in Italy and details published in the

Proceedings of the Academy of Sciences of Naples in 1889 indicated that the locality of origin was at Fortega. Here three implements were unearthed from a peat bog associated with a former lake dwelling. The nature of the original habitation may have encouraged Dr Meschinelli, who described the traps, to identify them as model boats.

This history of discovery, one of the most interesting to have centred around traps, was originally summarised by Dr Robert Munro, Secretary of the Society of Antiquaries of Scotland, in his book *Lake Dwellings of Europe*, published in 1890. By 1919, the list of discoveries had grown to forty-one and the geographical distribution had extended to include Denmark and two further sites in Ireland. Munro had originally concluded, from the similarities of form and discovery sites, that there must be a common function. Furthermore, he had been of the opinion that the nature of the discovery sites suggested that they were otter traps, rather than anything else. In his paper to the society in 1919, he included a communication from Mr Patrick Gillespie, who had associated Munro's earlier descriptions with an illustration of a cross slab at Clonmacnois in Ireland. The slab was sculptured with a variety of design patterns including some pictorial matter. One scene was of a deer having become hobbled by putting its foot through a construction so apparently like those described by Munro, according to Gillespie's eyes, that he could only assume that the treadle traps were indeed for capturing deer. The Clonmacnois stone dates back to the eighth or ninth century AD, and Gillespie advises that the treadle traps must have been deer traps of a kind known and used in Ireland at that time.

When writing of the Auqharney trap in 1922, Professor Reid suggested that it would be baited beneath the valve or treadle. He could not cite particular animals caught with it, as no bones had been discovered in the area from which the trap had been recovered, but in thinking of bait having been used, he was probably agreeing with Munro who described how an otter would push its head through the valve to get at bait. Nevertheless, Reid did agree that deer, as seen on the Clonmacnois stone, might be caught in these traps when treading on them. Gillespie, too, drew attention to deer being captured in the Far East by traps of similar design to those found in Europe, though the oriental versions were of bamboo.

The whole story has been brought up to date more recently by Holger Rasmussen, who has related the excavated traps to modern

Fig 4   A detail from the Clonmacnois stone, showing a stag caught in a
treadle trap

counterparts in eastern Europe. The modern traps, practically
identical with prehistoric treadle traps, were described by a Pole,
Moszyński, in 1929, but it was not until 1940 that Rasmussen made a
comparison between new and old. The modern ones were located in
Polesia, Masovia and Galicia, and in situations so similar to those
occurring several thousands of years previously that it was impossible not to believe that all were constructed in an almost identical
way and used for similar purposes. The Polish traps were set in
groups in marshy ground with valves pressed downwards, and were
used to capture roe and red deer, and even bears. The variation in
size of the traps was related to the kinds of animals being caught,
although the placing of them near to the known drinking-places
would be an important prerequisite for capture. The animals would
push their feet through the aperture of the main block, thereby releasing the spring and so becoming firmly secured and possibly dis-
abled.

This discovery and comparison explains why the ancient traps were found in bogs and in many cases grouped together. A group of nine was found stacked in an upright position near Larkhill bog at Ballyshannon, Co Fermanagh in Ireland, while groups of five were found at Laibach, Yugoslavia, and at Vicenza in North Italy. Groups of three to six were also found near Teltow, in Brandenburg.

The technique of using pollen analysis for dating purposes has been employed to determine the age of some of the traps. Traps going back to the late Bronze Age, about 1000 BC, were found at Drumacaladerry bog, north Donegal and Lake Gölen, Vastergotland, the trap from the last-named place now being on show in the Nordiske Museet in Stockholm. Traps from the latter part of the sub-boreal period came from Silkeborg, Denmark. We have already seen that they were also in use in Ireland during early Christian times, and quite recently in Poland.

Apart from age, another interesting factor associated with distribution can be observed by mapping all the known sites of recovery, ancient and modern. This appears to show conclusively that all the areas in which this kind of trap has been used are associated with deciduous forests, a fact confirmed by the materials used in their construction. Bogs in the circumpolar belt have provided prehistoric sledge-runners and skis, but no treadle traps. Had these devices been used in that region, no doubt they would have been preserved and recovered in due course.

The First Civilisations

The social evolution of early man was a slow process, but as populations increased so men came into ever closer contact with each other. Eventually they began to live in community, and so tribal life developed. Inevitably, some tribes became stronger than others and from time to time one would predominate as a ruling unit. So nations and civilisations grew up, especially where natural resources offered exceptional facilities for larger populations. Rivers in particular feature as foci for civilising influences, and great ones such as the Tigris, the Euphrates and the Nile have played important roles in the story of human progress. The same held good in North America and in colonising this continent Europeans infiltrated through river valleys such as those of the St Lawrence, Hudson, Mohawk, Mississippi, Red, Missouri and Columbia rivers, which had indigenous populations of Indians already settled there.

This association of early civilisations with rivers provided an opportunity for people to fish the nearby waters. So it is that fishing relics rank high among the artefacts unearthed by archaeologists, and traps, or remains suggesting them, have appeared from time to time. The Ancient Egyptians, depending on the Nile as much as do their modern counterparts, were also endowed with considerable talent for artistic expression. This they applied to the decoration of tombs, with the emphasis upon features of everyday life associated with the world from which the inhabitants of the tombs had departed. In this way we know that the Egyptians used fish traps and that their design was similar to that of many used all over the world today. The conical or elongated outer casing, presumably of basketry work and probably using reeds from the river, had an inner funnel, a pattern which has persisted not only for capturing fish, but also for lizards and other small creatures. The Egyptian artists showed that the traps were used either individually or in groups fastened to fences, or booms, stretching from the bank of the river. Again, this method of use in multiple units has persisted until recent times.

It is inconceivable that some of the animal traps evolved by earlier men did not continue in use up to the time of the Egyptians, but they have provided little evidence of these in their artwork. No doubt traps of all kinds were employed but did not rate as worthy of artistic attention unless featured in the hunt or chase; and we must remember that the Egyptians were possessed of a culture which had developed weapons so superior for hunting purposes that humble traps would find only a limited application. There is evidence, however, according to Old Testament chroniclers, that their near neighbours, the Israelites, used nets, traps, snares and pitfalls.

The apparent insignificance of traps as subjects for historical record is further evidenced by the scant mention they receive at the hands of Roman chroniclers, which is the more surprising when one considers the importance of wild animals in the lives of the Romans. Perhaps no nation or empire, before or since, has used wild beasts so extensively for exhibitions and sport, and although we can find relatively few indications of traps being used to capture the animals they must have then been as important in this form of hunting as they are now.

Probably pits and nets were the main trapping constructions used during Roman times. A common pit used for wildcats, such as lions, leopards and cheetahs, would have had a central pillar, sometimes of wood, occasionally of stone, to which the bait could be attached. The form of bait would depend upon the predators sought. For lions, a goat-kid or lamb would be used, but leopards would be attracted by using a puppy so fastened as to cause it to howl with pain. The pit would be surrounded by a stockade over which the lion or leopard would leap in search of its prey. When an animal was caught in the pit, a cage baited with meat would be lowered and the captured animal hauled up after being enticed inside. Sometimes wild hunting dogs would be caught by the same means, accidentally or deliberately.

Elephants, which were used extensively by the Romans both for show and as a means of transport, could be captured in Africa by horsemen driving a herd towards pits in artificially constructed hollows, *vallem manu factum*. Pliny suggested that elephants could be tamed by first starving them and then giving them barley juice. George Jennison thought that this might well have been fermented barley, ie beer, which elephants readily drink.

According to Pausarius, wisent, or European bison, were captured by being driven into fenced hollows, the bottoms of which were lined with oiled skins. Though seemingly a crude method, it is one which must have persisted for Raphael Volaterranus, in the fifteenth century AD, describes it as a means of capturing wisent in Lithuania, but without resort to slippery skins. Pits were also cited by Caesar for taking the wild oxen or aurochs in Germany, and animals such as bears were captured after being driven into nets by hunters.

Apart from the written evidence in literature of the period, there are a few surviving examples of graphic illustration. A Roman villa at Bona, in Algeria, has a picture preserved showing an African hunt in which horsemen are driving beasts into nets camouflaged behind a prickly fig hedge (*circa* AD 300). And at the British Museum in London there is a mosaic in which nets are shown submerged in shallow water, presumably to trap animals going to drink.

Other forms of traps are mentioned in literature from Roman authors. In *Xenothon* we find a description of the colthrop (*pedica dentata*), which was a trap used to catch beasts such as elephants, antelope and bears. Essentially it consisted of a noose in a frame, anchored to a log which made flight difficult. A rope trap for taking leopard is mentioned by Aelian as in use in Mauretania. The trap was set in a store-hut and was supposedly baited with rotten meat, although Jennison feels that this would be more likely to catch a lion—an animal noted for its habit of returning repeatedly to a kill, no matter how old, until it has been consumed.

Another interesting trap mentioned in Roman literature is the mirror trap, which depended on animals, such as tigers, rushing at their own image, thinking it to be a cub or an enemy. And both Didorus and Caesar mention the capture of animals—elephants in Ethiopia, and elk in Germany—by the simple process of half sawing through trees known to be favourite scratching or leaning posts. There might, too, be some validity in at least one of the methods of catching monkeys described by Cleitarchus and quoted by Aelian.

The first and least credible procedure narrated was that of hunters depending upon the imitative ways of monkeys to an extent whereby one pair of shoes would be put on by a hunter in full view of a monkey troop. A second pair of shoes would be left behind, but would contain a hidden noose. When a monkey put its foot into a shoe, the noose would be pulled tight by a drawstring held at a distance by one of the hunting party. The second method, still relying on mimicry by monkeys, consisted of hunters, in sight of the troop, daubing their faces with a black paste. A bowl containing black paste, but with added bird lime, would be left behind, whereupon the luckless monkeys would repeat the action, thereby sealing their eyes with lime and falling easy victims to the hunters waiting nearby. Whether or not one could depend upon monkey mimicry to this extent is doubtful, but Martial mentions bird lime as being employed in the arena to render bears helpless when they rubbed it on their faces.

The evidence available concerning the traps known to have been used by Romans, or peoples of other countries catching animals for them, does not suggest a high degree of mechanical effort being applied to their construction. And this is surprising when we remember the well-developed skills in civil and mechanical engineering for which the Romans were renowned. However, a number of bee-hive shaped mole traps unearthed from Roman sites do suggest that the Romans, keen gardeners in many cases, were as much concerned about mole hills as we are today.

If, from the end of the Roman Empire to the fifteenth century AD, there was a need to use traps to destroy pests, or to secure animals for other purposes, there is little documentary evidence to confirm it. There is a British record that in the late thirteenth century two 'foresters of fee', John le Wolfhunte and Thomas Foljambe, were given no duties other than to destroy wolves. Although few by comparison with former times, wolves were then still sufficiently numerous to menace preserves containing deer, and hence enjoyed no protection. The wolf-hunters were commanded to set traps each year during March and September. We also know that in the middle of the thirteenth century poachers in Britain used snares to catch deer.

Mouse Traps through the Ages

When we do find accounts and illustrations of traps in the fifteenth century, the type around which most interest is centred is the mouse trap. The *Oxford English Dictionary* suggests that the term 'mouse trap' first appeared in English usage during the last quarter of the fifteenth century, and certainly it is about this period that manuscripts and paintings indicate its advent. The types of traps illustrated show little novelty in design or function, but simply a scaling-down in size to suit the prey concerned. This apparent preoccupation with mouse traps suggests that mice had become too numerous to be tolerated without taking action against them, and no doubt the insanitary habits said to have been common in Europe during this time—the casting of scraps for animals from dining-tables and the general disposal of domestic waste into the streets—would encourage rapid multiplication of rats, mice and other vermin.

C. Roth has compiled a social history of the mouse trap as revealed by illuminated manuscripts published as codices of 'The Ancient Parable', or *Mashal La Kadmoni*, written by the thirteenth-century scholar, poet and physician, Isaac ibn Sahula. Roth explains that the circumstances of Jewish trade in the Middle Ages made it necessary for precautions to be taken against the risk of mice invading business houses. The codices of 'The Ancient Parable' were all produced by German or North Italian Jews, and the Italians would be familiar with their loan-banker kinsmen's methods of protecting customers' pledges, their only evidence of moneys advanced, against attacks by mice.

Two parables recorded by Ibn Sahula concern the mouse and the weasel. The weasel gives the mouse good advice, and when this is ignored the mouse is caught in a trap. The parables are illustrated in manuscript and printed versions of *Mashal La Kadmoni*, sometimes accompanied by rhyming couplets. Translated, these read:

> Here Mouse and Weasel together are met,
> And by their side the trap is set.

and

Here Mouse is snared, by greed you see:
But Weasel goes his way, still free.

Though the parables and couplets remain fairly constant, the illustrations in successive editions of the work clearly reflect the mechanical variations in traps over a period of some 200 years. The earliest examples, both dated about AD 1450, appear in manuscripts in the Bodleian Library; but the sources of origin, Germany and Italy, probably account for the difference in form. One of the German versions, Fig 5, thought to be made of some metal, gives the impres-

עיך דריוד יא ויעyvמ: מ:לקְ מ-ֿ דרדרY אי -ֿ ראYדYﬞ -ֿ יי יבֿ ד7ﬞ77

Fig 5   German steel trap, from manuscript of *Mashal La Kadmoni*, in the Bodleian Library, Oxford

sion of a steel or gin trap, and certainly appears to utilise some form of spring mechanism. Although the illustrations for this work are invariably crude, in this example the weasel is easily identified by its long neck and short, rounded ears. The two Italian versions, Fig 6, are live cage traps almost identical with Victorian-type mouse traps used in Britain. The body of the trap is a cage, at one end of which there is a trapdoor connected by a cord to one end of a release lever. The other end of the lever carries a hook which, in setting the trap, is attached to a bait rod inside the cage. With the hooked end of the lever held to the bait rod, the door is kept open, but movement of the bait rod by a mouse releases the lever and the weight of the door is sufficient for it to fall into place and seal the entrance. It is interesting to note that even in the fifteenth century the favoured bait for mice, if the illustration is interpreted correctly, was cheese.

Fig 6   Italian cage mouse traps, from manuscript of
Mashal La Kadmoni, in the Bodleian Library, Oxford

The other German trap is from the Bodleian manuscript of 1450, and two others in illustrations from a version in Staats- und Universitaetbibliothek, Munich, appear in Fig 7. These are all familiar deadfall traps, the Munich examples indicating a 'before and after' sequence. A more cumbersome type of deadfall trap is illustrated in a version of 'The Ancient Parable' dated 1493 and housed in the Bibliotheca Ambrosiana, Milan. Although this work was published in Northern Italy, the scribe responsible was thought to have been German. A version of 1693 was produced at Frankfurt-on-Oder and

Fig 7   Two deadfall mouse traps from a manuscript of *Mashal La Kadmoni*,
in Staats-und Universitaetbibliothek, Munich

the illustrations, from more modern woodcuts, showed a barrel
deadfall type of trap, but dome-shaped rather than rectangular.

A further source of illustration, also fifteenth century, is provided
by the St Joseph panel of the 'Mérode Altarpiece' triptych. This
painting, now in the collection of the Metropolitan Museum of Art,
New York, is attributed to the Master of Flémalle and dated *circa*
1430. It caused a considerable amount of controversy during the
last century, largely centred on the objects seen on the window
shutter of St Joseph's workshop, on the centre of his workbench and
being worked in his hand.

Roth mentions this painting in his compilation, and implies that
the objects on the shutter and on the bench are the same kind of
thing. A detailed examination shows that that on the window shutter
is unquestionably a deadfall trap of a double-pillar type, ie, the
weight, formed by a slightly-domed block of wood, slides down the
two pillars when the peg attaching it by string is released by a mouse
after bait. So, since wares are said to have been displayed for sale on
the shutters of Flemish shops of the period, it would seem that one at
least of St Joseph's skills was the production of mouse traps.

The object on the bench, however, though superficially appearing
like that on the shutter (it has a double-pillared structure), is a trap
of a different kind. Irving L. Zupnick, writing in the *Burlington
Magazine*, refuted any suggestion that it was a trap and went to great
length and much erroneous argument in explaining it away as a carpenter's plane. However, John Jacob, then at the Walker Art Gallery,
Liverpool, replied shortly afterwards with an account of a facsimile
made by one of his technicians. The reproduction was put to work in
the gallery and proved conclusively that it could catch mice. This
twentieth-century copy of a fifteenth-century Flemish trap was
exhibited recently at the National Museum of Wales, Cardiff.

Although it did not repeat its Liverpool success, there was no doubt of its potential when used somewhere other than in a sealed display case. Basically the trap, Fig 8, consists of a hollow trough from which the pillars arise. Between the pillars is stretched a twisted cord and this is wound to tension by a piece of wood inserted through a loop of the twist. This same piece of wood serves as a spring under tension from the cord and applies pressure to a pivoted board in the base. One end of the board is raised by a catch and a nail underneath holds the bait. A mouse entering for the bait will agitate the catch and release the pivoted board.

Fig 8   Facsimile of Mérode mouse trap, made at the
Walker Art Gallery, Liverpool

The third trap has not hitherto been adequately explained, so far as is known. It has been considered that St Joseph might be drilling holes in a piece of wood prior to constructing a cage trap, but in this event the holes would hardly be as extensive as they are. Another suggestion has been that a spike block, as used to torment Christ, is being prepared. Yet a third interpretation would have it that, with dowels in the holes, the object could be used as a maze into which a mouse could be lured—a fanciful if rather impracticable idea. The most likely identification is that the drilled board is a bug trap. The factual basis for this is a series of bug traps (picture, p 33), from

Poona, India, now in the collection of the Anthropological Museum, Aberdeen. These traps are placed near to beds in the hope that the artificial cavities will be utilised by bugs instead of the more generally favoured wall cracks.

A final comment from the Middle Ages confirms the trust placed in contemporary mouse traps, but suggests that efficient rat traps were either unknown or considered less effective than poison. This is revealed in Thomas Tusser's *Five Hundred Pointes of Good Husbandrie*, 1580, where the section for 'Huswiferie' in dealing with the 'Dairie' has this to say:

> In dairies no cat,
> Laie bane for a rat.

> Though cat (a good mouser) doth dwell in a house,
> yet ever in dairie have trap for a mouse.

The interpretation of 'bane' follows from the final couplet:

> Take heede how thou laiest the bane for the rats,
> for poisoning servant, thy selfe and thy brats.

The New World

While people in Europe at the end of the fifteenth century were concentrating on their mouse traps, Columbus was discovering America. There the North American Indians had developed a culture particularly suited to the country in which they lived, and one which was to serve as a model for the white settlers to follow.

The first Europeans to visit American shores, before the officially recognised discovery by Columbus in 1492, reported the use of furs and feathers as wearing apparel by the native inhabitants; not that the clothing covered the Indians' bodies extensively, but at least the articles designed and tailored by the squaws made for comfort. It seems likely that the Indians had been hunting and trapping furbearers for many years before their country was visited by Europeans; also they had exchanged pelts with each other in a form of internal trade. They were good judges of furs, but not of their value in European terms. The early white traders depended for many years upon the experience of the Indians, indeed the establishment and maintenance at all of a fur trade was probably due to the efforts by the Indians to find goods which would interest the visitors.

The questionable aspect of this new trade was the rate of exchange established. Without any doubt, the Indian was excessively exploited by the first European traders, who gave him no hint of the real commercial value of the skins brought for exchange. The payment proffered was seldom more than a few glass trinkets for bales of valuable furs. Mostly Dutchmen, the traders who founded Nieu Amsterdam, later to become New York, had had a long history of dealing with aboriginal people and had never shown signs of being conscience-stricken by the grossly unfair terms they offered in trading with them.

Within two hundred years colonisation was sufficiently advanced to make it profitable for the settlers' trading activities to be harnessed to a parent controlling company. As the result of an expedition led by de Chamberlain in 1608, a fur-trading post had been set up at Montreal under French direction, and when the Hudson Bay Company came into being in 1670 its stimulating effect on the fur trade was to have a profound influence on the future use of, and interest in, traps throughout the North American continent.

In the early days of the company's activity the traps used by fur traders were of various kinds, some being based on traditional principles but devised from materials conveniently to hand. The trapping skills already used by the indigenous peoples of the American continent, particularly those of the Indians and Eskimoes, were copied by many of the white trappers. At first, the skill of the white trappers lagged far behind that of the Indians, but by about the middle of the eighteenth century they had become equally efficient. Typical of Indian traps copied by the white men was the log deadfall. This consisted of one log held over another by a baited trigger and was used for larger animals. A similar device, but employing ice blocks in place of logs, was used by Eskimoes. Noose traps were also popular during the early eighteenth century. Some of these were automatic, being triggered by release of a bent sapling supporting a snare when a salted trigger string was chewed through. The spring noose using a sapling was particularly valuable as the prey was carried aloft into the air and so protected from ground scavengers likely to rob the traps.

The Indians used net traps into which game were driven. The nets were made of sticks, to which interwoven vines were fastened before string and wire became available from settlers.

Iron Trap Development

Meanwhile, in Britain, iron traps had been developing. Just how far back in history we would have to travel to find a hint of their origin is uncertain, but it is possible that the Iron Age men first began to make iron traps. Not until the sixteenth century do we find documentary evidence of their existence and then the elaborate design suggests that it was no prototype, but the descendant of a long line of less sophisticated models.

This first evidence comes from Mascall's book, which was published in 1590. Here he describes a variety of traps and the one shown in Fig 9 he described as 'The griping trappe made all of yrne, the lowest barre, and the ring or hoope with two clickets'. It is obvious that it was a double flat-springed trap of the kind now referred to as a gin, or steel trap.

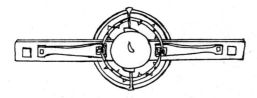

Fig 9   Mascall's iron trap (sixteenth century)

Carl P. Russell mentions a trap he examined at the Natural History Museum in Salzburg, Austria, which, according to members of the staff of that institution, was invented and used by fur-hunting Austrians in the seventeenth century. It was of a type which apparently persisted, for the design is similar to that on which C. Steiner & Schider of Salzburg were basing the traps they manufactured before World War II. Unfortunately, the original was lost with the rest of the museum contents as a result of bombing during the war. Fig 10 shows the form of this old trap, which was known as a jump trap, from the action of the central spring mounted within the jaws (when they are opened).

It is thought that the early British and French colonists arriving in North America could have taken traps with them, probably as a safeguard against pests. No doubt they would have included some of these early forms of iron traps, which later would provide the basis upon which future blacksmiths could make replacements and additions.

Page 51 (*left*) Combined
fall-trap and decoy bird
cage trap, as used by the
Chokwe people of north-
west Zambia; (*below*) a
sparrow net trap

Page 52 A goshawk trap: (*above*) dove is placed in cage as decoy; (*below*) hawk comes to trap and releases dove

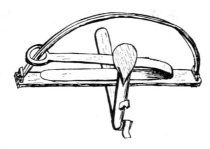

Fig 10　Seventeenth-century Austrian jump trap

Some of the early fur trappers, before the days of organised industry, would no doubt have used iron traps, and probably engaged local smiths to produce replicas of their favourites. Many examples based upon the English rat trap or gin trap have been unearthed from trappers' caches.

When trapping as an industry first became established, steel traps were imported, but later they were manufactured in North America and initiated what was to become a prominent commercial venture, especially in the United States.

The North American Trapping Industry
The trapping industry was widespread in North America. From north to south, the range was from the British possessions in Canada to below the Rio Grande in the Spanish Mexican provinces. From east to west, the area covered was from the Great Plains, east of the Rocky Mountains, to the Pacific coast. In opening up the country, the trappers pioneered routeways and preceded missionaries, gold miners and cattlemen. The geography learned by these explorers laid a foundation upon which future development could take place—many of the early fur-trappers' routes have since become national highways.

It might be wondered what kind of men these trappers were, and a good description has been given by Rufus Sage, who knew them at first-hand. He describes them as being dark-skinned from exposure, with features rough-cast and hardy. Their hair was long and coarse and often bushy, worn down to the shoulders and usually surmounted by a low-crowned woollen hat. All clothing was made by the trapper from raw materials acquired during the trapping season.

The main outer clothes were invariably of buckskin, fringed at the edges and seams with buckskin strings. Footwear consisted of deer or buffalo skin boots giving hard and durable service. The belt worn around the middle was an important item as it carried such vital necessities as butcher-knives and pistols. A bullet pouch hung from the neck and transversely across the body was worn a strap carrying powder horn, bullet mould, ball screw, wiper and awl. The man would carry a hardwood gunstick and rifle taking thirty-five balls to the pound.

Trappers were either 'company men' or *engagées*, employed chiefly by the Hudson Bay Company and later Revillon Frères, or 'freemen' (freelance trappers independent of the companies). The company men would work virtually for their bare existence, exchanging skins for essential provisions needed during the long season of isolation. The free trappers would control their own equipment, which might consist typically of a twin-lock gun, 100 flints, 25lb powder, 100lb lead, powder horn, double shot bag, skinning knife, tomahawk and four to six traps. The freemen often worked in groups to form a full-scale trapping expedition composed of fifty to a hundred men. Such an organisation could more easily attract capital investment and made possible closer operational control.

The 'season' varied according to locality. In the Rockies, it was chiefly during the spring and fall, but in some parts of the south and west, where there was less snow and ice, it would also extend into the winter period.

It was not unusual for a trapper to tramp a distance of fifty miles in the course of setting his traps. He would operate from a base camp, which served as a refuge during the winter to protect him against the hazards of climate, Indians and grizzly bears. If he lived in a community, he would also face the problems of quarrels with his fellows, not lightened by the frequent stresses of hunger, thirst, accidents and disease.

The life was certainly tough and demanding, with no luxuries. Except for scanty supplies of flour, tea, coffee and salt, the trappers lived off the country, with buffalo flesh as their favourite meat. An odd feature of this diet was that the trapper, once accustomed to buffalo meat, could not tolerate the flesh of other animals—a juicy ox-steak meant nothing to him. The rigours of the trapper's life during the pioneering period were intensified by the additional hardships endured in the course of opening up new country. In 1856,

Antoine Robidoux could account for only three survivors from a band of over three hundred which had entered the Rockies thirty years earlier.

When on the trap circuit, trappers would often hide away equipment and furs, borrowing the French word *cache* to describe these concealed stores. Much care was devoted to making the stores secure but, even so, they were frequently raided by Indians, or the contents damaged by floods. Up to 150 traps might be set on a 50-mile circuit. For small animals, steel traps would be used, but for larger ones a favourite was after the pattern of the English figure four, using logs.

The names of some of the first white trappers—men like Rogers and Kit Carson—have become almost legendary, but these pioneers eventually gave way to half-breeds, or *breeds*, who combined the white man's intelligence with the Indian's skill.

The Quarry of the Trappers

All kinds of animals were taken, but up to about 1845 one of the most eagerly sought was the beaver. A fashion in beaver-skin hats for men raised the price of pelts to between four and six dollars a pound, so that a good trapper could make $1,600 to $2,000 (£400–£500) a year, a very useful income in those days. The bottom fell out of the beaver-skin trade when silk importations and a new fashion for silk hats made beaver skins valueless.

Chittendon has given a detailed account of beaver trapping. He explains that the steel trap was in universal use and was highly effective in the hands of skilled hunters. Such a trap would weigh about 5lb, and during the early nineteenth century cost between twelve and sixteen dollars. The trap would be secured by a 5ft chain with a swivel to prevent kinking. At one time the steel jaws of the trap were covered with net to enclose the animal unharmed, as a live animal would provide a better skin than a long-dead one. In setting his traps, the trapper waded into the stream for some way in order to cover up his tracks, and the traps would be placed a little way from the bank in three to four inches of water. Each trap would be secured by stretching the chain to its full length and then fastening it to a strong stake driven into the stream bed, also a little way from the bank. A small twig was set immediately over the trap, projecting a few inches above the water surface, and the bait was fastened to the exposed end.

The bait was unusual in that it was procured from the same species of animal for which the traps were being set. It was beaver musk, known as castor or castorum, a granular, sticky substance costing about three dollars a pound, and possessed of an odour intensely attractive to beavers. An animal drawn by the scent would raise its mouth towards the bait and in so doing bring its feet directly under it. This would result in the feet treading upon the trap, so springing it and capturing the beaver. The instinctive reaction of a beaver in this situation is to dive down and conceal itself in deep water, but the restricting chain would prevent this and, after vainly trying to gnaw through it, the beaver would generally sink down, ultimately to drown. Even if the beaver succeeded in wresting the anchoring stake from the bottom, the reprieve would be short-lived, since the combined weight of trap, chain and stake would eventually exhaust the animal, which would then sink and drown.

Such was the demand for beaver skins that the species was almost made extinct by the time changing fashion decreed a respite from the ceaseless trapping that had gone on for many decades. Since then protective legislation has produced a great come-back and allowed beaver trapping—often as much a sport as an industry—to be undertaken today in some areas under controlled conditions. From time to time the beaver population explodes and trapping laws, which normally open the trapping season in mid-winter, are relaxed to allow trapping from the fall.

But when beaver were diminishing there were plenty of other kinds of animals to be trapped. The muskrat, which has provided many billions of pelts over the years, has never faced the threat of extinction as did the beaver. There are several reasons for this. First, the muskrat lives in swamps and although the development of farmland has driven out many fur-bearers, only the wholesale drainage of swamps is likely to endanger the muskrat's survival. Additionally, it is not a fussy feeder, and when one source of food fails it happily turns to another; also, being as contented in the water as it is on land, it never lacks a place in which to hide. Its greatest safeguard against extinction, however, is its ability to produce repeated litters of young—three to nine rats in a litter and three litters a year. To the trapper, ease of capture is always a strong recommendation and since he can expect twenty traps to yield twenty muskrats, the popularity of this animal for filling the odd day's trapping between more important work can be appreciated.

Another small animal hunted by the trapper was the skunk, and as an imitation of the sable its skin was of value, though only the Indian could tolerate the stench which polluted the air if the captured animal was handled too slowly. Finding a skunk in a pitfall, a white trapper would shoot it immediately, whereas an Indian, impervious to the smell, would take his time in order to secure a perfect pelt.

Like the muskrat and the skunk, raccoons would also be trapped during idle periods in the trapper's life. In the early days, 'coon skins had little commercial value, but in time their qualities became better appreciated and they were added to the professional trapper's list.

In the days before fur-farming became an established industry, a rarity highly-prized by trappers was the pelt of a mink. Living in swamps and rivers, mink have a weakness which can lead to their destruction—they cannot resist a fish, especially if it is for free. Knowing that mink were in the vicinity of a river, trappers would strew fish-heads around to induce false confidence and then follow with small fish-baited steel traps. But even though it may fall victim to a trap set by man, the mink is no mean exponent of self-defence and has been known to topple an attacking hawk with little apparent effort. The best time for trapping mink was between fall and Christmas, when the pelt was undergoing a colour change from red to russet; by the time a white carpet of snow had covered the ground, the mink's pelt had turned conspicuously to almost black.

Water is a favourite haunt for the trapper, for here he may find not only muskrat and mink, but also other fishers, such as otter and pekan. The pekan, or blackcat, like its smaller cousin the pine marten, can be distinguished from the true water dwellers by an absence of webbed feet. He is greedy and not at all fussy about his diet, being quite content to feed off the fish wreckage of an otter's hunt; although he hates the water as much as the otter relishes it. When opportunity lends itself, the blackcat will prey on any smaller creatures coming down to the water to drink, but because of his greed is himself an easy prey to the trapper, who needs nothing more than a snare or a deadfall to effect a catch.

Sometimes fur trappers would find a different kind of marten in their traps. Shorter than a pine marten and with bushier tail, the American sable has a pelt almost black compared with its cousin's coat, and is regarded as a rich prize.

Apart from the small fur-bearers, there were always the foxes.

Varying from one locality to another in North America, they might be red, black, silver or blue, but the fur trapper only really valued three, the black, the silver and the Arctic fox. To get the best pelts, he had to travel northwards into the polar ice regions, but if he secured first-class skins the financial reward was more than compensation for the privations he would suffer.

Of course there were also bearskins, but bear trapping has always been considered a hazardous occupation, often more a matter of necessity than desire. The professional trapper and hunter living in daily communion with nature has acquired a respect for Bruin which is not appreciated by the city man turned hunter and out for a day's sport in the company of professional guides. In California, bear-hunting during the middle nineteenth century was carried on for a variety of reasons, self-protection being high on the list. Bears were often trapped alive to be used for bear-and-bull fights, or even just for public exhibition. Bear steaks were regarded—and still are in some circles—as great delicacies, and the fat produced good oil when rendered. As the skins were prized as rugs and blankets, dead grizzlies were of considerable value and both wooden box and steel traps were employed to capture them.

The catch of a North American season was taken to fortified trading posts, where a system of barter prevailed. In 1825, however, General William H. Ashley introduced the 'rendezvous' system as a substitute for trading posts. This allowed for a change of site from year to year, no doubt in accordance with changes in the territory covered by the trappers. A 'rendezvous' resembled a medieval fair and this annual event, restricted to the Rocky Mountain area, frequently degenerated into a session of heavy drinking and general debauchery. Goods of all kinds were exchanged for skins, but the rate of exchange was such that the goods were often priced as much as 2,000 per cent above their cost. An item in great demand in exchange for skins, especially beaver skins, was a gun. The exchange rate was established as the number of skins which, piled up, would reach from stock to muzzle, a practice which led to the production of especially long-barrelled guns, popular in the Canadian North-West until well into this century.

A famous name associated with the fur trade was that of John Jacob Astor who, in 1808, started the American Fur Co, and so laid the foundations upon which the Astor millions were later built up. Many other private traders flourished throughout North America,

especially in the United States where, at one time, almost every bar-
tender in New York was said to be a skin merchant.

In Eastern Canada, centred around Quebec, trapping was mostly
in the hands of farmers. They were unskilled, both in technique and
skin evaluation, compared with professional trappers, but were none
the less extremely tenacious in striking a bargain and in demanding
best-quality skin prices for inferior pelts.

Furs and Fur Trading
The fur trade in the United States has dwindled considerably since
the beginning of the present century owing to changes in fashion and
the development of synthetic 'fur'. Yet there is still quite a thriving
industry and statistics for 1966 issued by the US Department of the
Interior show, for example, that during the previous season furs
throughout the country sold for a sum of $16,399,922, the values for
individual states varying between $3,720 in Connecticut and
$4,614,371 in Louisiana. It appeared that fur value was rising and
the average prices received by trappers over twenty-five states had
increased by 22·6 per cent in a year. True, there were variations, and
while bobcat, muskrat, otter, red fox, raccoon and coyote prices
were up, those for bassarisk (ring-tail cat) and civet cat (spotted
skunk) were down. Trappers obviously could not expect an even
return for particular kinds of skins, since in Idaho a lynx pelt could
fetch over $38.00 but it would only average just over $17.00 in
Montana.

A few figures for the catch of different species is revealing. The
muskrat was caught in greater numbers, by a wider margin, than any
other species; and the total for all but twelve states was 4,678,098.
Wolverine came at the bottom of the list, being taken only in Alaska
and Montana and amounting to 714 pelts. Beaver was caught in all
but eleven states; the highest number, 26,692, came from Michigan
out of a total of 185,461. After muskrat, the other giant catches were
for nutria and raccoon, 1,262,179 and 1,257,152 respectively. In
the case of nutria, 1,257,385 came from the state of Louisiana
alone.

From these figures it is obvious that the professional trapper in the
USA has to relate his anticipated catch to the state in which the best
yield is likely, though he has also to bear in mind the potential
variation in pelt value from one state to another. He may also be
influenced by the trapping legislation which, in the USA, can differ

from one state to the next. More details of this legislation will be given later.

Across the Bering Straits from North America, the Siberian fur trade had been flourishing for many years before Cabot had colonised Canada. The natives used many different devices for catching animals, some traditional but many particular to this region. The traps—snares, pitfalls and live-bait lures—were always hand-made, but the snare in various patterns was by far the most popular, being easily made from readily accessible raw materials and light enough to be carried in large numbers.

The animal most important to Siberian trappers was the Arctic fox. Before World War I, 20,000 skins a year were taken by dealers to Yakutsk and as many after the war were exported each year from the Chukchis districts. While the Arctic fox was taken with snares, or enticed by bait into pitfalls, its red cousin was too sly to be so easily deceived and could be taken readily only by shooting. Until one actually engages in the business of trapping, it is seldom appreciated how the intelligence of animals can vary remarkably between even quite closely related forms.

Farther west, up to the time of the Soviet revolution, there had been a considerable fur trade in Russia. After this period, mainly because of anti-capitalist feeling, dealing with American buyers ceased and the trade, together with the extensive trapping which supplied it, dwindled to extinction.

Elsewhere in Europe there was little organised trapping to supply the fur trade, so the commercial production of traps was directed more towards pest destruction and, especially for tropical markets, the capture of big game. In this field German manufacturers excelled before World War II, but a significant volume of production, especially of small traps, also came from France, Great Britain and Scandinavia.

An interesting speculation is how the currently popular spring breakback mouse and rat traps originated. There is no certain date of introduction, although available information suggests that they were not in use before 1850. From this time until the beginning of the present century the well established deadfall type of trap, and the equally favoured lever pattern, door release live trap, must have shared a market with the more modern breakback version. During the last fifty years the medieval-style traps have disappeared, except for those in the collections of museums and antiquarians.

Today, interest in traps and trapping is sufficiently widespread to give old traps an intrinsic value as collectable items, and sales of animal traps, especially in the veteran category, have been held from time to time even at such illustrious auction premises as those of Sotheby's in London.

CHAPTER TWO

Modern Manufacture of Traps

HISTORICALLY, a number of events combined to influence the large-scale commercial production of animal traps. Carpenters and blacksmiths made traps in small quantities, often as special orders, from before the Middle Ages. Some may have devised versions of their own and gained business through the reputation earned by their products, but trap-making was essentially a common task of husbandry so that mass production was unnecessary.

The industrial revolution created a new style of commerce. The installation of expensive machinery and the need to keep it in constant operation forced small iron and steel manufacturers to devise a variety of saleable lines. In a number of cases, following the patenting of more and more inventions created in a fever of industrial demand, new types of traps were produced as sidelines to more important items. A search for markets to absorb the new mass-produced traps from European factories resulted in sales to countries where the fur trade was at the peak of its prosperity and where time could no longer be spared to produce 'home-made' traps. On the North American continent, the early demand for the mass-produced article was met by imports but when, by the mid-nineteenth century, the demand increased, the development of their own iron and steel trade enabled Americans to start producing traps for themselves. From this period, in step with the ever-increasing importance of trapping in North America, many trap-manufacturing businesses sprang up, so that today the countries of this continent probably have more companies producing traps than any other single area of the world.

A current list compiled by the Bureau of Sport, Fisheries and Wildlife, a section of the Fish and Wildlife Service of the US Department of the Interior, gives the names of fifteen manufacturers of live traps, three manufacturers of mole traps, three for pocket gophers, four for rats and mice, three for snares and three for steel traps—all in the United States.

The Sewell Newhouse Trap

One of the early American companies founded to supply traps for the fur trade was that known as the Oneida Community, Limited. However, this anticipates a little, for the success of this company was based upon the expertise in trap construction developed by a Mr Sewell Newhouse.

In 1820, when Sewell Newhouse was fourteen years of age, he went with his family to Oneida County in the state of New York. Although not a newly colonised area, this central region of the state retained some features of frontier settlement. The Erie Canal was building, but travel was mainly by stage coach along ill-constructed tracks. In the forest-clad basin of Lake Oneida some of the larger game animals still abounded. There were deer and bears, packs of wolves roamed about, and small fur-bearers were common around streams noted for salmon. Several thousand Iroquois Indians, inhabiting reserves in this and neighbouring counties, lived a primitive life as close to nature as had their forbears.

Young Newhouse helped on the family farm, but found plenty of opportunity to indulge his passion for exploring the backwoods. In the way common to those who live side-by-side with wildlife, he became expert in tracking and developed the extra-sensory powers which make a good hunter. His need for efficient traps could not be met by purchase, for the farm was remote from sources of supply, so the boy had to devise some for himself. At the age of seventeen, with more experience in handling metals, he was able to produce up to fifty in a season, using a blacksmith's shop to fashion the iron parts and learning, from a chance meeting with a mechanic, how to temper springs made from worn-out axe blades. Though crude at first, his traps did catch animals and his esteem spread to his Indian neighbours, who were·happy to purchase traps, after a season's use, at 62 cents apiece. The proceeds from these sales provided new material for further traps and so, in a limited manner, the production of 'Newhouse traps' was under way.

Working on his own, or occasionally with hired labour, Newhouse manufactured traps in this fashion for the next twenty years. Production increased until he was able to turn out 2,000 traps a year, all to meet a local demand stimulated by his own reputation for successful trapping. This trapping was a seasonal relief from construction, and also gave him the opportunity to test new designs in the field.

As is usual with men of this type, Newhouse soon gained an almost legendary reputation for his feats as a woodsman, as well as being credited with outstanding athletic prowess, especially in running and wrestling. How much of this was fact and how much fantasy is difficult to establish, but one story relates how he tamed three big Indians, the worse for drink, when they attempted to force a quarrel upon him. In reality, though no doubt a strong man, Newhouse was known for his gentleness and was much respected by the Indians.

The key to the success of Newhouse traps was their faultless construction and certain action. He was far more concerned that they would catch animals than catch customers, so that while he sold as many as he could construct to the standards he set, it is unlikely that they would ever have gone into large-scale production had not a group calling itself the Oneida Community become established some two miles from his home. This was in 1848, and two years later Newhouse and his family became members of the group.

A few traps were made in the next year or two, but in 1855 there was a call from merchants in New York and Chicago, important centres in the now flourishing fur trade, for traps in large consignments. Sewell Newhouse and another member of the Community, J. H. Noyes, set about establishing a workshop capable of meeting the demand. Initially, there were only three hands and rather simple machines, but after a year a larger workshop was erected and more hands employed. Both Newhouse and Noyes, together with some of the machinists, devised new machinery so that eventually even the springs could be mass produced. Chain-making by machines was also developed and the production rate increased by leaps and bounds.

In 1867 the Community was able to publish statistics indicating that in the eight previous years they had manufactured three-quarters of a million traps, in eight sizes, ranging from a rat trap to a bear trap. By then, the labour force had increased to sixty at the busiest seasons and was processing 150 tons of American iron and steel annually.

As time went on the business expanded still further and new patterns and qualities of traps were introduced. Names such as

'Hawley & Norton', 'Victor' and 'Star' became associated with Newhouse traps and these are still household words not only in North America but in many other parts of the world as well.

The Community also did a certain amount of publishing, notably *The Trappers' Guide*, written by Newhouse himself and containing not only details of the traps manufactured, but also a wealth of information concerning the capture of animals, the treatment of their pelts for preservation, woodsmanship and a number of personal anecdotes.

Later, in response to a demand from ranch owners in the west, the Community introduced a special trap, their No 4½, for capturing wolves. To mark this they published a booklet, *How to Catch Wolves with the Newhouse Wolf Trap*, and this included a comprehensive methodology written by Ernest E. Thompson, government naturalist of Manitoba at the time.

All the traps produced by the Oneida Community were eventually manufactured by the American Trap Company in Pennsylvania. This subsequently became the Animal Trap Company of America, an associate company of the Woodstream Corporation of Lititz, Pennsylvania, which today appears to offer the greatest range of traps of any firm in the USA, including the still popular Newhouse and 'Victor' ranges.

The success established by the Oneida Community was forecast in this appendix to *The Trappers' Guide*:

> The influence of these little utensils, now so widely used, on the progress of settlement, civilisation and comfort, will occur to every observer. The first invaders of the wilderness must have other resources for immediate support than are offered by the cultivation of the soil. These are present in the valuable peltries of fur-bearing animals which are the occupants of the soil in advance of man. Hence the trap for securing them, going before the axe and the plow, forms the prow with which iron-clad civilisation is pushing back barbaric solitude, causing the bear and beaver to give way to the wheatfield, the library and the piano. Wisconsin might, not inappropriately, adopt the steel-trap into her coat of arms, and those other rising empires of the West —Kansas, Colorado, Nevada and Golden Idaho—have been in their germ and infancy suckled, not like juvenile Rome by a wolf, but by what future story will call the noted wolf-catchers of their times—the Oneida Community 'Newhouse Trap'.

If the Community had faith in its wolf trap, it had no less in its largest production, the No 6, or Great Bear Trap. This was rightly advertised not only as a weapon to combat bears, but also to catch tigers in India, lions in Africa and jaguars in South America. It did, in fact, enjoy international sales since its 16in jaws and springs each of 6lb weight were a match for all animals except, perhaps, the elephant. Even this beast was not immune, for though the makers did not claim that a No 6 would take it by the leg, they thought it might be taken by the trunk, and indeed this has occurred more than once. The justification for exposing animals to this kind of brutality is another matter, to be taken up later.

Fig 11   Newhouse wolf trap

The Colin Pullinger Trap

Though the export trade in British-made traps to fur-producing countries rapidly diminished, there was still a considerable manufacture of traps to catch vermin. Examination of British patent records from the middle of the nineteenth century reveals a remarkable devotion by inventors to designs for vermin traps, especially for catching rats and mice. Very few designs went beyond the patent application stage, but one which was successfully manufactured and proved highly effective was Colin Pullinger's perpetual mouse trap.

Pullinger, in common with many inventors of his time, was a jack-of-all-trades though, judging from the success of his mouse trap, it would be incorrect to say that he was master of none. A trade card issued by him *circa* 1860 tells us that he lived at Selsey, near Chichester in Sussex, and that he was self-styled as contractor, inventor, fisherman and mechanic. He listed his trades as builder, carpenter, joiner, sawyer, undertaker, turner, cooper, painter, glazier, wooden pump maker, paper-hanger, bell-hanger, sign-painter, boat-builder, clock-cleaner, lock repairer and key fitter, umbrella and parasol repairer, mender of china and glass, copying clerk, letter writer, accountant, teacher of navigation, grocer, baker, farmer, assessor and collector of taxes, surveyor, house agent, engineer, land measurer, assistant overseer, clerk at the parish vestry meetings, clerk to the Selsey police, and clerk to the Selsey Sparrow Club. Apparently he had also served at sea in the four quarters of the world as seaman, cook, steward, mate and navigator.

Selsey must have been much indebted to him, not only as a factotum without apparent equal, but as a genial employer. An item in the *West Sussex Gazette* for 2 January 1868 is headed 'The Annual Treat at the Patent Mousetrap Manufactory'. This reports a Christmas Eve party comprising fifty men, boys and friends enjoying traditional fare and more than usual rejoicing. The company apparently spoke highly of their employer and 'heartily and repeatedly cheered Mr Pullinger and his family'.

He also invented a rat trap and an improved mole trap, but these do not appear to have enjoyed the success of the repeating mouse traps, which, incidentally, he not only sold but also let out on hire.

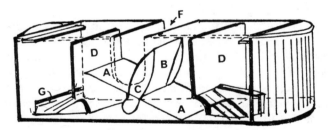

Fig 12   Pullinger's repeating mouse trap

The repeating mouse trap he invented is seen in Fig 12 and was known as a balance trap, from the action of the central pivoted lever. The trap is about 13in long with an end section 3¼in square. It is divided into three sections, a middle one 7½in long separating two end compartments by means of divisions D. Mice enter the trap through the aperture F, either at the sides or from on top. When set, the balance AA will be tilted down at one end and a mouse entering will step on the opposite end. Its weight causes the tilt to reverse and a vertical plate B above the lever, together with flanges C, prevents the mouse retracing its steps. The only way of reversing the procedure, while the mouse is on one side, would be for a heavier weight to press down on the other side. From the end of the middle compartment into which the mouse has been tilted there is, through partition D, a hole. This leads into a tunnel with wire bar roof sloping down towards the bars at the end of the compartment. The door is hinged to D and can be pushed up by a mouse attracted to bait in the end compartment. The door cannot be pushed up beyond the horizontal position owing to a restricting bar G (shown only on one side). Once the mouse has pushed through the door and this has dropped down again, the exit is cut off. The tunnel is too narrow to allow a first-caught mouse to escape when a second is entering. In the original trap, mice were removed via doors to one side of the floors of the end compartments.

When the patent for this trap expired, many imitations appear to have been marketed, but mostly these were inefficient compared with the original. An acceptable variation was made for a number of years by the firm of Duke, Waring, Crisp & Co, at their Soho wireworks, in London,

Other British Trap Makers

Another British firm founded in the second half of the nineteenth century was that of W. & G. Sidebotham. At their Graisley Works in Wednesfield, Staffordshire, they gained a reputation for manufacturing steel traps of high quality—the gin traps so popular among estate owners, keepers and farmers. As with Newhouse traps, those produced by Sidebotham's were of all sizes, since the firm catered not only for the home market but also for countries abroad, especially those in tropical regions which abounded in big game. Sidebotham's still manufacture traps but the gin is now illegal in England and Wales, and by 1973 will be illegal in Scotland for taking foxes and otters.

The firm of Gilbertson & Page was founded in 1873 and although it markets general merchandise in the interests of estate owners keeping game, traps have always been one of its specialities. The range produced includes cage traps for squirrels and birds, tunnel traps, mole traps and, since the Spring Traps Approval Order of 1957, the 'Juby' and 'Imbra' traps. The company also markets the Sawyer Vermin Trap manufactured by the Capjon Pressing Co of Wiltshire. These approved traps are regarded by the Ministry of

Agriculture, Fisheries and Food in Britain as humane killers, mainly for rabbits and ground vermin such as stoats, weasels, rats and squirrels. One other approved vermin trap is that made by A. Fenn of Redditch, an improved version of which, the Fenn Mk III, enjoys a fair amount of popularity with gamekeepers.

Another British trap-making firm, which has been established since 1895, is that of S. Young & Sons (Misterton) Ltd. Among the many goods their most intriguing catalogue offers to countrymen generally are a number of cage traps, of their own manufacture, for the live capture of fish, birds and mammals. This company also markets the traps of other manufacturers, together with such interesting sundries for trapping as trappers' sieves, trapping hammers, 'Young's Irresistible Bait' and 'Young's Fox Lure'.

The Verbail and Havahart Traps

In the United States, in the absence of Federal legislation outlawing steel traps as in Britain, manufacturers have not developed humane steel traps, but have relied upon cage live traps when humane capture has been necessary. There was, however, one interesting attempt to produce a humane steel trap by Vernon Bailey, well known as a former Chief Field Naturalist at the Department of Agriculture's Biological Survey Bureau and as a past president of the American Society of Mammalogists. Bailey was particularly concerned about the need for humane capture of animals and set about devising suitable traps after retiring from government service just before World War II.

The trap he invented was the Verbail Chain Loop Trap (Fig 13). In this trap, after springing, the pan is no longer required and drops from the bow, which holds the animal in the chain noose. The spring tension is not sufficient to injure an animal however much it pulls, yet it holds securely, and the more securely the more it is pulled. The safety factor is the bow string which absorbs the shock of any lurch by a captive animal, thus preventing a leg being broken or a stake uprooted.

The inventor and the firm marketing the trap, the former Animal Trap Company of America, claimed that unwanted animals, or furbearers not in prime condition, could be released without injury. Tests carried out by William Casto and Clifford C. Presnell were not so conclusively in favour of the trap for coyotes, as they found it less efficient and less humane than a steel trap.

Fig 13   Verbail chain loop trap

Another American live trap, the Havahart, comes from the All-cock Manufacturing Co which was founded over 130 years ago at Ossining, New York, a district better known for a human trap—Sing Sing gaol. Until just before World War II, the firm's production was almost exclusively devoted to laxative tablets. The war saw its resources applied to the construction of ammunition cases and bullet-proof fuel tanks for aircraft, and it was during this time that it employed as a sheet-metal worker an ex-patriot Bavarian, Rupert Merkle. In the 1930s Merkle had won an American Humane Society award for a box live trap and after the war he persuaded the Allcock company to manufacture a redesigned version of his prize-winning two-door trap, which was then called the Havahart trap. (Picture, p 85.) The family company, headed by Fox B. Connor, who has been a member of it for forty years, still makes laxatives, but 90 per cent of its business is now in traps, which net over half a million dollars a year.

The Havahart trap design is believed to be based on a seventeenth-century English version taken by gamekeepers to estates in Bavaria. The current version runs to seventeen models, ranging from one for mice to one for mountain lions.

CHAPTER THREE

The Traps of Nature

LONG before man roamed over the earth's surface, when lowly animals were supreme in their kingdom, Nature produced her own traps. Like all successful devices, these have persisted, and have a deadliness unmatched by any man-made trap. Many belong to plants, the first living colonisers of the earth.

Plants, like animals, need food to keep alive. Without the right kinds of foods they cannot grow, lack energy for even the simple movements they carry out, and cannot multiply. Most plants obtain their sustenance from soil, water and air and then carry out a chemical synthesis changing simple substances like carbon dioxide, water and mineral salts into plant body tissues.

Of the mineral salts which come from the soil, the most important to plant life are those containing nitrates, for without nitrogen no plant tissues could be made. Some soils, however, are deficient in nitrogenous salts, and in the rare places where this is so there can often be seen a curious alternative method by which plants obtain the nitrogen they need. Such plants, by adaptation of their leaves, have developed some extraordinary traps in which to capture small animals such as insects, spiders and perhaps slugs, and so obtain the nitrogen deficient in the soil but abundant in the animals' body tissues. This is the work of Nature, but contrary to her usual practice. Everywhere animals eat plants, and animals eat animals which have eaten plants, all to get, at first- or second-hand, the precious nitrogen sucked out of the soil. It is most unusual to find plants eating animals, but it does happen in these so-called carnivorous, or meat-eating plants.

Plants as Active Trappers

Members of this group of plants, unrelated except in the common activity of trapping animals, are found all over the world, but there

71

is one place in particular where all the different kinds can be found in abundance. This is in the area around Cape Fear, North Carolina, in the United States. Here is an area of 1,500 acres of savannah-like bogland—these plants are mostly found in boggy places—providing a flowering succession of animal-trapping plants from spring until autumn. It is renowned, however, for one in particular—the Venus' fly trap, exclusive to this coastal plain known as the Burgaw savannah.

When the United States was still a British colony, John Bartram sent the first sample of the Venus' fly trap to the mother-country. Botanists were astounded. Even Linnaeus, who had handled many thousands of plants during his life's work of classifying them, was amazed and described this one as 'a wonderful phenomenon'. Charles Darwin went further and called the fly trap 'the most wonderful plant on the earth'.

The wonder surrounding such plants inevitably attracted botanists from all over the world to North Carolina, and soon collectors with an eye to commercial exploitation were making serious inroads into the floral population. Today, it is by no means easy to find the plants unless one is accompanied by a local expert.

Despite its name, the fly trap is not exclusively tuned to catching flies. Like other trapping plants, it will capture anything small enough to penetrate its trapping device. Selectivity occurs only when digestion is necessary, and the plant's digestive juices, secreted from tiny glands in the leaf surface, will not flow in response to inanimate objects. The fly trap will catch a small pebble, but it will not attempt to digest it. The main food probably consists of small ground beetles and ants, but the spectacular seizure of a fly alighting on its trigger mechanism possibly accounts for its popular name.

The Venus' fly trap is a squat, green plant with a rosette of leaves spreading from three to six inches across. During the flowering season, aerial stalks raise the blooms above the prostrate plant, but always the terminal portions of the leaves, modified as traps, open and close to satisfy its nitrogen-hungry interior.

As seen in Fig 14, the basal part of each leaf is similar in shape to that of a primrose, but the upper surface is shiny and the edge has small spines. The modified outer third is the business part. The upper surface here has a rosy hue from countless glands and the spines are much longer. The midrib of the leaf acts as a hinge, so allowing for the necessary movement. Each half of the trap has three

Fig 14   Venus' fly trap: (a) the whole plant—note the glands on the trap
leaves; (b) detail of a trap leaf, showing a captive fly

stubby trigger hairs, and contact with these produces an electrical
stimulus which releases the moisture from turgid peripheral leaf cells.
This normally-present moisture resists the tension of woody tissue
in the midrib and keeps the leaf open, hence removal of water allows
the leaf to shut. The speed of closure varies with temperature, but in
bright hot sunlight a leaf can close tight shut from full open in one
second. This is a useful regulator, for the hotter the environment the
more active will be the insect prey.

Spines at the edges of the leaf trap enmesh to prevent an enclosed
insect from escaping, although the very tiniest are able to get out if
not immobilised speedily enough by the secreted juices. F. Morton
Jones, in a letter to Darwin, agreed with him that economy of effort
might be the reason for allowing small creatures to escape, and
thought that the size range of trapped insects could vary from the
maximum a leaf could hold down to a quarter of an inch.

The leaves are usually open at an angle of between forty and fifty
degrees, although they can extend to as much as eighty degrees.
Stimulation of the trigger hairs may take a little time; a single contact will not provide enough stimulus for closure, but once the
stimulation threshold has been reached, the leaf snaps shut. It
remains bowed for a while, but over a period of anything from half
an hour to twelve hours gradually flattens, squeezing out digestive
juices, as if from a stomach, first to immobilise the animal and then
to digest it. These juices have anaesthetising properties and a formic

acid content, which serves as a steriliser, prevents decay from occurring within the trap chamber.

Experiments have shown that if a piece of raw meat is so placed that
half is trapped within the leaf and half remains outside, that outside
will decay and become rotten while the portion inside remains fresh.
Similarly, a piece of rotten meat placed inside a leaf will lose its
odour.

The digestive juices dissolve every part of an insect except the hard
skeleton of chitin. When absorption of nutrient matter has taken
place and only the shell is left, pressure builds up in the peripheral
leaf cells again and the enmeshed hairs disengage. The leaf then
gradually opens, and the plant is ready for its next meal.

More widespread in both tropical and temperate climates are
plants of the butterwort family. Extracts from the leaves were used
as antiseptic salves by Alpine shepherds, and this ointment known
as a 'butter' gave the plant its name. These plants also have a low
habit, producing a central flower from within a prostrate rosette of
leaves. The upper surfaces of the leaves, like those of the fly trap, have
glands, concentrated at 25,000 to the square centimetre, which produce a sticky fluid and a digestive juice. Insects visiting these plants
soon adhere to the leaf surface, whereupon the leaf edges curl over
and roll the prey towards the centre. The flow of digestive juice com-
pletes the process, again leaving only the chitin.

The trio of actively trapping plants is completed by the sundew
family, of which over a hundred species are known, the greatest concentration in one area occurring in Australia. In the sundew, the
leaves have a different modification, since the terminal portion of
each is button-like, with up to 150 tinted tentacles over the surface.
The tentacles at the centre of the button are short and stubby while
those at the edge are long and hair-like. Each tentacle has a swollen
tip and from this exudes a drop of sticky fluid with the tenacity of
glue. It is the mass effect of these glistening droplets, like sun
shining on dew, which prompted the name by which the plants are
known.

When an insect alights on one or two of the bulbous-tipped tentacles, hairs close over the hapless creature and push it into the
centre of the button. More fluid is then ejected so that the stupefied
animal is eventually drowned in a pond of mucous. The length of
time taken for this to happen varies, but averages about fifteen
minutes. The trap of the sundew may then remain closed over its

victim for several days while the digestive juices play their macabre role.

Two factors stimulate the closure and trapping process—mechanical pressure and chemical sensitivity. A pressure of 1/70,000 grain will start the reaction, and Darwin discovered that 1/20,000,000 grain of phosphate solution would also serve as a stimulus. Neither one of these two stimuli alone is sufficient, since reaction to both chemical substance and pressure is essential. A pebble on its own will not cause stimulation, nor will distilled water, but milk or beef broth has an immediate effect, which suggests an ability to differentiate between edible and inedible substances.

Plants as Passive Trappers

In contrast to the actively trapping plants the pitcher plants are passive trappers. Whereas we can draw a comparison between fly traps, butterworts and sundews, and the snapping spring-motivated precision of steel traps, the pitcher plants, like the man-made pitfalls, just wait until a chance victim drops into their watery pools. Even then subsequent events appear submissive rather than aggressive, though the process ends with the animal losing to the plant just the same.

The pitcher plant trap is a trumpet-shaped leaf, formed by union of the outer edges. The trumpet edge is shiny and as slippery as an ice rink, so that inquisitive insects are doomed the moment they alight on the rim. And to make doubly sure, the inside of the pitcher is covered with recurved downward-facing spines, which frustrate any efforts an insect might make to retrace its ill-considered steps.

Among the different kinds of pitchers are various devices to ensure that the desired result is achieved. Two American pitchers, *Sarracenia minor* and *Darlingtonia californica*, have a structural design which prevents the escape of winged insects, such as flies or moths. Over the trumpet hangs a hood, in the centre of which there is a translucent spot. The upward-flying insect attempting to escape is attracted by the light penetrating the 'window', flies towards it and is knocked back. *Sarracenia minor* further ensures an adequate food supply by providing a trail of nectar to lead insects up the side of the tube on to the treacherous rim.

Insects are attracted by nectar and scent, and although these are normally associated with flowers they also occur in the modified leaves of pitchers. The pitchers are also often coloured, which serves as an additional attraction to insects.

The insides of the trumpet tubes are part-filled with a fluid containing anaesthetising elements said to be more powerful than novocain. There are also sterilising and digestive fractions as well. Presence of prey in the chamber stimulates the flow of fluid, and experiments have shown that raw meat. beef broth and milk will all accelerate this flow. But there is no response to cheese, milk casein or raw egg-white.

F. Morton Jones, working with J. S. Hepburn, discovered a relationship between amount of fluid flow, stimulant and length of exposure. Fragments of raw meat brought about a 15 per cent increase in the fluid volume in a pitcher. Beef broth, after stimulating for five days, was shown to have caused a 387 per cent increase in volume. Milk, after one day, had caused a 120 per cent increase, but after seven days the volume had increased by 1,242 per cent. Oddly enough, acids and alkalis have no effect on fluid flow, but, as in the stomachs of mammals, they are soon neutralised inside the pitcher.

The canopies mentioned as occurring over the trumpet heads of some pitchers will prevent overflow of the fluid content during heavy rain, However, in the sphagnum bog pitcher, *Sarracenia purpurea*, where there is no canopy, the fluid does overflow in rain but, nevertheless, the plant still flourishes along 2,000 miles of American coastline northwards from Florida.

There are some odd relationships between insects and pitchers. One might expect any six-legged arthropod to have an inbuilt warning system after millions of years of co-existence with plant traps. But nature does not work in this way. Seemingly, the reproductive rate of these insects more than compensates for losses so that, willy-nilly, the average insect is allowed to fall for the ruse every time. Even so, just as some men flirt with danger and yet manage to avoid it, some insects have found ways of benefiting from the presence of plant traps. Spiders have found it expedient to lurk near the traps, so getting their meals with less effort. An ant, *Cremostogaster pilosa*, is frequently caught in the pitcher traps and yet, given a dried-out and disused pitcher, will use it as a nest.

A carrion fly, *Sarcophaga sarracenia*—a singularly appropriate name—lays its eggs among the digesting insects inside a pitcher-tube. The young larvae, or grubs, hatching from the eggs are immune to the fluid and feed and grow on the decomposing insect matter. When the larvae are full grown they burrow their way through the side of the tube, drop to the ground and there pupate until, eventually, the adult fly emerges from the pupa.

Perhaps even more remarkable is the larva of a mosquito, *Wyeomyia smithii*, which spends its life in the pitcher fluid. Mosquito larvae do habitually remain in naturally occurring water, but the pitcher plant fluid is a long way removed from the neutral environment of a pond, and these larvae even manage to survive the freezing of the pitcher fluid in winter.

Edwin Way Teale, author of *North With the Spring*, thought that these insect-eating plants were almost animate in their sensitivity, and spoke of them as 'things apart from the stolid unconsciousness of ordinary plants around them'. Certainly they have collected together a cunning armoury, involving jaw-like leaves surrounded by a dental fringe of spines, mazes of spikes, leaves which close like a remote-controlled trap door, and adhesive surfaces a hundred times stronger, relatively, than man-made glues.

Spiders and Webs

If Nature has favoured some plants with equipment to catch animals, she has also provided most hunting animals with ample resources for capturing their prey. Claws and teeth are well recognised weapons, but we sometimes forget the efficiency of the spider's web, a superb trap as well as a marvel of engineering skill. Yet the whole process is the automatic product of a natural computerised spinning machine.

All spiders are carnivores, and hunt instinctively for their food, even to the extent of being cannibalistic. The main differences between them depend upon whether they track down their prey, or wait passively on, or by, a web. Our interest here is in the web-builders.

There have been attempts to show that different spinning achievements—tubes, sheets or orbs—have an evolutionary sequence. This has not been proven and it is not necessarily significant, since each device is effective in the context in which it is used. Any order of treatment used here is not meant to reflect progressive development.

Trapdoor spiders were first described in 1756 by Patrick Brown in his *Civil and Natural History of Jamaica*. Over a hundred years later, in 1873, J. T. Moggridge provided a more comprehensive analysis of the types of tube traps produced. He described four variations. The first was a straightforward cylindrical tube in the ground, lined with a tube-web and having a thin 'cork' door. The second was very similar to the first but possessed only a wafer-thin door. The third variation had a double door—a thin one at the surface and another part of the way down the tube. The final complication was a tube capped on the outside with a wafer door, but then, a short way down, a second tube ran obliquely to the first and also had a wafer trapdoor at the intersection. All of these traps, and even more complicated ones which have been discovered since Moggridge's description, belong to spiders in the Ctenizidae group, which includes the tarantulas.

Such traps are made by the spiders digging into the ground with their chelicerae, or jaws, which in these creatures have fringes of comb-like spines specially adapted for burrowing. The tube sides are sealed with a mixture of saliva and earth, which is also waterproof, the final stage consisting of the application of a layer of silk. The burrow is increased in size as the spider grows, and the trapdoor seals the entrance when necessary.

The trap is used both as a nest and as a hide for the spider. In the simplest type, where the tube is uncapped, the spider waits until an insect comes near the hole, then rushes up and drags it in. Where tubes have lids sealed on the outside, as in *Atypus affinis*, the only British representative of the group Mygalomorpha, the spider waits until a victim such as a woodlouse, worm or crawling insect moves over the tube surface. It then pushes up through the silk of the purse-web and pulls the prey through. This process, while giving the spider greater protection than an open burrow, does necessitate repair of the silk capping after each meal. The ultimate stage is provided by use of a hinged trapdoor. The stimulus to the spider is the same—movement of a creature over or near the door; in this instance, however, the spider pushes open the door, drags in the prey and allows the door to drop back into place. In some tropical trapdoor spider burrows, the door has two holes on the undersurface mud lining and these serve as grasping points for the spider to use in pushing it open.

More obviously apparent and certainly more universally occurring are the familiar spider webs stretched in various ways above ground. Some are found on the ground, a number occur among tall grasses, and others are suspended among bushes. The common cobweb is a familiar feature in the corners of rooms, across window frames and in door openings, and though these webs may appear superficially similar, they are, in fact, of four or five different kinds.

In all cases the silk is a natural product of the spider, produced from special glands and spun by devices called spinnerets. The structure of the web is specific to particular groups of spiders, each of which constructs its web according to a pattern laid down as a blueprint in the creature's nervous system. Instinctively, an individual will invariably build in a certain way, making little or no allowance for unusual situations. Silk is produced by all spiders, but not all use it in web construction. Some of the more primitive forms use it mainly for building protective cocoons for their eggs, or for making nests not intended to serve as traps but only as retreats.

It has been suggested that insects developed wings in order to escape from ground-hunting spiders, and that spiders, in turn, produced sheet and orb webs to trap insects in flight. There is no proof for this theory, but it is an interesting speculation, and certainly, except for the larvae of some of the caddis flies and the ant-lion, spiders are the only animals, apart from man, to have developed traps as a means of capturing prey.

A group of webs, known as calamistrated webs, shows an interesting development in web construction. These are webs formed from silk produced by special glands in cribellate spiders—the glands are referred to as cribellum glands and have perforated plates, in front of the spinnerets. From the glands, silk issues and is combed by rows of spines known as calamistra and found on the penultimate segments of the fourth pair of legs. The wavy adhesive band of silk, combed out, is overlaid on two strands of silk produced by the spinnerets, resulting in a fibre of great strength and extremely high adhesive properties.

Calamistrated silken webs are common household features. In Britain, spiders of the genus *Ciniflo* produce them as sheets in cellars, on gate posts and in wall crevices. The sheet is irregular, but has a hole, or retreat, for the spider to live in.

Those we call cobwebs are enlarged versions of calamistrated webs. The sheet is bigger, sometimes triangular in shape, but the apex is always curled up to form the spider's retreat tube. With a larger sheet there is a greater catch. The term 'cobweb' has been given a number of derivations. The 'cob' part has been suggested as an archaic term for head and the 'web' part as a term for trap, but exactly how the combination as 'head trap' is meant to be applied remains uncertain. A more likely derivation is an Anglo-Saxon and Flemish term 'kobbe' for spider and Anglo-Saxon 'wefan', or Old

English 'webb', meaning to weave. A free translation of a combination of these terms—'spider's network'—provides a more meaningful interpretation. The common house-spider in England, *Tegenaria domestica*, is a good example of a cobweb spider.

A non-calamistrated version of a tube and sheet web is found in another house-spider, *Agelena labyrinthica*, associated with out-of-doors situations in Britain. During June and July, when the spiders are immature, they produce webs on the ground. In the autumn, they move up into bushes and produce a web which has above it an additional tangle of threads. These seem to provide an extra facility for ensuring successful food capture, since insects flying into the aerial barrage of threads will drop into the web below, where the spider is waiting in the nearby tube.

The next stage in web development could have been a direct extension of the above double trap. It is a kind known as a hammock web, and the commonest exponents of this art of building are the spiders known as 'money-spiders'. These are members of the family Linyphiidae and are responsible in summer for fields full of shining silvery webs, covering small depressions in the ground. As the aerial thread tangle has been discarded, it might be thought that these spiders would find victims hard to come by, but this cannot be so as the group is the one most abundant in Britain. The answer, no doubt, is that the undergrowth of fields provides a large population of wandering ground-living creatures all too easily trapped in the gossamer sheets.

We come now to the webs which are admired most of all, both by observers uninitiated in the delicate manipulations responsible and experts who, though they understand the spider's skill, still marvel at the elaborate product of such a simple nervous control system. These are the orb webs.

Sometimes the orb web is referred to as a 'cartwheel' or 'geometric' web, and both descriptions are apt. To behold the shimmering silk creation of a garden spider in the early morning sun, whether naked, rimed with frost, or sparkling with thousands of adhering diamond dew-drops, is a joy to be remembered. No wonder that the work of these tiny creatures has inspired poets and saved kings.

Two spider families are involved in spinning orb webs, the Tetragnathidae and the Argiopidae. The commonest individual in Britain is the garden spider, *Araneus diadematus*, but other species are found all over the temperate and tropical areas of the world. Whereas many spiders responsible for other kinds of webs only repair and replace them casually from time to time, orb webs are built afresh every day, sometimes twice a day, and may well be repaired during the day as well.

The time taken to fashion an orb web is, on average, half an hour to an hour, and it can be spun at any time of day, although a particular species is usually consistent as to when the work is done. *Araneus diadematus* spins at dawn, whereas *A. sexpunctatus* works at sunset.

However intricate the web may appear, there is no conscious deliberation or consideration on the part of the spider. In attempting to explain the significance of this instinctive behaviour of spiders, Theodore H. Savory in his book *The Spider's Web* suggests that a conscious act would make allowances for variations in site and the web would be adapted accordingly. Likewise, consciousness of actions performed should allow for improvement in technique and economy of effort as time progresses, whereas spiders achieve none of these benefits of experience. Every web they spin is the result of the same set of actions, it takes the same time to complete, and if it has a varied form it is merely the result of limitations imposed by the environment. Nevertheless, automated though the spider's work may be, it remains a wonder of creation by any standards.

The form of an orb web is seen in the picture on p 33, and a diagrammatic representation of one-half of a web appears in Fig 15. From these, some of the fundamentals of construction may be grasped. First, it should be noted that a spider starting an orb web never utilises a ready-made framework. For instance, if a square wooden frame is provided in the laboratory, boundary threads are spun as a first stage and will adhere at suitable points to whatever structures are employed for attachment. The purpose of the boundary threads is to provide a flexible and elastic surface for resistance to pressures exerted by movements of spider and prey on the purposeful part. The remainder of the web consists of radii, linked to the boundary, and spiral threads interconnecting them.

There is a definite sequence of events. The first thread spun is the uppermost one, or bridge thread, which is fundamental in determining the ultimate form. From it two frame threads, one on each side, are produced, and there may or may not be a thread below corresponding with the bridge thread—some webs, for example, are triangular.

The radial spokes of the web wheel do not meet in the centre,

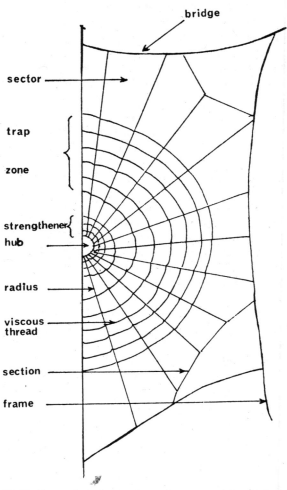

Fig 15   Half of an orb web, to show the construction (after Savory)

and a careful examination of any orb web will reveal that there is a hollow hub. The space between two radii is called a sector, and the sectors found in one part of the frame are called a section. The extent of the radii may vary and in some cases stop short of the boundary thread, from which a further bridging thread may stretch.

Spiral threads link the radii, and in the half section of Fig 15 it will be seen that these connecting threads form concentric rings, rather than spirals. Three to five turns form the central of three constructions of spiral threads and this is used as a strengthening region. The second spiral, not shown in the drawing, is built as a temporary platform, while the third or main spiral is being developed. As the main spiral threads are laid down, those of the second spiral are removed.

The third spiral, the most important part of the web, is described as a viscid spiral because it is formed from sticky threads to which adhesive droplets, from special aggregate glands, are attached. This is the trap zone. The spider usually retires to a hiding place, but is in contact with the hub by means of a signal thread which transmits any movement of the trap zone caused by a captured insect.

When the spider is in its retreat during the daytime one or two of its forelegs rest on the signal thread, but as night falls it will emerge and move towards the hub of the web. This alternation between centre and periphery of a web may also be related to age of the spider, its state of hunger and either the dryness or dampness of the atmosphere.

When an object comes into contact with the hub of the web, the reactions of the spider vary according to the nature of the stimuli. If an inanimate object falls on to the web—a petal or leaf for example —only a feeble and momentary stimulus will reach the spider, which will then pull on radii linking with the object, and detect its position according to weight resistance. Eventually the spider moves forward and approaches the object, feeling it when close enough with one of its forelegs. Inedible material trapped in the web will be cut out and allowed to fall. If the disturbance was caused by an object which subsequently fell through the web, or if it was caused by a puff of wind, the spider pulls on radii in different directions but, finding no weight resistance, retires to its retreat.

When a live object is trapped and struggles to free itself, it creates a series of vibrational stimuli which evoke a more rapid response by a spider. It turns to face the disturbance and then moves rapidly towards it, until it can touch the victim. The nature of most objects falling into a web is analysed by means of a 'taste-bite', and those which are inedible or do not stimulate taste are removed by cutting them free of entangling threads. However, if the object is distasteful, the spider appears distressed, moves to the edge of the web and 'spits' out the offending matter. If the taste investigation was by means of a leg, the spider's response is to clean the limb by passing it through its jaws.

Approved food captures are invariably moved from the capture point to the spider's lair, after first enshrouding the prey in a silken cocoon. Sometimes the prey is given a second bite, and it is then either carried in the mouth or attached by a thread to the spinneret and finally dragged away. The method chosen depends upon the weight of the insect captured. Experiments indicate that objects weighing around eighty grammes will be carried on a thread, and a hind leg may be used to provide additional support.

Caddis Flies

Mention has already been made of caddis flies as another group of animals which build their own traps. Not a true fly, the caddis is a winged insect belonging to a group known as the Trichoptera. They are listed under various names, such as sedges, silverhorns and Welshman's buttons, and are best known in the adult stage by anglers who imitate their form in artificial flies in order to lure fish. There are three groups which are active trap-builders, and these are species of *Hydropsyche*, *Philopotamus* and *Plectronemia*. Like spiders, these insects have silk glands, but these are located in a part of the jaw of the grub or larva. The larvae of caddis flies live in freshwater and most of them construct tubes to protect the unarmed parts of their bodies and either wait within for food material to come drifting through the water, or else move over plants upon which they also feed. In these tube-builders, a basic tube of silk is produced and on to this are sealed pieces of all kinds of matter imaginable, such as sand granules, leaves, leaf fragments, stalks, pieces of stick and even shells of small snails.

The trap-builders utilise their silk-producing ability to construct underwater web traps, not unlike those of some spiders, and these webs, or nets, are stretched between rocks or submerged vegetation. Nearby, the caddis larva has a tube, also made from silk, and waits inside it until the net has sieved off enough material from the flowing water to provide a meal. It will then emerge and skim off the captive and edible material. Such a trap can only be wholly effective in flowing water.

Young net-spinning larvae construct their first net soon after hatching from eggs. Thereafter, nets are made fairly regularly, as

Page 85 (*above*) The Havahart No 2 box-trap; (*below*) a Monmouthshire mole trap

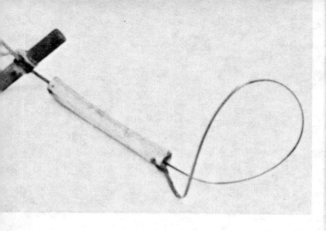

Page 86
(*above*) Eskimo squirrel snare; (*right*) a
guillotine-type mole trap; (*below*) string of
Burmese snares for jungle use

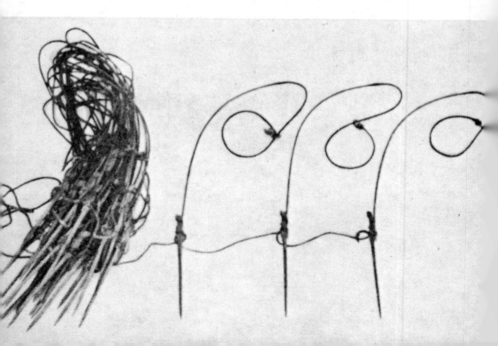

they are damaged or become too small to capture enough food for the rapidly growing grub.

The Ant-Lion Larva

The only other animal which produces a trap is the ant-lion, a neuropterous insect with the scientific name *Myrmeleon formicarius*, which lays its eggs in sandy areas suitable for digging by the larvae which will eventually hatch. The name 'ant-lion' belongs, strictly, to the larva only, and is derived from the combination of its chief characteristics—an appetite for ants and a ferocious appearance when on the attack.

The trap used by the ant-lion is a pitfall, and it is formed only at night (Fig 16). Construction starts with a circular outline traced in the sand to mark the boundary limits of the pit. Thereafter, the larva uses its head and mandibles (cutting jaws) as shovels, so that as it

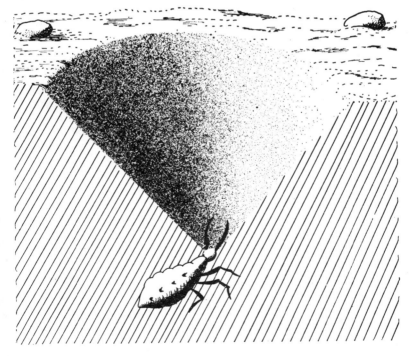

Fig 16   The pit of the ant-lion, *Myrmeleon formicarius*

backs away from the edge and throws sand out, a pit is gradually created. When the pit has been completed the larva buries itself in the bottom, leaving only a pair of mandibles, its chief armament, exposed.

Food capture occurs when ants, common in the areas where ant-lions are found, topple over the edge of the pit. The dislodged sand accelerates their precipitation towards the bottom, and the larva lends a hand by jerking away more sand with its head. Finally the victim is seized in the knife-like mandibles and held until all its juices have been sucked out.

The length of time spent by the ant-lion larva in its pit is uncertain, but in some instances it is thought that development towards the adult stage may take a year or two.

The pitfall trap of the ant-lion larva was, as we have seen, probably one of the first types of animal trap to be copied by primitive man and, living as he did so much closer to nature than his modern counterpart, it would have been surprising indeed had he failed to notice and copy some of the many examples of naturally occurring traps around him.

CHAPTER FOUR

Man-Made Insect Traps

COMBAT between man and his fellow animals can take many forms and occur for many different reasons. If the competition tests man's skill and provides an element of danger and adventure, it is regarded as sport. This may also render an incidental service in reducing pests, but should the pestilential level become too high to be thus indirectly controlled, direct organised action then becomes essential.

Within the world of insects there are many forms which, because they bring disease to man, destroy his food, or undermine the health of plants and animals under his care, must be regarded as pests. At this point insects become both enemies of man and victims of his concerted efforts to destroy them; even so, the battle is not one-sided and man's resources are frequently stretched to the limit. Traps of many kinds have been devised to aid man's struggle against insects, but whilst these can be effective measures for dealing with minor irritations, particularly on a domestic scale, when faced with an insect foe of large numerical strength man now places greater reliance upon chemical insecticides. For, dangerous though the side-effects of these may be, they are faster-acting and more efficient than any trap yet devised.

Apart from their limited use in pest control, traps are also used by those whose job it is to collect insects for research purposes, not to mention the legions of amateur collectors, some of whom later extend their range of interest and become qualified entomologists. For this purpose, especially when the insects are required alive, trapping can provide a convenient and even selective means of procuring them.

Methods of Trapping Insects
The methods employed depend upon three principles. The simplest method, but restricted to ground-living insects, is that of the pitfall trap, which may be baited or unbaited. The second method utilises a

bait of some sticky substance, while the third involves the use of light.

The sight of a moth circling round a lamp as if unable to tear itself away, naturally suggested that light possessed certain properties attractive to some insects. This theory, plausible though it may appear, was found to be untenable when, in 1950, two brothers called Robinson carried out comprehensive tests involving the relationship between insects and light. And because so-called light traps are important in the field of insect capture, it is worthwhile briefly considering the discoveries of the Robinsons and subsequent workers.

Insects and Light

It would appear that there are two properties of light which have significance in regulating the movements of insects in the vicinity of a source. One of these is the power of the source, which is usually expressed in units called lumens. The other, related to the first, is surface brightness, or the power per unit area of surface, expressed in lumens per sq cm. It follows that a light surface with a high surface brightness will be one of high power and low surface area.

The Robinsons found by experiment that an increase in the power of a light source could result in recovery of more insects, but only of the same species as recovered by a similar source of lower power. An increase in surface brightness, though not necessarily increasing the total number of insects caught, would result in a greater number of species being found. They also noted that insects would appear to fly towards a single light source in an otherwise dark area whereas, with multiple light sources, there was no precise directional movement by insects to any one source.

Part of the explanation given by the Robinsons suggests that, in relationship to insects, a light source produces two concentric field areas. The outermost is the range, expressed by its radius, within which insects are sensitive to it through their compound eyes. The innermost sphere (a sphere if the light source is high, but a hemisphere if the source is at ground level) is an area within which an insect will be deflected from its normal flight path—towards the light—and, according to the Robinsons, this is an area of dazzle.

Insect physiologists, such as Wigglesworth, have shown that insects, which have compound eyes containing many light sensitive facets, so direct their flight as to keep the light source in line with certain illuminated facets, ie, at a certain angle. The change of direction, or the deflection, which occurs closer to the light is made in order to maintain that angle between the light source and the facets.

The compound eye of an insect is a fascinating structure, because each behaves as if it were made up of a number of smaller eyes, hence the name. Seen under a microscope, the eye surface appears to be made up of a mosaic of regular circles or hexagons (circles when there are few and hexagons when there are many). Each unit of the mosaic is the facet to which reference has already been made, and it is produced backwards into the eye as a cone-like structure. Because each unit produces a separate image, the mass effect in one eye is a series of images which juxtapose to produce a mosaic picture rather like a newspaper photograph seen through a magnifying glass. Proof of this was provided eighty years ago by a German, Exner, who actually took a photograph using the eye of an insect.

The Robinsons' experiments showed that insects travelling through the outermost zone, and not entering the inner zone, would eventually pass out of the light's influence. They also showed that any apparent differences in behaviour between the sexes in response to light was related only to differences of flight activity, viz night-flying females and daylight-flying males of the same species.

It is well established that only insects belonging to the ecological area in which a light occurs will respond to it. For others the light source will not be an attracting force as the area has nothing to offer, ecologically, for insects which do not belong to it. Ecology is, of course, the study of the inter-relationship of animals and plants within a particular environmental situation. Generally speaking, a given combination of plants, animals and topographical area will constitute an ecosystem which will remain stable in terms of its inhabitants, although by no means static.

The spiral flight path which insects follow when approaching close to a light brings them down until, eventually, they seek a shadow area and settle to inactivity, as indeed happens in daylight with night-flying moths. So when the Robinsons set out to apply their theory of the relationship between light sources and insect movements to the design of a trap, they realised the importance of providing unavoidable shadow areas within the trap casing. And to this was due the apparent success of the Robinson trap, compared with the relative failure of earlier light traps.

'Sheeting'

The earliest use of a light source for capturing insects was known as 'sheeting', because the light was used in conjunction with a white sheet. In its simplest form, a sheet was laid on the ground and a light, such as a hurricane lamp, placed on top of it.

The advantages of sheeting are cheapness and portability; its disadvantage is the inconvenience of having to stand by all the time, otherwise insects which have crawled into shadow areas will then turn away from the light and fly out of its influence. It is also important that the sheet shall be so placed that insects approach it upwind and, when hung vertically, that a fold overlaps the surface of the ground, otherwise falling specimens will be difficult to distinguish.

Box Traps

When insect collectors tired of constantly watching a sheet, they sought a more effective trap and the idea of a box trap was probably suggested by seeing insects flying through open illuminated windows. The simplest box trap can be made by replacing the sixth side of any closed box with two overlapping sheets of glass, as in Fig 17. Any

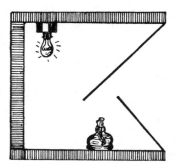

Fig 17   Insect box trap

kind of light source can be used, and an anaesthetising, or killing, mixture may be placed within to ensure capture of incoming insects. Unfortunately, this device has a number of disadvantages, for although it can be left unattended, at least overnight, its light source is unidirectional and it has, therefore, to be positioned in the most suitable direction for catching insects in a given area. And if the area is new to the collector, this direction may not be easy to assess. It also has the drawback that insects may well trample on one another and the more hardy ones, unaffected by a weakening killing bottle, can escape when daylight replaces the relative darkness of an artificial source.

In 1929 W. A. Hiestand described a moth trap which overcame some of the disadvantages of a conventional box trap. This construction (Fig 18) had the merit of a multi-directional light source and

Fig 18   Hiestand's insect trap

a funnel device into which falling insects would be overcome by fumes arising from the killing bottle below.

The Rothamsted Light Trap

A combination of the box trap and the Hiestand trap is found in the Rothamsted light trap devised by Dr C. B. Williams. The first versions were used by Williams in the Egyptian desert in 1923, and various subsequent modifications related mainly to the use of different light sources, such as an acetylene-vapour flame, a petrol-vapour flame and electric light bulbs.

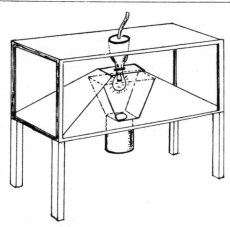

Fig 19   Williams' Rothamsted light trap

As seen in Fig 19, the basic construction is a wooden or metal floor and roof, each about 22½in square, kept apart by 12in metal rods at each corner. These have screwed ends and nuts above and below the boards keep them secured. The floor has a central 2in hole leading to a killing jar of the Kilner type. The roof has a central 4in hole over which the appropriate light source is suspended. The trap units are sheets of glass, eight in number. Four sheets form an outer truncate square pyramid reaching to within 2in of the roof. The remaining four make up an inner, smaller and inverted pyramid which acts as a funnel leading to the killing bottle. The traps in use at Rothamsted have employed 200W electric incandescent bulbs as light sources, and Williams favours tetrachlorethane in a plaster-of-Paris base for the killing bottles.

Entomologists at Rothamsted found these traps efficient and economical to run but, as with all the traps so far discussed, there were inevitably shadow cones into which insects could move and so escape the influence of the light source.

Mercury Vapour as Light Source
The Robinson brothers' trap was designed not only to overcome the the shadow-zone effect, but also to utilise a far more efficient light source. Their ideal was to discover a source of infinitely high power and infinitely low surface area, and their compromise was to use a continuous running discharge lamp with mercury vapour as the source

of ions. The principle of the mercury-vapour bulb is that the outer glass bulb contains an inner tube holding the mercury vapour and linked to a supply of electrical power. When the supply is switched on, it causes ionisation of the mercury atoms and, because few of these exist at first, the initial glow is dim. As the process is self-generative, the numbers of ions and hence the strength of current gradually build up and the lamp becomes brighter and brighter. In practice, a limit has to be applied to brightness level or the lamp would burn out, and this is achieved by using a choke in conjunction with the lamp. A special lampholder is also used to take the three-pinned bulbs—so made to prevent insertion in a normal socket.

The Robinsons found this lamp of great advantage compared with other light sources, when used in traps of the type already discussed. Their impressions were qualitative, but quantitative calibration of the respective merits of incandescent and mercury-vapour light sources were made by Bretherton during a period of years up to 1953. Though his experiments were not controlled with the scientific precision one could wish for, they did achieve results showing irrefutably that the MV lamp had more effect for most species of moths than other forms of illumination. Furthermore, when used in a Robinson trap the results were better still. There were species variations, but in some instances, eg amongst the Noctuae, use of an MV bulb in a window trap showed a threefold increase over the number of insects taken with an ordinary bulb, and when the MV bulb was used in a Robinson trap the increase leapt fourteen-fold.

The idea behind the Robinson trap was to harness the downward-spiralling path of insects moving towards a light source, and to achieve this the light source was set in such a way that its top would be level with the drum framing (Fig 20). From the light source, there radiate a number of vertical metal vanes, each so shaped as to produce a cone when all are in place. When spiralling around the lamp, insects will move downwards and eventually strike a vane, whereupon they will drop into the trap below.

Following Williams' lead, the Robinsons used tetrachlorethane released from an electrical evaporator as an anaesthetising source, but modern collectors generally prefer to provide material within the body of the trap to encourage natural settlement of the trapped insects. The most favoured material consists of broken sections of the papier mâché, or fibreboard, egg-packing sheets used by egg distributors.

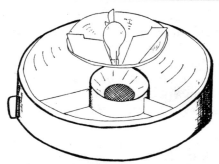

Fig 20   The Robinson light trap

Use of light traps, especially the MV Robinson types, has resulted in the capture of vast numbers of insects, which naturally raises the question of potential imperilment of species survival. Writing recently in *The Field*, Denzil Ffennell reported having taken 33,000 moths in a light trap during 1968. Of these, he had kept 250 for his own and other collections and released the remainder. He described how birds congregated near the trap when a haul was being sorted and, although rare catches were taken to safe places for release, he estimated that a third of the year's catch—all common ones—would go to the birds because it was not possible to release them in selected areas. Claiming to have done this for a number of years, he justified the harmlessness of the practice on the grounds that 50 per cent of a catch are males, that 50 per cent of females caught would have already bred, and that the total, anyway, would be but a small proportion of the number normally taken by predators. His one fear was that news of taking a rare species would be flashed around on the entomological bush telegraph and bring in many lamps to the area, thus making extinction of the species more likely. On the other hand, it was argued that by catching a number of a rare species and releasing them together, there might be a greater chance of their pairing and founding a new colony than under normal conditions.

However, because it was so easy to collect specimens with an MV lamp, Ffennell suggested that new collectors should not be allowed to use it until they had had time to learn sound basic field techniques. It is also worth noting here that moonlight has been shown to influence the effectiveness of light traps, since some insects, mosquitoes especially, are more attracted by moonlight, when this is coincident with light trapping, than the light source used in the trap.

The Hungerford Underwater Trap
Before leaving the subject of light traps, it is interesting to note that three Americans have described a version constructed for use under water. This is the Hungerford trap and it was devised to collect water beetles, water bugs and the larvae and nymphs of dragonflies and mayflies. The form of the trap is based on the box trap, but has to be adapted to maintain a working light underwater and prevent any silting-up of the trap entrance. The details of the trap are shown in Fig 21. Galvanised iron flue piping, about 21in in length, forms the

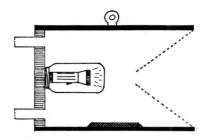

Fig 21　Hungerford underwater light trap

body of the trap. One end has a copper gauze funnel using gauze of 40 meshes to the inch; the opposite end has a wooden plug containing four short lengths of 1in pipe, the outer ends of which are covered with the same type of gauze as used in the funnel. To the centre of the plug is fastened the lid of a Kilner jar and this, in turn, has the screw end of an electric torch fastened to it. Within the body of the trap is placed a lead sinker and above this, on the outside, an eye for attaching an anchoring line.

In use, the torch is fixed inside the Kilner jar and switched on. The trap is then lowered into the water and anchored to a suitable buoy, the trap preferably being so balanced that the funnel end tips slightly upwards. When the trap is recovered, it is tipped on end to allow drainage through the 1in pipes and concentration of the catch.

The trap can only be left for a few hours during the night, as the batteries quickly become exhausted. The authors used a 6V car battery, the current being fed to a 6V bulb through an insulated cable, but the battery had to be recharged after ten hours' use, and battery decay was accelerated by continual re-charging over a short period. There is also some risk of current leakage, and shorting could produce a dangerous current of 50 amps. Under no conditions should a mains electrical supply ever be harnessed to a trap of this kind.

'Sugaring' and other Adhesive Traps

One of the oldest methods of capturing insects is by the technique known as 'sugaring'. This has been applied more specifically to the capture of night-flying moths, but has also proved useful for all types of insects at all times of the day. Essentially, a fermented sugar bait is painted on to suitable surfaces, the effectiveness of the trap depending upon the bait being attractive and sufficiently sticky to hold captive any insects coming into contact with it. The surfaces used can be natural ones, such as tree trunks or branches, fences and walls, although specially-made surfaces are favoured by some collectors, particularly in areas where suitable natural surfaces are scarce.

The formula for the sugar mixture varies from one collector to another and, usually, experimentation results in a mix which proves successful in the hands of a given individual and for the particular species being sought. In the *Handbook for Collectors* issued by the British Museum, a formula suggested employs 2lb sugar, 1lb treacle, half a pint of beer and a little rum. The mixture is boiled until it acquires the desired consistency and, with strict attention to culinary art, some collectors judge this by taste!

Armed with a satisfactory brew and a supply of suitable surfaces— pieces of cork, hardboard or wood—the collector lays a trail of sugared patches in the area to be investigated. A circular route allows for periodic round trips of inspection. Insects to be collected are removed, preferably with a special aspirator, and stored for a day before killing. This is to allow exudation of undigested sugar solution, which, if allowed to remain in a freshly-killed insect, will spoil the specimen from a collection point of view. Care should also be taken to ensure that the sugar patches are so placed that vapours of fermentation are carried downwind.

One can, of course, discover naturally occurring sugaring patches, and sap oozing from tree trunks and branches will often be found to attract and trap insects. Similarly, water holes in damaged trees may contain decomposed substances which attract insects, and inspection of such natural traps will often reveal species to be found in no other way.

The use of sticky devices of all kinds has been exploited commercially, mainly for dealing with insect pests. The sticky fly-paper was a familiar sight in shops and domestic premises before DDT and other chemical insecticides came into general use, and fruit growers sticky-banded their fruit trees to trap insects climbing up the trunks. A home-made version can be devised by painting strips of paper with a mixture of heated spruce gum and linseed oil. In areas where fleas abound, particularly in tropical countries, protection from their attentions when in bed can be achieved by placing sticky paper on the floor round the bed.

Home-made Traps
Cracks in floorboards and walls are common sites for many insect pests such as fleas, bed-bugs and cockroaches, and various home-made traps have been devised to counter the attacks of these insects. Standing bed-legs in tins of oil is one method of preventing bugs from climbing up to the bed, and the provision of portable shelters for insects seeking seclusion, either during periods of inactivity or at certain stages of their life history, has been frequently utilised as a means of trapping them.

S. N. A. Jacobs, editor of *The Entomologist's Record*, has told the author of a trapping device he used during World War II to capture the larvae of *Ephestia elutella* in grain stores, where the insect was a pest. It consisted of strips of corrugated cardboard, 3in wide, fastened with pins at a distance of 1ft below the ceilings. The trap was operated in September, at a time when the larvae were due to go into diapause, a period of arrested development in some insect life cycles at the onset of a cold season, akin in some respects to hibernation. When this stage is reached with *Ephestia* larvae, they cease feeding and climb walls in search of suitable hiding places, for which purpose the corrugated card was obviously ideal. After migration had ceased, the strips could be removed and destroyed.

Pitfall Traps for Insects
Pitfall traps for insects follow a similar pattern to most others of

this type. They are designed to take ground-moving insects, such as beetles, various bugs, earwigs, cockroaches, crickets and grass-hoppers, and can consist of any suitable container sunk into the ground to rim level. Glass jars are preferable as they do not suffer deterioration from exposure and have slippery inner surfaces which defeat attempts by insects to escape by crawling out.

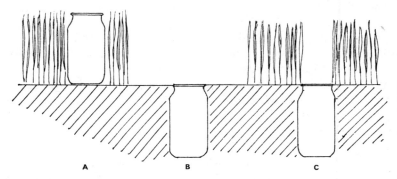

Fig 22   Greenslade's experiment in the use of pitfall traps for insects

In an attempt to discover the best method of siting a pitfall trap, Greenslade placed his jam-jar traps in three different positions. The first (A) was on the surface with the rim coming close to the top of the herbage ground cover. The other two traps were both sunk in the ground so that the rim was at ground surface level. The difference was that in one case (B) the herbage was cleared down to ground level all round the trap, while in the other (C) it was left high around the trap. Results showed that traps sited as in (A) had a low catch, trapping only insects habitually moving over the herbage. Traps sited as in (B) had the best catch, being less fouled with debris than in trap sites of the (C) type.

The trap may be baited or unbaited, but a suitable bait, provided it is not left indefinitely and is appropriate for the species sought, will encourage more visitors. Baits can be divided into two main cate-gories, those intended for insects such as carrion and dung beetles, and those for seekers of nectar and fruit juices. Apart from natural material, there are a number of synthetic artificials which sometimes have even higher volatility than the naturals. Many baits, such as stale beer for domestic flies, have been handed down through centuries of usage. Molasses, or sugar syrup, has long been a favourite for cockroaches, and Beirne, with reference to Canadian and American species, has suggested the addition of fusel oil to diluted molasses.

Pitfall traps should always be covered to prevent the trap filling during rain and to discourage the attentions of insectivorous creatures such as frogs, toads and lizards. A heavy piece of wood or stone supported over the mouth serves very well for this purpose.

With some baits used in pitfall and other traps there is a progressive process of decay which attracts different species at different stages. One can, therefore, expect to find a succession of captive insects, and frequent visits to such traps are essential.

Wire Cage Traps
In addition to pitfall traps, various types of wire-cage traps have been produced for taking insects. The principle upon which they work is attraction to bait in a shallow container, with the cage above preventing escape by upward flight, the normal reaction after feeding.

One such trap which makes use of this instinctive escape reaction of insects has been devised by Dr René Malaise of Stockholm. Known as the Malaise trap, its design is similar to that of a large tent and it relies upon the tendency of insects to find their way into a tent, particularly in the early evening, and to spend daylight hours climbing the inside of the walls trying to get out. In some respects, this method also involves elements of light-trapping.

The trap is constructed (Fig 23) of fine-mesh netting (mosquito-

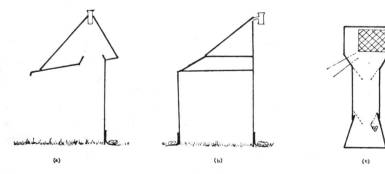

(a)   (b)   (c)

Fig 23   The Malaise trap

netting would be ideal) of any colour. The more recent versions built by Malaise have had an opening 12ft high and 6ft wide on one of the four sides of the lower compartment. Above this is a conical compartment with a baffle funnel leading to a killing bottle at one corner.

The killing bottle (c) was specially made by Malaise to fit on to a brass tube so inserted as to project out of the terminal tip of the trap. The bottle consists of three sections screwing one on to another. The top and middle sections each have a funnel extension dipping into the compartment below. An ethyl-acetate evaporator hangs from the lower funnel.

Insects in the tent move towards the off-centre apex and then into the killing bottle, heading towards the light penetrating the grille of the upper section. Slightly anaesthetised, they fall into the middle compartment where complete anaesthetisation follows. When they fall into the lower chamber in moist climates, they can remain in a relaxed and protected state for up to a week.

The siting of the trap, as with box-light traps, is important. The opening should face downwind to provide for upwind-flying insects, or a double tent may be used—comprising two separate lower compartments with openings facing different directions but linked to a common upper section—in order to accommodate wind directional changes if a trap is to be left for a long period.

For the most part, the Malaise trap is non-selective and its success depends largely upon standing it in the path of flying or crawling insects. It should, therefore, be placed in an area where insects are likely to abound, and suitable places for general collecting would be near to hedgerows, patches of water, areas of tall grass, edges of woodland, and on pathways between clumps of highly scented or otherwise attractive flowers.

Radiant-Energy Traps

Radiant-energy traps have also been designed to destroy irritating night-flying insects, and would be most useful in warm climates where this particular pest problem is a very real one. These traps, available in the United States, make use of battery-powered units which generate black heat and propel a fan. Below the fan and heat unit is a reservoir of detergent water into which the insects, attracted by the heat, are propelled by the fan and there drowned. Small units operate indoors, but larger ones are made for use on patios or near to swimming pools.

Page 103 (*above*) The Duffus mole trap showing left side set and right released; (*below*) a wooden full-barrel mole trap

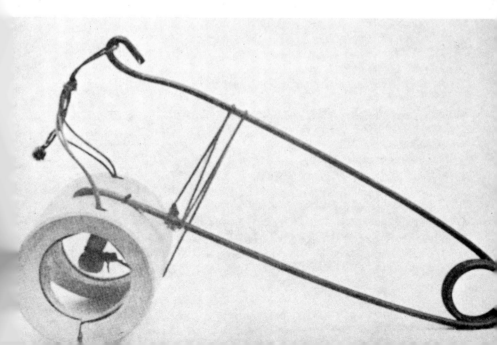

Page 104　(*above*) A single-hole guillotine mouse trap; (*below*) a three-hole spring-loop mouse trap

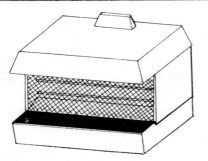

Fig 24   A radiant-energy trap

The Formalin Fly Trap

Before World War II, the British Museum (Natural History) recommended the formalin fly trap. This consisted of a bottle with a narrow neck filled with a solution of formalin, made up from half a pint of lime water, a teaspoonful of formalin and a dessertspoonful of sugar, topped up to one pint with water. A circular piece of blotting paper was placed on the open neck and two blotting-paper wicks were dipped inside. Rooms in which a trap of this type is used should not be occupied, as the fumes can be noxious.

In recent years some work has been carried out to find ways of

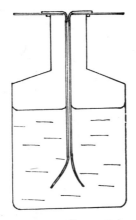

Fig 25   A formalin fly trap

trapping mosquitoes, mainly with the object of sampling populations for medical research purposes. A number of traps, not so far described, have been employed, the pioneering work having mainly been undertaken in North America, and an interesting series of traps was designed by Johnson and Taylor (1950–5) which depend upon the suction force of an extractor fan. These comprise a horizontally-mounted electric fan which draws air through a fine mesh cone and into a cylindrical magazine mounted at the base. The apparent value of such a trap is its facility for collecting unbiased samples of insects flying in the air above. In the case of mosquitoes, the best results have been achieved when the mouth of the trap has been located more than 1ft above the ground surface. Segregating discs with insecticide-impregnated pads can be arranged to drop down inside the magazine at pre-set intervals and so isolate portions of the catch at desired time periods.

Of two American traps which have proved popular for capturing small insects, one is the 'Trinidad' trap with a mosquito-gauze covered framework which allows entrance at one point only. The other consists of a metal cylinder with gauze funnels at either end, but with the apex of the funnel open. Both types employ mosquito-proofed cages, usually with live bait inside, though carbon dioxide gas produced by sublimation of dry ice has been found to be an effective alternative.

CHAPTER FIVE

Fish Traps

A RUSE used to attract an animal into a machine, be it bait or reliance upon that animal's natural curiosity, puts such a machine into the category of traps. But when we come to consider the methods used for taking fish, it is not always quite so easy to decide which is a trapping device and which is not. Are we, for example, to include fish-trapping as an aspect of fishing? It is certainly not one of the techniques employed by sporting fishermen, yet commercial fishing frequently depends upon the use of traps.

Another difficulty arises when we consider the expression 'to fish'. We think here of something active, perhaps a way of taking fish by sweeping them into a net or by playing them on a line. But an angler who leaves his line with its lure dangling almost motionless in the water is coming very close to setting a trap. The distinction, admittedly, is narrow, but it does exist. When the angler feels a bite he goes into action, and if he does not harry the fish and tire it, he may not only lose the fish, but bait, hook and line as well.

A true fish trap functions in quite a different way. To begin with, it is usually secured in the water, sometimes as a permanent structure, certainly at least for several hours. The fish is lured to the trap in one of the conventional ways and, having entered, finds little opportunity for escape. There it must stay until it is recovered by the owner of the trap. Another characteristic feature of fish traps is that almost all, except for some of the most modern commercial ones, are live traps.

One of the confusions about fish traps arises because some of them make use of nets, whereas nets are generally associated with active fishing. Seine-netting might be considered as a trapping procedure, because fish do become trapped, but the physical hauling of the net ashore to secure the catch tips the scale in favour of classing it as an active fishing process. A stake net is usually considered a trap, yet its principle is not unlike that of the seine net, except that it remains static and holds its catch until this is released.

To add to the dilemma, there is also confusion as to what can be regarded as fish. If the fish trap was used only to catch fish as defined scientifically, all would be well, but when we talk of fishing and include such animals as lobsters, crabs, shrimps, crawfish and the vast assortment of shellfish, definitions begin to lack precision. The names 'crawfish' and 'shellfish' are misnomers, because although they both include the noun 'fish' they are no more related to real fish than a worm or an elephant.

Notwithstanding all these oddities of English language usage, let us attempt to clarify the situation. In this section only devices functioning in a manner generally accepted for traps will be included, and only those traps which, apart from true fish, take underwater-living backboneless animals. From this it follows that fish traps as a group will not include treadle traps or underwater snares used to catch wading and swimming birds and mammals.

Primitive Patterns

A point of particular interest in any study of fish traps is the way in which so many of them developed into a common pattern, even those made many centuries ago and in many different parts of the world. The commonest material used for fishtraps has been brushwood or withies, plaited together to form baskets. The shape of the basket has varied from time to time and place to place, although most frequently it has been roughly conical with the wider end bell-shaped. From the bell, an inner funnel leading into the body of the trap provides an entrance for fish, and, by its shape and position, inhibits any escape.

In Chapter Two mention was made of osier creels discovered from Stone Age times. Their pattern and apparent method of usage have remained unchanged, particularly among more primitive and rural communities, up to the present day. An example of a fishing trap in use by the Mendi people of the Congo region of Africa follows very closely the pattern used hundreds of thousands of years ago and bears a striking resemblance to the putchers used in the Severn estuary, in England.

Crab and Lobster Pots

Lobster, crab and prawn fishing have all been carried on for centuries, using traps predominantly—though they are more frequently referred to as pots or creels. Crabs and lobsters are generally found fairly close in to the shore but crawfish, where they occur, usually live farther out in deeper water. These animals are particularly associated with rocky-bottomed coasts, where they lurk in the safety of rock crevices and have to be lured out by suitably baiting the pots lowered from the fishermen's boats.

Around Cromer, off the Norfolk coast of Britain, crab pots were formerly made of netting stretched over wooden or iron hoops. The pots were 1ft 9in long and 1ft 3in wide, and at either end was a funnel through which the crabs would enter in search of bait. This was either smaller crabs known locally as 'toggs', or flat fish called 'butts'. Crabs were removed from the pots through a side door.

In south-east Scotland and north-east England, according to Michael Graham in *Sea Fisheries*, traps for crabs and lobsters were known as creels (or creeves). They were of varying design, but were invariably made from wood and twine. In Northumbria, such traps were closely associated with a regional type of fishing boat known as a 'coble', few of which remain operating at the present time.

In the south of England, particularly in Cornwall and Devon, the pots have a more consistent design. They are of basketwork, fashioned from withies to give a dome on top of a flat base. From the top of the dome the characteristic funnel leads to the interior. Such pots are sometimes called 'inkwell pots', but more recently barrel traps have come into use on Cornish coasts.

Along some parts of the south coast of England and around some areas of the Welsh coastline are to be found variations of a French

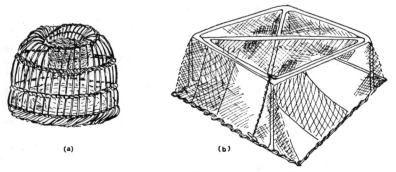

(a)   (b)

Fig 26   (a) Inkwell pot; (b) Leakey pot (folding creel)

pot. F. M. Davis, writing in *Fish Investigation* in 1937, described one
seen at Beaumaris, on the Menai Straits, which had ends formed
from the rims of bicycle wheels to which were attached old broom
handles giving a cylindrical design. The hoops of the funnels were
fashioned from the rims of pram wheels.

American lobster pots were frequently wicker baskets, similar in
design to the northern British creel, but larger. They measured about
3ft long by 2ft wide, were flat-bottomed and the ends and top were
arched. Each end was open to allow lobsters to make their way in,
but the openings were surrounded by short flexible pieces of wood
which prevented escape when they closed behind the lobster. A door
was let into the top to allow the catch to be extracted. Pots were
baited with the offal of fresh fish, weighted by a stone placed inside,
and secured by a rope from a piece of lightweight wood serving as a
buoy. They were lowered into the water at the low-water mark
during a season lasting between March and July, and were visited
each morning to collect the catch.

Experimental Pots
More recently, the Bureau of Commercial Fisheries at Gloucester,
Mass., has been experimenting with plastic-covered steel lobster pots.
These have inside dimensions of 5ft by 4ft by 2ft, and weigh 138lb.
The Bureau considers that these new pots have considerable potential
in opening up offshore fishing as they have a longer life than conventional pots and, if lifted every twenty-four hours, the catch can be
as much as 20lb a haul, although even 10lb would be a profitable
proposition.

Another interesting experiment has been the fitting of zinc anodes
to wire crab pots used on the east coast of USA. By preventing
corrosion this has given a threefold increase in the life of the pots,
which now last an entire season.

Around the end of the nineteenth century a thriving lobster fishery
was centred about Christiansund, in Norway. The Norway lobster
(*Nephrops norvegicus*) was the species caught and it was taken in
novel pots made from old casks. The open ends of these were covered
with boughs, but a hole was left for the lobster to gain entrance. The
usual bait was herring. In other regions of Norway, osier pots similar
to those used in Britain, were employed.

Lobster fishing was also a thriving industry off Irish coasts at the
end of the last century. The severity of winter weather conditions

restricted the fishing to the summer months and the comparatively small pots used caught lobsters up to about 5lb in weight. Any larger ones taken were those found clinging to the outsides of the pots.

Attempts have been made in recent years to develop the Irish crab industry, and in this connection the Fisheries Development Division of the Irish Sea Fisheries Board has investigated the relative properties of a number of pots in use elsewhere in the world.

Comparing the American parlour trap with the barrel trap, the English east coast creel and the Leakey folding creel (Fig 26b), the American parlour trap proved best on a number of scores. Though weighty, it better withstood the heavy seas experienced in the testing area of Schull. Its low catch of sub-legal-sized crabs compared favourably with the best of the other pots and its overall catch was the highest.

Only the use of locally available materials could have enabled crab and lobster fishing to survive as a one-man or family occupation, as it did on so many coasts. The vagaries of weather and its effect upon sea conditions constituted a recurring hazard while pot-making itself was a constant chore made necessary by the frequent loss of pots at sea. Some delightful pen-portraits of men who sought their living in this way have been given by Leo Walmsley in his novels of life among the lobster fishermen on the north Yorkshire coast of England.

It was an obvious if slight development from the use of individual wickerwork basket traps to placing them in groups, and most lobster and crab pots are now seeded in clumps. Prehistoric records indicate that fixed booms carrying rows of basket traps were even then in use, and certainly there is evidence of their having been employed in Britain in Saxon times. Such banks of traps have been described as 'fixed engines', and their use for catching shrimps and salmon is recorded in the *Domesday Book*.

Fixed Trapping Device
The breeding cycle of the salmon has a particular significance for the use of fixed trapping devices in river areas. The salmon spends part of its life in freshwater rivers and part in the sea. The change in location is associated with changes in its sexual cycle, and must also involve physiological changes to enable a fish used to fresh water to tolerate a high salinity in the sea. The salmon begins its life as an egg in the gravelly bottom of a freshwater river. When the egg hatches, the

young fish spends some time in the native waters feeding and growing. The length of time varies according to the location of the river, but after a year or so it is ready to leave the river and head out to sea. In Britain, the young smolts, as they are called at this age, are generally about two years old when they leave the rivers, usually between March and May.

The time spent in the sea is for feeding and growth is rapid. A two-year-old smolt leaving the river may be only five or six inches long, yet after only one or two years in the sea it may have grown to a length of eighteen to twenty inches and weigh more than 4lb. At the end of four years in the sea the fish may reach a weight of 40lb, and in Canadian waters it is not unusual for some fish of that age to scale over 100lb.

After their year or more in the sea, the salmon return to the rivers to spawn, and in many cases it would seem that they re-enter their natal rivers. This is the 'salmon run' and in Britain it can take place at any time from March to June. The fish are now prime and it is at this pre-spawning stage that they are fished and trapped. Fishing and trapping licences are issued to allow for catches before the spawning period, but the season closes when spawning is imminent.

In Britain, Western Europe and Eastern Canada, the salmon is *Salmo salar*, the Atlantic salmon, which returns only to the rivers of the western coasts of European countries and those of the east coast of Canada. The corresponding species in the United States and Japan belong to the genus *Oncorhynchus*, the Pacific salmon, and include *O. tschawytska*, the King, Sacramento, Chinook, Tyee, Columbian River or Spring salmon; *O. kisutch*, the Coho or Silver salmon; *O. gorbuscha*, the Pink or Humpback salmon; *O. nerka nerka*, the Red, Blueback or Sockeye salmon, and *O. keta*, the Dog or Chum salmon. All these different species migrate, as their names suggest, up west coast rivers, but the time varies from mainly spring for Sockeye, Coho and Humpback salmon, to the fall for Dog salmon.

In the United States, there is a species very similar to the Sockeye salmon, known as the Kokanee salmon, *O. nerka kennerlyi*, which is a non-migratory form. The Sockeye has an unusual feature to its life cycle in that the newly-hatched young, before reaching the stage when they would have grown enough for their move to the sea, migrate from the river into a lake feeding it and there they feed for up to two years in relatively static water.

With these migratory movements in mind, it can be appreciated how well a fixed engine will work when placed in the pathway of salmon imbued with an urgency to ascend rivers for spawning.

Along the Severn estuary and Bristol Channel, these engines were particularly prominent. On the Gloucestershire and Monmouthshire side of the Severn, the construction favoured was of wickerwork, but on the Somerset side netting was used, although the general construction followed the same principle.

Putchers and Putts

These installations were designed to capture shrimps and salmon, and it must have been a profitable venture for even in 1851, according to C. M. Yonge, they were yielding £10,000 annually. He attributes their reduction in numbers to a general decline in inshore fishing owing to competition from the expanding deep-sea fishing industry in the latter half of the nineteenth century.

Two kinds of installations have been used in the Severn area. Those for catching salmon are called *putchers*, and those used for both shrimps and salmon are known as *putts*. In all, about 11,000 were in use in 1860.

Putchers are conical in shape and made of basketwork. They are about 5½ft long, 5 to 7ft in diameter at the mouth, and are made up of three regions. The front, called the *kype*, forms the bell-shaped mouth and leads to the central region or *butt*, housing a valve of split withies. Behind comes the *forewheel*, which also possesses a valve and is closed terminally by a wooden plug. (Picture, p 34). The kype is fastened between stakes, usually six in number, but the butt and forewheel are held in the clefts of Y-shaped stakes. Putts are arranged in rows, but sometimes groups of two are spaced at intervals (Picture, p 34).

Both kinds of fixed engines are set to face upstream, the intention being for them to catch fish drifting back on an ebbing tide. There is, however, one instance of their being used facing downstream to take fish on the flowing tide. This was at Goldcliffe, at the mouth of the River Usk. Here there were at one time 1,200 putchers facing upstream and 900 facing downstream, so that this fishery had the best of both tides.

Inevitably, fish other than salmon would be caught in either putchers or putts; in fact, all kinds of marine organisms have been recorded from the catches taken. Putts are so constructed that larger fish, particularly salmon, could be trapped in the central zone or butt, while shrimps, and occasionally prawns, could pass through to the forewheel. That is detachable from the butt, so that the catch could be emptied by removing the plug and pouring it out.

The 1968/9 annual report of the Severn River Authority lists fifteen licences as having been issued during the year for operating fixed engines. The numbers of instruments involved included ten putts and 3,905 putchers. The salmon caught by fixed engines during the same period were 1,137, the greatest number, 436, having been taken in June 1968. The bulk of the salmon ranged in size from between 7 and 15lb, but 180 taken were over 15lb in weight.

During the year ending March 1968, the Usk River Authority licensed 127 putts and 2,900 putchers. In the same period, 823 salmon were caught in fixed engines, which included eight driftnets.

Weir Traps and Stake Nets

A variation of the practice of using a weir of multiple traps was tried at Swansea, Lynmouth, and a number of other places. Here a portion of the shore would be enclosed with a fencing of brushwood or wickerwork, so that when the tide retreated salmon and other fish were prevented from drifting back beyond the weir.

In other areas, stake nets, mostly patterned on the seine principle, have been used as weir traps. The first recorded use of stake nets in Britain was in the Solway Firth in 1788. Here, at a place called Newby, near the mouth of the River Annan, stake nets were positioned inshore because people had noticed that salmon nosed their way along the coasts in an endeavour to discover their natal rivers. In the 1820s, these traps had become popular and were numerous around the British coasts by 1850.

However, when fixed engines of any kind were set up the salmon resources of the rivers concerned were drastically reduced, and they were eventually prohibited in England following the recommendation of a Commission of Enquiry in 1860. In Scotland, laws were passed in 1862 and 1868 which attempted to conserve catches, but they were not very effective and stake netting went on largely uncontrolled.

Trap or Dredge Nets

M. Herubel in his book *Sea Fisheries*, gave an account of traps used around the French coast and in the Mediterranean up to 1912. Two types occurring frequently were those known as a *casier* and a *diable*. Both worked on the principle of pots used for catching eels or crabs. The *diable* was used in the Seine estuary for catching shrimps, sprats and herrings, and consisted of a bag of netting about 20ft long and supported on a wooden frame 16ft by 6ft 6in. The frame was anchored and weighted to keep it below water and its position was marked by floats.

Other forms of trap nets or dredge nets, known as *filets-dragues*, were used extensively. They were enclosures of network moored at the water surface by anchors. Off the Newfoundland coast they were used to fish for cod, off the Norwegian coast for salmon, and in the Gulf of Marseilles for mullet. They looked like enormous spouts, having vertical sides and lower portions which sloped away obliquely.

Eel Traps

Special traps for catching eels have been developed, particularly in Europe. M. E. Varley, in her book *British Freshwater Fishes*, mentions that because eels were so popular as food during the last century, there were eel traps in practically every millstream in the south and west of England. When operated by individuals, these traps mostly took the form of wicker-basket funnels, very much like the orthodox fish traps known from early times. On the River Severn, however, the eel traps were of netting, still funnel-shaped, but up to 50ft in length. The terminal portion, known as the 'cod', was long and narrow and had a non-return trap. As in other parts of Europe, the trapping was a seasonal practice coinciding with the autumnal migration of silver eels downriver.

The story of eel migration is a reversal of that for the salmon, for whereas salmon feed in the sea and return to the rivers for spawning, eels feed in the rivers for a number of years before they obey a breeding urge and move out into the sea. We know that salmon vary in the distances that they travel out to sea, but the saga of the eels tells of journeys over thousands of miles to the breeding grounds. Those from rivers in Western Europe appear to travel as far as the Caribbean to spawn in the Sargasso Sea, where they meet cousins from the east-flowing rivers of North America. Eels from rivers on the east coast of southern Africa travel up to Madagascar for spawning. The extent to which eel larvae hatching from eggs on the spawning grounds return to rivers, or even countries, from which their parents travelled, is still a mystery which has not, as yet, been completely unravelled by scientists.

A commercial fishery for eels was located below Lough Neagh, on the River Bann in Northern Ireland, but there were few commercial traps elsewhere in Great Britain and the total yield of all of them would be less than 100 tons. Today, eels are still very much favoured as food in Europe, even more so on the Continent than in the British Isles, and important eel traps are located in the Baltic, around the French coast, and on the shores of the Adriatic.

Bertin, in his famous work on eels, describes how in Europe, at points where eels assemble before leaving the rivers on their autumnal migration to the sea, barriers are erected to catch them in nets, generally located at the outlets of lagoons or pools. Along the French Mediterranean coast such traps are known as *bordigues* and consist mainly of pasks or labyrinths of wickerwork, sometimes of wattled reeds.

On the Adriatic coast are the famous *lavorieri*, especially in the *valli* of Comacchio, situated in the branches of the Po delta. The fisheries here yield 1,000 tons of eels annually. The system for catch-

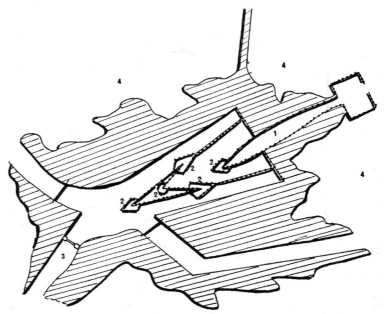

Fig 27   Eel traps as used on the Adriatic coast; (1) canal leading from the lagoon (*valle*); (2) eel traps; (3) canal leading to the sea; (4) lagoons

ing them is elaborate (Fig 27), consisting of a number of trap units placed between a *valle* (lagoon) and the canal leading to the sea.

Tunny Nets

On the Mediterranean coasts, especially in the regions of Provence, Algeria and Tunisia, *madragues* are used for catching tunny. These are nets composed of a number of chambers and attached to stakes. On either side of the net is a weir or tail (*coda* or *queue*), with a total length of about a mile. The net will be 1,000ft long and 230ft wide and has a terminal portion, the death chamber (*corpo*), where fish caught are clubbed to death.

Weir Traps

In the nineteenth century the river systems of eastern Canada were packed with fish traps, and even more elaborate weir traps. The catch sought was salmon, but here again, as in Britain, the decrease in river resources was such that the Canadian government eventually introduced legislation banning the use of weirs.

In Eire, as in other countries, there has been a close correlation between the development of hydroelectric schemes and river fishing, particularly for salmon. The Thomand weir provides modern trap-fishing and was part of the Shannon hydroelectric project completed in 1927. The weir is 480ft long and is supported on twenty-two concrete piers. Fish are directed from this into a central channel, within which there is a particularly interesting innovation. They have to pass over a grid which carries an electric charge so that the fish are stunned and killed. This produces a more marketable product than when the conventional blow on the head is applied.

Miscellaneous Fish Traps

A fish trap rather different from all the others we have yet considered was created by W. Hamilton Gibson, an author, who was much concerned with popularising the use of traps, especially among small boys. In his book of *Camp Life and the Tricks of Trapping*, published in 1881, he provided an extensive range of traps, mostly of the homemade variety, to occupy the interests of American boys whom, he thought, had a different outlook as regards hobbies and pastimes from that of their English counterparts.

His fish trap was one of his many variations of the double-box snare which, in turn, was a version of the spring-loop mole traps popular in Britain during the nineteenth century. It was made from a length of stove pipe, though presumably rainwater drain pipe or a piece of land drain would serve equally well. It should be a foot long and have a hole drilled through at a point midway between the ends. In line with this hole, but at points about 1in from each end, two further holes should be made. If these holes are considered to be on the top of the trap, then a further two are drilled about 3in apart on the circumference running round the pipe from the central hole. Through these last two holes a spring sapling is placed as shown in Fig 28. To the spring is attached a piece of cord or wire, divided into three just above the surface of the pipe. A short piece passes through the central hole and is knotted inside with a knot small enough to pass through the hole. The other two ends of cord pass through the holes at each end to form nooses inside, around the inner circumference of the pipe. The last operation is to devise a short stick, on one end of which bait can be fastened. This is pushed from inside so that it holds fast in the central hole and at the same time prevents the knotted string, which keeps the spring bent, from slipping through.

The trap is set up with suitable bait on the stick and a stone placed inside to weight the whole and hold it at the bottom of the water. The bait stick should be adjusted to hold with a degree of firmness appropriate to the fish being sought. Incoming fish will dislodge the stick which, in turn, will release the knot and allow the spring to straighten. This action will pull tight the nooses and so secure the intruding fish.

Of course, if the trap is weighted and set on the water bottom it is going to catch mainly bottom-living fish, although this depends to some extent upon the type of water concerned. In a lake, with relatively little surface water movement, trout will be bottom feeders, often nosing into mud and among rocks, so that a box trap could offer some temptation for them. Shallow lakes in rich agricultural areas will have soft muddy bottoms and the bottom feeders, in Britain, will be cyprinid fishes such as carp, bream and tench. A trap baited with molluscs—freshwater mussels, for example—might well attract trout, and also eels.

To catch fish in turbulent waters, it might be essential to anchor the trap by attaching it to a heavy stone by means of a reasonable length of cord, and then trying to keep it in a mid-depth position by a further piece of cord linking it with a buoy made from a small empty oil drum. This might well catch larger trout and possibly pike, although these fish, being more predacious than their juniors and preferring active prey, would be less likely to scavenge on dead and static bait.

Because of the different habits of fish, as regards both the kind and depth of water they populate and the nature of the food they take, it is essential to have traps of different sizes and shapes placed in different trapping situations.

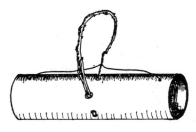

Fig 28   Box trap for fish

Portable fish traps of all kinds have been manufactured commercially, and a number of these are still on the market. Wire-mesh eel or fish traps are marketed by S. Young & Sons (Misterton) Ltd. In 3ft and 4ft versions, they are barrel-shaped with funnels from each end. It is recommended that these are set during the months of April to October, although in mild seasons the period may be extended into December. The traps are baited with half a dozen large worms, pieces of offal, or the entrails of herrings, and the bait should be enclosed in a muslin bag or hole-punched tin. During the summer, shallow runs between weeds are good places to set them, but deeper pools are preferable during colder months.

A variation of this trap is the Suffolk version. It is straight-sided, but oval in cross-section, has one funnel from one end and a second in line a third of the way in. The opposite end has a door through which to extract the catch. (Picture, p 34.)

Pike and Minnow Traps
For catching different varieties of fish, special adaptations of these basic patterns are used. For example, a variation for pike is based on the Suffolk trap, except that it is flat-bottomed and has a wide and expanded funnel extending beyond the main body of the trap.

Another version for catching minnows, based on the barrel-shaped eel trap, is marketed in Britain by Young's, and in the United States, as Gee's Improved Minnow Trap, by Havahart. This is interesting as having two identical halves secured together at the centre, and useful because the halves can be fitted inside each other for easier portability.

The Star Crab Trap

Another trap sold by Havahart is the Star crab trap. This has an ingenious action, is extremely portable and works well. Its one disadvantage is that it requires operating, and for this reason can only be considered marginally as a true trap. It consists of a square-mesh grid as a base from which are hinged four triangular mesh sides. These are linked with a system of lines which allows the four-pointed star shape, assumed when the trap is flat on the sea-bed, to be pulled into a four-sided pyramid. This action is controlled from a boat. The trap is baited and the operator, on feeling the line move as the bait is pulled, hauls on the rope, quickly closes the trap and brings it to the surface. If the sides could be sprung and released automatically when the bait hook was grappled, this could become a true trap. Seeded in groups and marked with floats, they could be more efficient than conventional pots, since crabs and lobsters seek out the bait much more readily over a flat surface than if they have to enter a three-dimensional container.

That fish traps are not always selective in their catch is demonstrated by an interesting report from Dr G. O. S. Reid. Writing in *The Field*, he told of finding a kestrel in a wire-mesh fish trap upended on the bank of the Darwell reservoir in Sussex. He wondered what had induced the bird to push through the 4 to 5in opening of the funnel, as there were no indications that any bait had been left in the abandoned trap. The bird, alive and uninjured, was released through the trapdoor.

CHAPTER SIX

Bird Traps

WHEN a bird can find its way into a fish trap, and when, as the writer can testify from personal experience, they are frequently caught in mammal traps, it might seem pointless to create traps especially for taking them. Nevertheless, a great deal of research has been directed towards bird-trapping, especially by government departments concerned with pest control.

Existing types of traps for birds can be divided into two main categories. The first group includes all those, home-made or manufactured, which are designed to take birds singly. The traps in the second group are those intended to take birds in large numbers, either in the course of pest destruction or for scientific activities such as ringing. Both categories include examples of traps which are selective to a greater or lesser extent; and each can be subdivided on the basis of the size of birds involved—arbitrarily, if not precisely, into those for small and large birds respectively.

Single-Catch Traps

The first example here is perhaps the simplest trapping device in any category. This is the use of bird lime, probably one of the oldest of trapping methods, whose possible use during Roman times has already been mentioned.

In common usage, the term 'bird lime' is often, but wrongly, applied to the excreta of birds, no doubt because this is frequently whitish in appearance and associated with twigs of trees, on which bird lime has traditionally been used.

Used in its correct context, it refers to any viscous material employed for capturing birds, and most often, this has been extracted from the twigs of certain trees. In Britain, holly twigs have been favoured more than anything else, whereas in North America the bark of slippery elm is the usual source. The extract is prepared by

121

boiling chippings of the selected wood or bark for some long time and then mashing the product. Grains of wheat or other cereals may be added to provide a more glutinous substance, and the extract can be used on its own, though additives are often included. Linseed oil is now commonly used but in former times goose-grease was popular. The mixture, whatever its composition, is stored cold and softened by heat before using.

Bird lime has always been associated with the placing of limed twigs upon trees, the idea being to seize birds which perch. A number of variations, both in the recipes and in the mode of application, are given by Willughby in the *Ornithology of Francis Willughby*, edited by John Ray. It first appeared in an English edition, with notes on fowling, in 1678.

W. Hamilton Gibson in *Camp Life and the Tricks of Trapping*, published in 1881, describes two methods of using bird lime. The first involves the use of an owl as a decoy, and though he does not say whether the owl is a live or stuffed one, he talks of fastening it into the crotch of a tree, so that one hopes he is suggesting the latter. The decoy is surrounded with limed twigs, and when small birds come to attack the owl in its daytime roost they are captured while entangled in the festooning twigs.

Gibson's second method of using lime is intended for capturing humming birds, and here the lime is painted on the insides of flower bells known to be visited by these birds. Success depends upon birds pushing their heads and long curved beaks into the flower trumpets while searching for nectar. Once in contact with the lime, they are unable to escape. Gibson recommends lime made by forming a gum from chewing grains of wheat, claiming that this is easily removed from birds' feathers afterwards.

The ethics of trapping birds, or any other animals for that matter, by the use of bird lime are questionable. In Britain, it is one of many methods prohibited by law, except for certain specified purposes and for which licences must be obtained.

Deadfall Traps

Other primitive methods for capturing birds include deadfall traps, of which there are many variations though one of the best known and most widely employed is the English brick deadfall. Intended mainly for small birds, and particularly ground birds such as seed-eaters, the principle is simple and the requirements few. Four bricks, a few twigs and suitable bait are all that is needed. The set-up is shown in Fig 29. Brick D is disturbed when the Y-shaped hazel twig is moved by a bird seeking bait. If the edge of brick D is allowed to catch on brick A, the trap will catch alive, the birds being confined to an enclosed space under the brick. If the edge of brick D is not so restricted on its fall, the trap will function as a true deadfall. Though generally well known, details of this trap were given to the writer by Lt-Col G. B. Donald, who knew of a Kent rabbit-catcher who used it to trap sparrows for feeding to his ferrets.

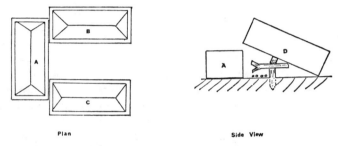

Plan   Side View

Fig 29   English brick deadfall trap

Logs can be used in place of bricks to achieve a similar result or, slightly more elaborately, a split-pole or wire cage can be set up to fall, after release of a trigger, over a bird seeking bait. As seen in Fig 30, the cage is released when a bird pecks at the bait tray. This is fastened on to a twig having a square notch at its tip suitable to hold around the base of the cage. A spindle stick, having one short and one long limb, secures the opposite side of the base with the short length. The long length is suspended over the Y-notch of the upright stick in such a way that it exerts sufficient pressure on the bait stick to keep the trap set. This trap is most likely to catch single birds but when set for quail, for example, has been known to catch a small flock.

Avian deadfall traps are successful when the release mechanisms used are in accord with the movements and feeding habits of the birds concerned. Since in most cases the trap release depends upon the use of a bait stick or lever, and because such traps are commonly set on firm ground, it follows that ground-feeding birds are most

Fig 30   Log-cage deadfall trap

likely to be caught by this means. If seeds of plants such as maize, peas or the larger grasses are used, they will attract pigeons, doves, pheasants and partridges. Carrion-feeding birds, such as crows and vultures, would be attracted if meat were attached to the bait stick. In countries with a hot, dry climate, carrion bait must consist of a whole animal with its gut split open. Flesh unprotected by a skin of fur or feathers quickly dries out in such conditions and loses its attractive odour-producing qualities.

Trap Cages
A step beyond the fall cage as an automatic trap for birds is the trap cage, also found all over the world and known to have been used for many centuries. Said to be a favourite trap among bird catchers, it was extensively used to capture song-birds in tropical countries, where there has been considerable commercial exploitation of these creatures.

The example illustrated on page 51 is one which is used by the Chokwe people of north-west Zambia and combines the normal fall-trap type of cage with a decoy cage—a not uncommon principle. Initially, using a bait such as millet, it is used as a fall trap until one bird has been caught and put into the lower compartment, when it becomes a decoy cage. The illustration shows the intricate construction from a wooden framework with meshing made of reeds. The materials will vary from one locality or racial group to another, but the design remains remarkably constant. In size, the cage is about a 12in cube and the hinged upper lid drops when a bird perches on the bait bar at the top. A lower door, or removable internal partition, allows for placing the call-bird in the lower section of the trap. A version manufactured to catch bullfinches is marketed by Gilbertson & Page Ltd, in Britain, where bullfinches may only legally be taken for the purpose of ringing by a licensed ringer and then subsequently released, or for aviculture by an aviculturist licensed to take wild birds.

An interesting ethnic trap is one used in Syria and, as with most traps used by rural communities, it can be assembled from readily available materials. The articles used here are wooden twigs, twine, horse-hair and the rib-bone of a goat or sheep. Two bows are made respectively from the rib-bone and a bent twig tautened by a multi-strand horse-hair spring. This is wound by the straight twig and the bows kept apart by a small peg held to the spring by a cord. When the peg is dislodged by a bird seeking bait placed around it, the bows snap shut and secure the bird. This trap is quite big enough to capture partridges, moorhens and birds of similar size and habits.

Automatic Net Traps

Once given the idea of a containing structure, such as a cage, and a spring mechanism to effect the catch, it was not long before automatic net traps appeared combining these features. One simple version among a number which are being manufactured at the present time is seen in the picture on page 51. This sparrow trap is made from wood, wire and netting, with a pressed-metal bait tray. The baseboard has a wire spring across its centre and this carries a wire-framed net. A trigger held by a staple at the back of the baseboard is secured delicately in a hole punched in the bait tray. Birds touching the bait tray release the trigger which, in turn, allows the net to clap over them. The heavy baseboard reduces the need to anchor the trap. This version comes in different sizes allowing larger breeds of birds, such as crows and pigeons, to be taken. It is important that small models are not too small and the spring width not less than 18in. Springs should be renewed annually.

A crow trap uses the same principle, but employs a double wire frame and net, one-half of which is staked to the ground using metal pegs. These traps have the advantage of being lighter in weight and less visible. Both versions are marketed in Britain by S. Young & Sons, Ltd.

A far more robust structure is a 'hoodie' crow trap, with double springs activating the net. This is supported by a steel frame and the whole trap is based on a strong steel bar which can be secured to the ground by pushing steel pegs through drilled holes. This trap is available from Gilbertson & Page, Ltd. Carrion crows and hooded crows in Britain are regarded as different races of the same species, but are separate in breeding range and differ in appearance. The hooded crow is readily identified by its grey mantle and underparts. Their habits within their own ranges are similar, but whereas the carrion crow is more commonly found as a lone bird or in pairs, winter-visiting hooded crows tend to be gregarious. Despite its name, the carrion crow's diet is not confined to dead livestock; it will take injured animals, live frogs and toads, birds' eggs, and molluscs such as slugs and snails, also vegetable matter, especially grain and fruit.

The culminating development of spring net traps is in the goshawk trap, used extensively in Continental Europe, especially in connection with falconry. It has been introduced to Britain for the same purpose and can be seen by visitors to the Falconry Centre run by Phillip Glasier at Newent, in Gloucestershire. Its superiority over other forms of net trap is in the incorporation of a decoy cage. The illustrations on p 52 show two stages in the use of this trap. A dove is used as a decoy and placed in the cage below the trap, which is then set. The cleverness of the trap becomes apparent at the next stage. Drawn by the decoy, the hawk will come into the trap which closes immediately; however, the mechanism of trapping the hawk automatically releases the decoy which 'homes' to its dovecote. The trappers waiting nearby see the dove winging home and know that a hawk has been taken and is waiting to be recovered.

The goshawk is rather like a large sparrowhawk and frequents wooded areas and forests, both on low ground and on mountains. In Britain, it is the race *Accipiter gentilis gentilis* which carries the vernacular name, but in North America it is a different race, *A. g. atricapillis*. A special feature of the bird, and one which has appealed to falconers, is its ability to use its short wings and long tail to advantage in weaving its way between trees and other obstacles. When taking its quarry, the goshawk waits until its prey is perched and then makes a sudden dash. It is this very habit which proves its undoing when it comes across a decoy in a goshawk trap.

Pole Traps
Spring traps of the kinds described, which take the catch alive, are

basically humane and, if carefully set and regularly visited, birds caught in them come to no harm. There are, however, less humane spring traps of another kind which do not kill immediately and which can cause immense suffering to captive birds. These are pole traps, which are nothing more nor less than gin or steel traps attached to wooden poles. Until 1904, when by parliamentary legislation their further use was forbidden in Britain, they had been used extensively by gamekeepers to control attacks by sparrowhawks, kestrels and crows on young pheasant chicks. No doubt because they were reasonably effective, they have never gone completely out of use, and from time to time inspectors of the Royal Society for the Protection of Birds discover instances of their use. Writing in 1913 about *Wildlife in Wales*, George Bolam described them as 'relics of barbarous times'. He mentioned that in the course of one year it had been recorded that a single pole trap had caught a buzzard, a cuckoo and a song thrush. Not a great haul, perhaps, but what a senseless waste of wild life when no discrimination is made between pests and harmless animals.

Noose and Snare Traps

Another such bird-trapping device which operates inhumanely is the noose or snare. Sometimes it will kill fairly quickly, yet at other times, through careless construction or setting, it holds its catch alive for long periods in a way which induces injury and suffering. In its simplest form, the noose is used to catch ground-running birds— a poacher's weapon supreme—by placing it on habitually used tracks, or in hedgerows and gaps in fences through which birds pass. It can be made slightly more humane by using a swivel between the anchoring peg and the snare wire. If an animal is caught in the noose, its struggles will not cause as much injury as when the noose is used without a swivel.

All manner of adaptations and incorporations of the noose have been developed. One given to the writer by Mrs Rachel Woodward of Chester had been used with great success by her father when poaching pheasants. She thinks the particular pattern was a design of his own and was called by him 'the hangman's trap'. In this, a bent sapling serving as a spring hangs over a hole dug in the ground. From its end hangs a line, at the end of which is a noose laid on the ground surface and surrounding the hole. A second string, farther back along the sapling, hangs down through the noose and has a forked twig at its end. This twig is held lightly, with the sapling under tension, in the notch of an upright peg pushed into the ground at the bottom of the hole. Bait, such as corn or oats, is strewn under the forked twig. The noose, ideally, is camouflaged with leaves. Pheasants putting their heads through the noose to take the bait dislodge the forked twig which releases the tension on the spring. The noose is jerked upwards and the bird swung aloft as on a gibbet. Mrs Woodward is prepared to concede that the trap may not be original, as indeed in essence it is not, being similar to the so-called 'bait set snare' used by North American Indians and described by A. R. Harding in his *Deadfalls and Snares*. Even so, her father may well have developed the trap on his own initiative, for we have seen how the same patterns in traps reappear repeatedly and independently among peoples all over the world and over many centuries.

Tilted Platform Traps

Pfizenmayer, writing about the lives and activities of people in Siberia, described two traps in common use there just after World War I, both of which had the same basic mechanism of a tilting platform over a basket. One was used for taking woodcock and consisted of a tall basket secured in the fork of a tree branch. Over 5ft high and 4ft wide at the mouth, it had a lid formed from an oscillating board. On one side of the upper surface was fastened a mesh-covered box containing bilberries. The woodcock, alighting on the board and leaning over to get at the fruit, would tilt the lid and be pitched into the basket.

The second version, found where heathcock were more common, as in the southern Yakutsk district, used a basket made as a funnel by driving staves 5ft long into the ground. Two more staves, longer than the others, were placed upright in line at a short distance from the basket. Each had a Y-shaped fork at the top and a third pole, long enough to project over the basket, was secured to them. A piece of cord hung down from the end over the basket, was passed through a central hole in a circular platform and knotted underneath. Berries were scattered on the upper surface of the platform and birds landing in search of food would be tilted into the basket as before. Both these traps could catch a number of birds at a time as the baskets were quite capacious. During winter, with snow covering food plants, the bait would be particularly attractive.

Box Traps

Box traps have been developed for catching various kinds of birds, and these can either function automatically or be hand-controlled by a hidden observer.

There is little difference between the automatic box traps designed for birds and those for mammals; indeed the writer has frequently found birds caught in traps he had put out for mammals. Similarly, a colleague, plagued with a rat molesting his hen runs, regularly set a box trap in his garden and although he eventually caught his rat, for a long time the only regular catch was a robin. This often had to be released several times a day, having become what trappers describe as 'trap prone'.

A box trap of the automatic type produced especially for birds, is the Potter trap, or a modification of it by W. M. M. Chapman, in which a drop-door, supported on wire slides, falls when a prop from a treadle is dislodged by birds seeking bait at the rear of the trap. (Fig 31). It is suggested that multiple versions of this trap could be useful but, in practice, they are often all sprung when one door drops into place. It is, therefore, better to use a number of single traps in the same locality, especially if early-caught birds are to act as decoys.

The Potter trap is designed for small birds, pigeon size and below, although partridges and pheasants have been taken in one. It is particularly useful for trapping small birds which have become a nuisance in a private garden, or it could be used for small-scale ringing work. Small seeds, as supplied by pet stores for feeding wild

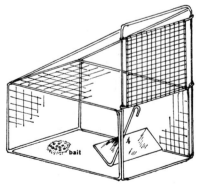

Fig 31   The Potter trap

birds, can be used as bait for seed-eaters, while other kinds of birds, such as blackbirds and thrushes, will be attracted by pieces of chopped fat, especially during winter. Birds like starlings, although relatively greedy, are shy of strange contraptions and are not easy to trap.

The Chardonneret trap, though basically a deadfall trap, is interesting, in having been adapted to take warblers by using water as a bait. The mechanism, seen in Fig 32, is self-explanatory, but the tricky feature is the method of keeping the water moving. This is achieved by hanging a punctured can filled with water directly over the water dish, so that drops from the can fall continuously on the surface. The trap is placed near bushes so that birds may approach it step by step, and for greater effect it is painted a drab green or brown and given a netting floor to allow the natural ground to show through.

Warblers are mostly shy and secretive birds and will not approach a trap unless they can do so by moving towards it from a succession of covers. For this reason the trap should not only be camouflaged near to a bush, but actually placed in a clump of bushes. Warblers such as reed warblers, will be more easily attracted in marshy and aquatic habitats if the trap is masked by reeds. The fact that dripping water from the trap does attract warblers is surprising, because they are normally cautious of anything moving.

Hand-controlled box traps in their simplest form consist of a netting cage with the door at one end lifted up and secured by a

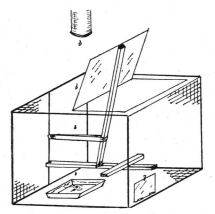

Fig 32   The Chardonneret trap

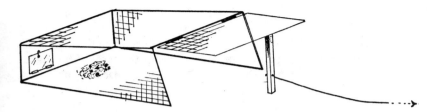

Fig 33   Hand-controlled box trap for birds

prop-stick (Fig 33). A long cord is fastened to the prop and held by an observer concealed at a distance. The birds are attracted by bait, and the advantage of this type of trap is that it need only be released when birds of the desired species are inside. A disadvantage is having to remain in the area for long periods of time while supervising the trap.

Pheasant trapping

Several traps have been designed to take pheasants and, from their nature, one could well imagine that all were products of the poacher. One example, said to be the invention of a Victorian poacher, is quoted by Charles Chenevix Trench. A champagne bottle is rammed neck-down into soft snow sufficiently firmly to leave an impression of the bottle after it has been removed. The hole left by the neck is filled with soaked dried peas. A pheasant will lean over and be able to reach the peas on top, but there will come a stage when it topples over and gets its head fast in the hole. A similar method, but using a jam-jar buried to its neck in a furrow, has also been quoted as a means of catching pheasants, by D. K. Caldecott.

Pheasants have been known to take bait from rat traps of the gin type without springing them, because of the delicacy with which they are able to peck seeds or similar bait from the bait plate. Utilising this knowledge, poachers in the late eighteenth century sealed peas to the bait plates of rat traps, using hot pitch. A gentle peck not being effective, pheasants would attack the peas more fiercely and so spring the trap.

Pheasants and partridges are particularly associated with partly cultivated ground having light soils. They prefer well-watered districts providing that there is ample cover nearby, since they like to run for shelter or crouch in cover, rather than take to the wing. The presence of young crops is always a temptation to them, more particularly if these are graincrops, peas or beans. Traps placed in a ploughed field, between the furrows, can be effective as the roots of former crops lifted by the ploughing will attract the birds. Although pheasants are more shy and wary than one might suppose, they are also excessively greedy and suitable bait scattered as a lead-in to the trap as well as on the bait plate will usually overcome their natural timidity.

Multi-Catch Traps

The single-catch trap has its attractions, such as portability, flexibility in siting a number of them, and specialisation for particular species. But there are also occasions when it is advantageous to be able to catch a large number of birds at a time.

In the past, most multi-catch traps were directed towards pest control of flocking birds and the capture of large numbers of birds to be used as food. They are no longer used in Britain for the latter purpose, but an additional use nowadays for such traps is for scientific research, particularly in connection with bird ringing (known as banding to Americans) and migrational studies.

The majority of them are live traps and they have the advantage, especially when used for pest destruction, that even though they cannot be selective those birds which are not wanted can be released unharmed.

The Clap-Net Traps

One of the earliest multi-catch bird traps known to have been used was the clap-net trap. This was described inadequately by Mottram in the early seventeenth century and more carefully by Willughby later in the same period. It could be used on its own, but was more frequently operated in conjunction with call-birds as decoys. Such traps are always released by hand control by a hidden observer.

Clap nets can be either double or single, that is they are made from either one or a pair of nets. Modern trappers prefer the single variety as it can be operated more speedily than the double and, of course, is less heavy to carry about. The single version shown in Fig 34 can be purchased, but would not be difficult to make. Clap-net traps range in size from small ones of 9ft by 4ft, up to a giant, 20yd by 20ft, described by Peter Scott and used by him for catching geese. His net needed torsion springs to assist the drawcord, but the smaller sizes can be thrown quite satisfactorily without this complication.

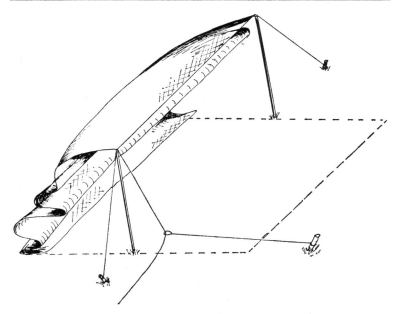

Fig 34   Single version of tne clap-net trap

Construction involves two lightweight poles, each half the width of the net to be used and with a hole drilled a little way up from its base. A rounded and greased leather bootlace is threaded through the holes and secured to an eyed metal peg or skewer thrust into the ground. The poles are thus hinged and located the net's length apart. A continuous cord serves as a guy for each pole and as a means of securing one edge of the net. The other edge of the net, the long side in each case, is pegged to the ground half its width from the poles. Better still, its edge should be pegged in a shallow trench and then covered over to provide a seal. The drawcord must be several yards in length, long enough to carry it to a suitable cover for the operator. The cord branches at the pole end and this is contrived by fastening the ends of the drawcord and two shorter cords to a brass ring. One of the short cords goes to a peg along the line where the moving edge of the net will fall, but placed just clear of the net's landing point. When the drawcord is pulled, a tension will be created between the top of the pole and the peg sufficient to bring the net over.

With the trap unsprung, the catching area is unimpeded and

therefore attractive, when bait is provided, to otherwise trap-shy birds. This type of trap is recommended for wading birds and is suitable for use on the mud flats where they are to be found. Some common waders which could be effectively caught with clap nets include curlews, whimbrels, godwits, sandpipers, stints, phalaropes and stilts. Many of these are found on sandy seashores and muddy estuaries as well as on the shores of inland lakes, but some are also commonly found along the banks of streams and rivers, especially if the rivers are tidal.

Sparrow Traps

Many multi-catch bird traps make use of a wire-mesh cage entered through funnels of one type or another, and can be used to catch birds from sparrow up to duck size. The simplest versions, called sparrow traps but by no means restricted to catching sparrows, come in a variety of patterns. A popular style consists of a half-cylinder, with a base measurement of 4ft by 2ft. It is made up of ½in wire mesh stretched over a heavy wire frame, there is a door at one end and funnels along the sides lead to the interior. Fig 35 shows the 'Eclipse' pattern, produced by S. Young & Son, Ltd. The so-called Government sparrow trap, designed by the Ministry of Agriculture, Fisheries and Food in Britain, is very similar but operates more like a fish trap. A funnel at one end leads into a floorless compartment, and across the middle there is a partition carrying a s̄cond funnel in line with the first. This leads into the second compartment which has a mesh floor.

The Frankfurt ringing station has produced yet a third version. This is a cylinder of mesh, placed on end, with three funnels leading

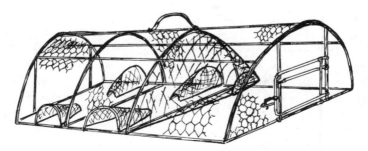

Fig 35   The Eclipse sparrow trap

inside from the perimeter at the base. Here water is used as a bait and placed in a saucer overlapped by the inner ends of the funnels.

These traps can be modified to catch ducks. P. A. D. Hollom, writing in the *BTO Field Guide,* describes one which is very like a fish trap, having a funnel at each end of a half-cylinder of wire mesh placed on a floating wooden platform. A slightly different type is used by the Eley Game Research Station at Fordingbridge, in Hampshire. This consists of a rectangular wooden-framed and wire-netted cage with funnels leading from opposite ends to the interior, which is partitioned into two compartments. The difference in use is that Hollom's version is floated initially without the upper cage in position, to encourage feeding from the platform. The Fordingbridge trap has sliding lids which are removed during the pre-baiting stage. Buoyancy is achieved in both traps by using empty petrol or gasolene cans strapped under the base, and cut maize is a suitable bait. These traps are approximately 6ft by 4ft at the base with funnels 12in high on the outside and 5in high at the inner end.

Aviary-type Traps
For catching birds larger than sparrows, especially members of the Corvid family, such as crows, rooks, magpies and jackdaws, large size aviary-type traps are employed. They can be sited almost anywhere, and gamekeepers use them to attract bird pests away from pheasant-breeding stations. Fruit growers place them in orchards, hoping to prevent attacks on their crops, and even domestic gardeners have resorted to them on occasion. Experiments have also been undertaken by the Ministry of Agriculture, Fisheries and Food to assess their value in catching feral pigeons on the flat roofs of buildings, and this same ministry has produced a whole range of plans with constructional details to assist those who wish to capture larger birds for one reason or another.

There are four different plans for making traps to catch rooks, jackdaws and carrion crows, known respectively as Mark 1, Mark 2, Mark 3 and Mark 4.

Although these aviary-type traps have been designed to remove pestiferous birds, they are, of course, largely unselective. Generally speaking, smaller birds would not be effectively trapped because the entrances for larger birds would also be large enough to allow little birds to escape. Blackbirds, thrushes and starlings, and perhaps redwings and shrikes, might be cohabitants of areas in which crows,

rooks and pigeons are found, and so could be trapped, the advantage
of these traps being that such birds could be released.

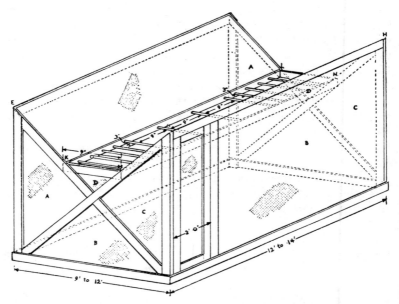

Fig 36   Rook, jackdaw and carrion crow trap of the Ministry of Agriculture, Fisheries and Food: Mark 1 ladder-trap version

The Mark 1 MAAF trap is of the well-known and universally
popular ladder-type. It can be made from roughly planed deal, 2in by
2in, painted with any good wood preservative other than creosote
and should not be less than 9ft by 12ft and 6ft high. All surfaces
except the space occupied by the ladder, KLMN in Fig 36, should be
covered with 1in galvanised hexagonal wire mesh. The ladder is 9in
wide, the first five rungs at each end being 3in apart. The remaining
rungs are 9 in apart, so leaving 9in open squares in the centre. A 2ft
wide door is made on one side to allow the catch to be removed.
      A live decoy bird, such as a hen, can be used under existing British
legislation, providing it has supplies of food and water, is untethered
and is left no longer than twenty-four hours at a time. Alternatively
bait, such as grain, dry bread or food scraps, can be employed. The
idea behind the trap is that once birds have been encouraged to enter

Page 137
(*left*) A man trap of the type used in World War I; (*below*) a typical notice used in the eighteenth and early nineteenth centuries to give warning of man traps

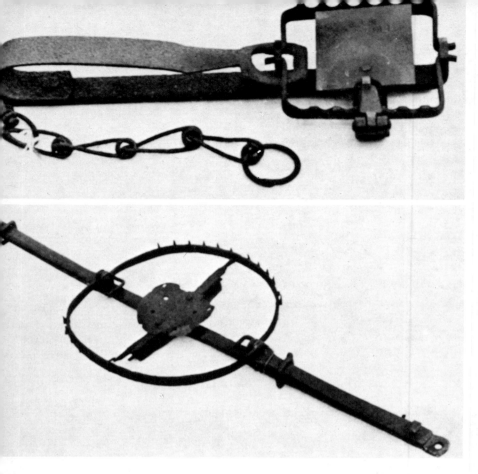

Page 138   Examples of gin traps: (*top*) rabbit gin in set position; (*centre*) fox gin; (*below*) bear trap

it and drop to the floor, they appear to be unable to fly up and out of the entry holes. To encourage entry, which may not be for several days or weeks in the first instance, the trap should be placed near trees or other perching structures to facilitate a gradual approach by the birds. The Ministry advises that captured birds should be taken out and destroyed at dusk, not in broad daylight.

The reason for this is simply that many birds would be especially wary if a trap appeared to have human association, more particularly if people entering were seen to bring out captive birds. It should be remembered that what may appear to be an empty bush or tree could be concealing thousands of keenly observing pairs of avian eyes. Anyone who has tried his hand at bird photography, using a hide, will appreciate the significance of this. The Mark 2 trap is a large cone version, and Fig 37 shows its general construction. Basically, it is a

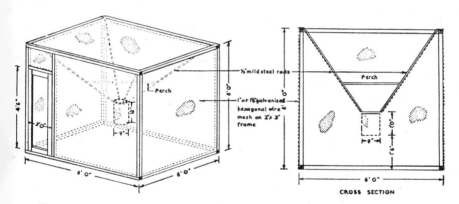

Fig 37   The MAAF Mark 2 rook, jackdaw and carrion
crow trap. Cone version

6ft cube of 2in by 2in deal wood framing, the four sides of which are covered in 1in wire mesh. The hopper at the top is formed by bolting four ½in mild steel rods to each of the top corners and spot-welding or wiring the other ends to a 9in diameter steel ring. This supports the entrance sleeve of ¾in wire mesh which should be 1ft long and reach to within 18in of the bottom of the trap. There is, as in the Mark 1 version, a 2ft wide door on one side. Siting, baiting and general usage follow the pattern described for the Mark 1 trap.

The Mark 3 trap (Fig 38) has the same general dimensions and

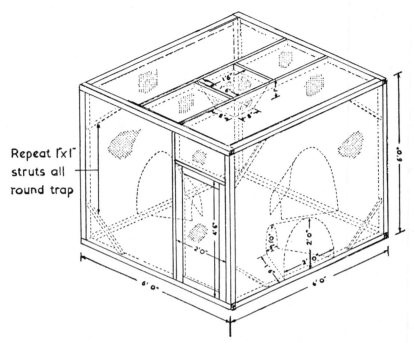

Repeat ⌈×⌉
struts all
round trap

Fig 38   The MAAF Mark 3 rook, jackdaw and carrion crow trap

construction as the Mark 2, the advantage here being stronger framing by means of struts at the corners. It also allows of greater diversity in use than either of the previous versions as it can provide entrances in alternative positions to suit the preferences of different types of birds. This is achieved by fitting a cone at the top and funnels at ground level. The top entrance tends to be selected by jackdaws and the side entrances by carrion crows, while rooks will enter through either position.

The last pattern produced by the Ministry for these birds, the Mark 4, is constructed of the same materials as the other models, but is 12ft by 6ft at the base. The major difference is in having the top covered only by 4in rope sheep netting. Fitted tightly at first, it is allowed to assume a natural sag and then requires no funnel. When carrion crows, particularly, are troublesome, the suggested bait is a dead hare or lamb.

Pigeon Traps

The feral pigeon trap used by the Ministry measures 6ft by 4ft at the base and is 5ft high. If it is to be used on the flat roofs of buildings in urban areas, it is recommended that it should be made in three sections for easier access through doorways. As seen in Fig 39, it is

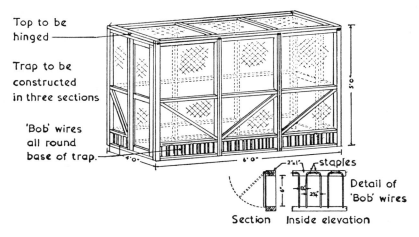

Top to be hinged

Trap to be constructed in three sections

'Bob' wires all round base of trap.

staples

Detail of 'Bob' wires

Section   Inside elevation

Fig 39   The MAAF feral pigeon trap

covered all over with 1in galvanised wire mesh, except for an area at the base of the sides, 6in high, where 'bob' wires are inserted. The detailed diagram shows how these are constructed on the inside from inverted U-shaped pieces of 10swg welding wire stapled to the wooden framework. In this way they are so hinged that while they can be pushed inwards from the outside, the reverse action is impossible providing the limbs of the U-section overlap the bottom batten of the trap.

In urban areas, the traps should be located wherever a flat roof is conveniently near a source of annoyance from pigeons, but in rural areas they can be sited on the ground. At first, they are left with the doors (diagonally opposite) open and the roof detached, or swung back if hinged. When birds are entering and leaving freely, the top is put on and finally the doors are closed a day or two later.

The different siting for traps used in towns and in rural areas is for one obvious reason—it would be impractical in urban areas to have large aviary traps on the ground, since even in parks it is unlikely that they would be left undisturbed to do their work. It is also common in built-up areas to find pigeons perching on the tops of tall buildings and although they will descend to feed, a glance upwards—say in Trafalgar Square, London—will show how many more there are perched up aloft. In relatively quiet rural areas, pigeons are inclined to spend more time feeding on the ground, and the traps are also likely to be left free from interference by people.

The bait suggested for such traps is a 4:2:1 mixture of New Zealand maple peas, small whole maize and wheat. Some of this is placed sparingly around the outside of the base and some inside. Water is provided, together with wooden boxes laid on their sides as shelters.

Inevitably, from time to time, a pigeon trap will receive a visit from a homing pigeon. If it has a ring with a code indicating a homing union, it could be handed over to a local fancier who would no doubt arrange for its return to the appropriate body.

In all these large aviary-type traps, a collecting-box can be built-in to facilitate the culling of captive birds. A wire netting partition is built at a distance of 2ft from one side of the cage and extends three-

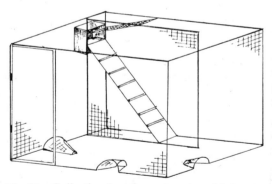

Fig 40   Collecting-box for aviary-type bird traps

quarters of the length of the cage. At the closed end, a collecting-box is placed as shown in Fig 40 and a funnel of netting leads up to it. The collector enters the trap and drives birds into the funnel. When they are in the box, a door is released by a controlled cord at the open end of the partition.

The Heligoland Trap

A similar principle is used in a special trap known as the Heligoland trap, a name derived from its use in catching migrating passerine birds in the Heligoland area. It is particularly useful where an area visited by migrant birds offers no natural cover.

Bushes are planted to lead towards a large wire-netting trap (Fig 41), which has an entrance about 24ft by 8ft, funnelled by wire-netting wings 15–20ft long. These wings guide the birds towards the opening, inside which water has been placed to attract them. The trap angles away sharply from the wings for about 20ft and then turns through a similar angle until its width is only about 3ft 6in. The floor of the final section tapers upwards to the catching box. Between the first and last sections of the trap there is a swing door controlled by a cord from the entrance. The catching box has a lid which can be raised parallel with the roof of the trap. The trap height is about 6ft.

The purpose of the trap is mainly to facilitate the ringing (or

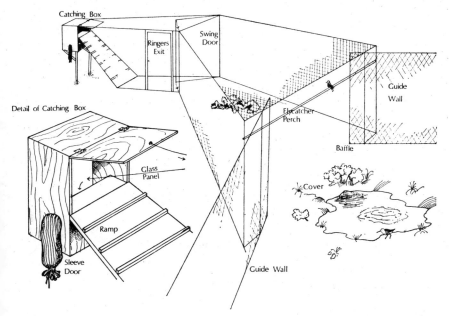

Fig 41   The Heligoland trap

banding) of birds. The ringer (or bander), walks from bush to bush towards the trap, flushing birds as he goes. When they are in the trap they are urged beyond the swing door, which is then released. After a bird has found its way into the catching box the lid is released by a remotely controlled cord, and the bird is attracted towards the rear by a glass panel at the back of the box. Two sheets are arranged so that the upper one slopes downwards while the lower one is vertical. The birds, fluttering against the upper sheet, slide down to the base and dip below a platform extending from the door two-thirds of the way towards the back. Below the platform, leading in from each side of the box, are sleeves for recovering the birds from outside. These can be woollen or heavy-gauge nylon stockings with the feet cut off. Birds will not be able to find their way out of these stockings and they are convenient devices for extracting them.

A door at the side of the last section of the trap allows the ringer to enter without going through the swing door. The guide walls are of 1in wire mesh, the main funnel of ⅝in mesh and the last section of ½in mesh. If a wire is stretched across the trap entrance, some 18in below the roof, it will deflect the birds downwards and act as a perch for flycatchers.

On the island of Skokholm, off the Welsh Pembrokeshire coast, a trap has been employed for catching dunlin. These birds frequent pools and the trap (Fig 42), is placed on a nearby mudbank. It consists of a wire-mesh funnel formed over hoops, made of stout iron

Fig 42   The Skokholm dunlin trap

rod, which extend beyond the floor level so as to secure the trap in the mud. The funnel entrance is 2ft 6in wide and 2ft high, but tapers to 9in at the end of the 6ft run. At a distance of 4ft 6in from the mouth of the trap, a partition with a secondary floor-level funnel leads to the inner section.

Birds are 'walked' by a ringer into the trap and, once in the outer section, are rushed to drive them through to the inner section from which they can be removed for ringing by means of a trapdoor on the roof. It is helpful to provide a guide wall sloping away from one side of the trap mouth for a few feet at a height of about 6in.

Decoys for Wildfowl

The Skokholm dunlin trap has certain features similar to those of a decoy used for ducks and other wildfowl. Its shape is remarkably like the traditional pipe of a duck decoy, though much smaller, and the method of rushing the birds into the trap is the same as that adopted by a decoyman or dog.

Decoys for ducks have a long history, which has been chronicled with great thoroughness by Sir Ralph Payne-Gallwey. As his book is now difficult to come by, it is worthwhile retelling some of the history he relates.

The name 'decoy' is thought to have originated in Holland where these constructions were probably first made. The Dutch speak of an *endekoog*, or duck cage, whereas older writers in English frequently refer to a 'duck coy' which, rendered into current usage, would mean 'duck trap' or 'duck cage'.

While it was the Dutch who brought the presently-used forms of decoys to Britain—they were invited by English kings and estate owners to construct them to Dutch patterns—duck-gathering ponds had been in use in Britain at least from the time of King John. These early decoys took the form of a pond, usually quite large, from which nets acting as wings led towards the funnel. When rushed, the ducks would be unable to take off because of the obstruction offered by netting wings.

These early decoys were operated by estate owners, particularly monastic institutions, both as sources of food for themselves and as commercial enterprises. They also, it would seem, offered an easy means of culling wildfowl when left unsupervised, for there is a record in 1432 of an armed mob which took 600 ducks from a decoy belonging to the abbot of Crowland monastery.

Daniel in his *Rural Sports*, mentions one drive at a decoy in Spalding, in Lincolnshire, which produced 3,000 ducks, and Willughby describes a drive carried out by 400 boats on Deeping Fen yielding 4,000.

The drives were mostly carried out during the summer before the ducklings had acquired their flight feathers and when the adults were moulting. This resulted in such a heavy toll of ducks, including a large number of young, that their numbers began to drop alarmingly and, in an attempt to counter the situation, an Act of Parliament in 1534 forbade the taking of ducks between 31 May and 31 August.

The diarist, Evelyn, records in his memoirs for 29 March 1665 that Charles II was then finishing a decoy in St James's Park, the designer-in-charge being a Dutchman, Sydrach Hileus, who had been specially brought over for the purpose. Evelyn mentions that ducks were *enticed* into it, so that it was probably the first British decoy to function as we now understand them to do.

Once the design proved itself there was a spate of building all over the British Isles, with the exception of Scotland where none appear to have been constructed. The most prolific building took place in the eastern counties, especially in Lincolnshire, where the flat land and plentiful supply of ponds naturally provided these basic requirements for a decoy. At one time there were as many as 110 decoys in East Anglia, spread over the counties of Lincolnshire, Norfolk, Suffolk and Essex, out of a total of 188 in England and Wales. The total in Ireland reached twenty-two.

The heyday of their use was during the eighteenth and early nineteenth centuries, but by the middle of the last century their number had been considerably reduced. Writing in 1886, Sir Ralph Payne-Gallwey could list only forty-three still being used in England and Wales, and three in Ireland. Since then, their numbers have diminished even more sharply. Though there may be a number of old decoys in a state of decay, the writer knows only of two in use, one at Slimbridge on the Gloucestershire side of the River Severn, and the other at Peakirk, in Northamptonshire, both of which belong to the Wildfowl Trust.

There has recently been a restoration of the Boarstall Decoy in Buckinghamshire, thanks to the efforts of the Wildfowlers' Association of Great Britain and Ireland. It is not known when the original was constructed, but Kennet wrote of it in 1815 as a 'fine decoy for wild ducks'. It was still in use in 1886 but at some time thereafter it was abandoned, though never completely destroyed. Completion was scheduled for 1970 as a contribution towards European Conservation Year.

The decoy at Orielton, in Pembrokeshire, was begun in 1868 on an artificial lake first created in 1820. It became important as a ringing centre between the two World Wars, but was abandoned after World War II, although the research station there is still active in other fields.

Slimbridge decoy, as now used by the Wildfowl Trust in Britain, was built in 1840 between the Gloucester–Berkeley canal and the River Severn, on what are called the New Grounds. It has played an important part in the ringing programme of the Trust's research centre.

Decoys for wildfowl have also been used in the United States, where the traditional pattern has been similar to that used in the days before Dutch designs appeared in Britain. Hamilton Gibson described what he called a wild-duck net and which consisted of a single pipe built in the shallows at the edge of a lake. A somewhat unusual feature was a large square enclosed section, or pound, at the terminal end of the pipe, inside which live decoy ducks were placed. The wild ducks could either be driven into the net, or enticed by the decoys. It is recorded that at the end of the last century large numbers of wildfowl were taken annually by these methods and devices around Chesapeake Bay.

Gibson wonders why ducks travelling into a decoy pipe never seem to consider turning about and flying out the way they came, but it is, of course, upon this pattern of behaviour that the success of this type of trap depends. To make doubly sure, the birds' own natural curiosity is supplemented by driving, or enticing them ever deeper into the trap, and certainly when one bird out of a number can be persuaded into a funnel, the remainder will follow.

How a Decoy Works

To understand how a decoy of the Dutch pattern works, it is helpful to know the meaning of the nomenclature associated with it.

A decoy is always worked under the control of a decoyman, and its success as a trap depends largely upon his actions and his control of a dog, together with his knowledge of the birds and the immediate surroundings. The dog used is always called 'Piper', since he works along the *pipes*, which are long curving channels as extensions of the pond. These pipes are covered by netting stretched over *hoops* of wood or iron.

The *screens* are panels made from reeds and placed at intervals along the pipes. They allow the decoyman to remain concealed whenever this is necessary in the process of enticing the ducks.

The *head shew* is a spot between screens at which the decoyman first appears behind the ducks. His actions frighten them and they move farther along a pipe into which they have already been lured.

The breast wall is made from one or two screens flanking the right of the entrance to the pipe. It shelters the *breast wall landing*. This, as well as the *back-wing landing*, consists of smooth banks on the flanks of the pipe entrance, and its purpose is to tempt ducks into landing. Once landed, the ducks are said to be *banked*, and are then considered to be at a suitable distance for decoying along the pipe nearest to them.

The *draught* of a pipe is that part of the pond which narrows in front of a pipe.

Halfway along each pipe entrance are *reed edges* consisting of small beds of reeds designed to provide places for waterfowl to hide in.

Between the high screens are connecting low ones called *dog jumps*, designed to allow the dog to negotiate the length of a pipe when decoying.

The *yackoop* (a corruption of 'wake-up') is a special dog jump between the breast wall and high screen. It is the dog's movement over this which attracts banked ducks and urges them into activity.

The extreme end of the pipe, where it has become very narrow, is known as the *tunnel net*. This is detachable in order to recover the ducks trapped in it at the end of a decoying manoeuvre.

Decoy ducks are tame ducks kept at a decoy to attract wildfowl into the pipes.

Food is the grain used for feeding fowl along the pipes.

In order to mask the odour of clothing and the breath of men visiting the decoy, a piece of burning turf or peat is held on a stick, and this is referred to as *turf*.

The pattern or plan of a decoy can vary a great deal and may have to conform to local topography. It is a personal decision on the part of the designer, who must understand the likely movements of wildfowl coming to the area. The number of pipes can vary, but a high-yielding decoy will usually have three or four. Simple versions have been used with only a single pipe and over-ambitious patterns have employed as many as eight.

A decoy pond can be anything between one and three acres in extent, but is always shallow and seldom deeper than 3ft. Each pipe will have a mouth width of up to 20ft and a length of about 70yd. At the tunnel net it will have narrowed to 2ft in width. Similarly, the height of the entrance may go up to 18ft, but reduces to 2ft at the end. Water depth in the channel of a pipe will be about 18in at the mouth, but only a few inches at the extremity.

The screens are usually placed along the left-hand side of the pipe at a distance of 2 to 3ft from the channel bank. They are approximately 6ft high and 12ft long and so arranged that there are about a dozen, overlapping in echelon pattern for two-thirds of the pipe length. All these features are seen in Fig 43, which could serve as a plan for the construction of a decoy.

The art of decoying is only acquired with lengthy practice and tutoring by an experienced master, so it is little wonder that, in the past, decoying was passed on as a family tradition. One of the most famous decoy families in England was that of the Skeltons, who originated at Friskney, in Lincolnshire, but whose descendants spread to many areas of Britain from about 1807 onwards.

In luring ducks from the pond and along a pipe, the dog is under the decoyman's control and responds to whistles directing its actions. Being exceedingly inquisitive, ducks react quickly to a dog appearing suddenly from behind a screen along a pipe, at a short distance from the entrance. They swim inwards to get at the dog and, when enough are enticed, the decoyman suddenly appears at the head shew. This frightens the ducks, which rapidly paddle deeper into the funnel. Meanwhile the dog has concealed itself behind the screens, and the same procedure is successively repeated until, finally, the birds are flushed into the tunnel net.

At one time it was traditional for a decoyman to wear a red coat, in the belief that this gave him a more frightening appearance, and scattered grain was sometimes used as an alternative or additional means of enticement.

Some of the largest traps ever to have been used, decoys are live traps but they seldom capture automatically. A lone duck might find its way into a tunnel net through curiosity and a reluctance to turn about, but they can only be really effectively used when operated in the fashion described.

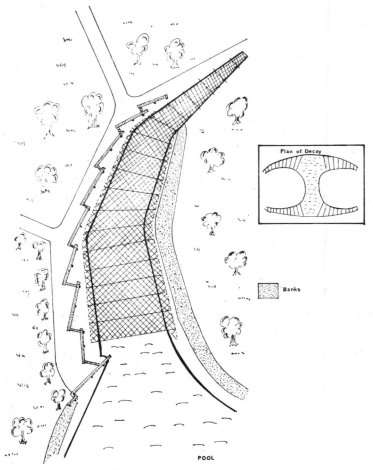

Fig 43   Diagram showing a plan of a decoy pipe.
(*Inset*) Plan of a four-pipe decoy

A Flood-lit Trap

Although it does not cover as much ground as a decoy, the flood-light trap developed in the United States is bigger in gross size of the trapping device. The trap consists of metal frames with lightweight small-mesh netting spread over them. At the mouth, the frame might be as much as 30ft square, but succeeding frames would diminish in size, so forming a funnel, maybe 60 to 80ft long. Beyond this would be a long, low black tent.

The trap is set up at a night-roosting place frequented by large flocks of birds and floodlights are placed in the mouth of the trap, which should face the roosts. The lights are switched on, and men walk towards the mouth flushing the roosting birds and driving them into the funnel, to be captured inside the tent. Strongly gregarious birds which flock at night roosts would include rooks, jackdaws, starlings and, of course, house sparrows.

Hoop-fence Noose Traps

In Siberia, wildfowl, and ducks in particular, are caught in large numbers using a simple technique. When the Indigirka river overflows its banks small islands are left standing out of the water, and these the native Yakut huntsmen encircle, at a short distance inland from the water's edge, with a willow-wand hooped fence. The hoops overlap (Fig 44) but at certain points there are gaps wide enough for a duck to pass through.

Fig 44   Siberian hoop-fence noose traps

When the ducks come ashore to sun themselves or for the night, they seek gaps in the fence, each of which has a cunningly contrived plaited horse-hair snare fixed to it. Ducks passing through these are killed, and a fair number can be caught during a single night for, oddly enough, surviving birds do not seem to be affected by the presence of corpses in the snares.

On the banks of the Orinoco in South America, the local Indians use an almost identical method—yet another example of similar methods being adopted independently by primitive peoples living great distances apart.

CHAPTER SEVEN

Mammal Traps: 1

ONCE mammals and birds had emerged as divergent forms of the hitherto dominant reptiles, they were destined to become the supreme colonisers of land and air respectively. And had it not been for the evolution of the human mammal but a short while ago in the earth's long history, who knows in what direction ultimate animal supremacy might have travelled?

Some scientists consider man's appearance to have been a chance phenomenon: conversely, theologians attribute his arrival on earth to divine planning which had ordered the programme of earthly progression towards this climax. The possibility of his not remaining in this apparently unassailable position does not concern us here, except perhaps in speculating on the traps which could be engineered for him by an as yet unknown foe.

Early man, a little unsure of the competition he might meet, was cautious in sizing up the opposition and took no chances. No doubt he soon realised that his most dangerous opponents were the animals closest in relationship to himself, and it is almost certain that among the first defences he built were traps—mammal traps.

It is important at this stage to be quite sure as to the kind of animals with which we are concerned when we use the term 'mammal'. The mammals are often spoken of as 'animals', which they are, but using the term in a sense which suggests, for example, that birds are not animals. Unfortunately, one hears zoologists, who ought to know better, often talking about 'birds and animals' when, in fact, they should be saying 'birds and mammals'. How then are we to get our terms sorted out? In the first instance, if we have something living we could ask ourselves if it is a plant. If we are sure that it is not but know that it is alive, then it has to be an animal, for living things, except for ultramicroscopic forms which are difficult to place in a certain category, have to be either plants or animals. With this

153

clear we must then realise that an animal can be worm, crab, insect, snail, sea urchin, fish, frog, snake, bird or mammal. The mammal, therefore, like a fish or a bird, is simply a special kind of animal. What makes it special, in the way that feathers are special in a bird, is a combination of many physical and functional features, but those most readily recognised are the presence of a coat of fur or hair and an ability to give birth to live young, which can then be suckled at the breast. It is from this last feature that the name for the group comes, since breasts are technically known as mammary glands. It should be noted, incidentally, that there is one group of mammals which does not produce live young, but lays eggs instead. This is a group known as the Monotremes and includes the duck-billed platypus, a primitive mammal living in Australia. Despite the fact that these animals lay eggs, they do have mammary glands and when the eggs eventually hatch the newly emerging young are suckled by the mother.

Of course, mammals are not all alike and just as birds can be divided as a group into smaller assemblages, such as falcons, ducks, owls and larks, to name only a few, so mammals include such creatures as horses, cattle, dogs, bears and seals. The last named group, and also whales, might at first appear to be misfits. It is true that, superficially, they appear to be more like fish, but they do really have fur, which is evident on close examination, and they do suckle their young.

From the early days onwards men spent more time and energy on designing mammal traps than on any other kinds. It is not, therefore, surprising that this is the largest trap category, not only in distinct varieties but also in the total numbers produced. Yet despite their many patterns, mammal traps can all be assigned to one or other of five groups. These are pitfall traps; deadfalls; snares; spring traps (which are sometimes associated with snares) and cage or box traps. In one form or another, these five groups have been represented among the other categories of animal traps, but it is not unlikely that the idea of using them to capture other animals was prompted by their original success in taking mammals.

Pitfall Traps

It is appropriate to consider this kind of trap first, because, as we have already seen, it must have been man's earliest device for capturing animals by remote control.

In its simplest form, it is just a hole in the ground into which, with

Page 155 (*above*) A Fenn trap being set in a tunnel; (*below*) detail of trap

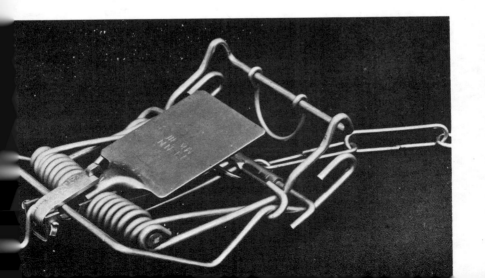

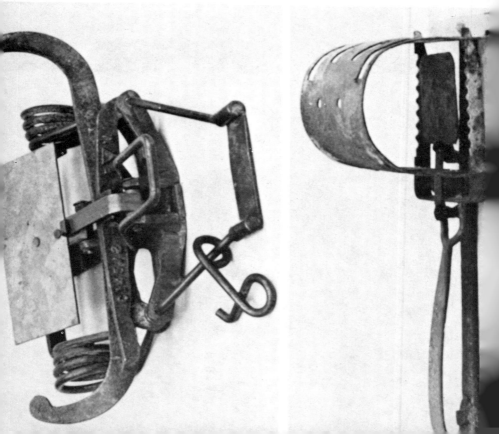

Page 156 (*above left*) The Juby trap; (*below left*) the Everitt rat trap; (*above right*) squirrel taken in Imbra trap in two-piece tunnel

luck, an unwary animal might stumble and become trapped. The natural overgrowth of pits by vegetation, and the consequent advantage of concealment, would soon have impressed the first men and suggested the possibility of digging their own holes and providing them with artificial screening. This technique is still in use all over the world, not only for catching animals, but also men and their machines in time of war.

Primitive societies depend upon pitfall traps, large and small, for capturing dangerous animals. Elephants have been victims of these pits from the time of the woolly mammoth, while modern ivory poachers still find them effective and discreet.

From this simple pattern, all manner of elaborations have developed; especially those designed to entice the animal into the pit, rather than rely upon the relatively few occasions when a wild creature's natural alertness is caught off-guard. An example of such a lure is the trap used by Eskimoes to catch Arctic foxes, and its success illustrates the advantage of understanding the habits of animals and harnessing these quirks of behaviour to the design of the trap. For the Arctic fox trap depends for its success entirely upon the natural greed of these animals, which is such that trappers can depend on them rushing for food, regardless as to where it is placed.

The trap is a box-shaped pit dug in frozen ground, or in the great depth of ice which covers lakes. The pit has perpendicular sides, is about 8ft deep, and its mouth is covered, except for a small opening about 2ft square, by blocks of ice. A foot below ground level there is placed a wooden platform balanced on wooden pivots secured to the side-walls. This platform holds the bait—fresh meat or fish—which is so secured that the platform remains level.

Seeing the bait, a hungry fox will discard any caution it might otherwise observe and jump directly on to the platform, so upsetting its balance and tipping the animal into the pit. The platform rights itself again ready for the next fox to come after the bait, and such a pit can catch a number of foxes one after another (Fig 45).

Prof J. G. D. Clark has mentioned the discovery in recent times of pits in ice for catching reindeer, and it is thought that urine was used as a bait. He suggests that in all probability traps like these could have been used in Glacial times.

A variation of the Arctic fox trap which can be adopted for catching small mammals consists of a simple wooden box with a platform just below the mouth as in the fox trap. The platform should prefer-

Fig 45   Arctic fox trap

ably be made of thin steel sheeting and should have loops of steel welded on opposite sides to receive the nails or metal rods acting as pivots. Bait is fixed to the platform, which swings over when an animal jumps on to it. When rodents are likely to be taken, it is a good plan to line the inside of the box with tin plate, otherwise the animals might gnaw their way through the wooden sides. A barrel can be similarly adapted and, with about a foot of water in the bottom, makes a good multi-catch rat trap.

An even cheaper pitfall made from a barrel dispenses with the pivoted platform and uses a sheet of paper instead. To ensure a good catch, the paper is stretched across the top, tied to the sides and damped, but left intact for a day or two. Fresh bait is placed on top as rats gain confidence and remove it. After a while, when the rats appear to be feeding regularly, the paper is coated with gum arabic and the bait sealed to it. The paper is then cut with a razor blade across the centre in the form of a cross, the gum ensuring that it remains taut. The now-confident rats will not hestitate to jump on to the paper, but will drop through it into the water in the bottom of the barrel, the cut paper then reverting to its former appearance in readiness for the next hungry visitor. These simple traps have been known to clear rat-infested premises in a short time. An improvement might be to place a wooden plank, as a projection over the top of the barrel, from the walls of a building such as a barn. If the plank is linked to a natural rat-run, it will provide a ready-made pathway to the trap.

Rats are creatures of regular and recognisable habits, so that although they are cunning in the extreme and wary of traps, a thorough knowledge of their normal reactions to given situations helps the trapper considerably. One especially noticeable trait in common brown rats is their unwillingness to come out into the open. This applies even inside buildings, where they will hug the walls when moving about. If they are moving over roof rafters, they leave characteristic scuff marks on the upright joists around which they have to travel. Similarly, where sacks of grain or other edible materials are stored, there are tell-tale black scuffs on sacks or boxes around which they move on their regular routeways. If they want to cross from one side of a building to another, they will prefer to use overhead crossbeams, and this habit can be turned to good account in trapping by extending a beam from a wall to come over bait lying on the ground. The rat will attempt to reach the bait from the beam, so that if a trap is placed on the beam the rat is most likely to be caught.

Although they can swim quite well, rats will skirt water if at all possible, rather than cross it. They have keen hearing and a good sense of smell, so that traps are unlikely to be sprung in noisy areas or where there are any smells which rats find offensive. They are particularly sensitive to human smell and to that of predators, such as cats, dogs and ferrets.

The 'Pied Piper' and other Rat Traps

Two variations of pitfall traps for catching rats are described by A. Moore Hogarth in his book *Rats and How to Destroy Them*. One of these is known as the 'Pied Piper' trap and is in the form of a tunnel, the outside of which is used by poultry as a feeding hopper. It can be made of steel, should be about 30in long and 4in square in section, and the centre of the floor has a loose but pivoted section 12in long. The tunnel is fitted over the mouth of an oil drum sunk into the ground. The drum has removable lids for all but the section occupied by the tunnel, or the trap and hopper can be made so as to fit over the drum completely.

At first, the floor in the tunnel is secured by pins pushed through the sides and under each end of the pivoted section. The inside is filled with a liberal supply of bait—corn grains or barley seeds with a dressing of aniseed—and left until rats are feeding regularly. The fixing pins are now removed and the rats will then be precipitated into the drum, which should have a foot of water in the bottom.

Similar to the barrel traps are those dug as pits 5ft deep, but with sides sloping outwards from the mouth, ie, the floor has a greater area than the mouth. The mouth is covered with a wooden lattice. The floor is strewn with chaff and on it is placed a jar with a narrow neck containing a mixture of honey, maize, and hempseed. Rats jump down but cannot get the bait from the bottle, and it is claimed that they will eventually turn cannibal and devour each other, the one eventually found presumably being like the sailor in the 'Yarn of the Nancy Bell'.

Remarkably like the Pied Piper trap is the tunnel trap which at one time was used in Monmouthshire for catching moles. A model of the trap situation is illustrated on p 85. Like the rat trap, this has a wooden tunnel with a pivoted false floor, but in this case the tunnel is set in a mole tunnel known to be in use. The earthenware pot—like a crock—is buried directly under the false floor. These pots were specially made and had holes at the neck through which string or wire could be fastened to hold the tunnel secure. The bottom was filled with water, and if rain and drainage water seeped in, holes half-way up the sides of the pot prevented the water level from rising any higher. Thus moles would never be able to ride upwards to an escape level during a rainstorm. Incidentally, and contrary to a commonly-held belief, moles *can* swim.

Yet another use for pitfall traps is in catching rabbits, a method which has been used in Britain and also in Australia. They could only be used in conjunction with rabbit-proof walls or fences, and at certain points in these, small holes or *meuses* were made, just large enough for a rabbit to penetrate. Immediately inside the holes were the pitfall traps, or what were called 'tip traps' because they worked like the Pied Piper. Sometimes these pitfalls were set in runs on the outside of a rabbit-proof fence to catch rabbits running up and down in search of an opening.

Rabbits, unlike rats, lack an instinctive awareness of traps, though they share with rats a tendency to keep to regular pathways, dictated in the case of European rabbits by the network of underground tunnels and surface boltholes which make up a warren. Among the rabbits and varying hares of North America—as with European and African hares—there is no burrow system, but instead a series of covers in tall grass areas, among brushwood or in snow, known as forms. But in both cases there are the well-worn paths between boltholes or forms along which these animals habitually travel, though they sometimes make slight detours or produce dead-end side trails. The regular paths, obvious to the trained eye of a trapper, provide a perfect site for traps.

Rabbits and hares are perhaps among the easiest animals to trap, despite their acutely sensitive hearing and keen sense of smell. Moreover, their acute sense of hearing can be used to advantage by trappers who, having placed traps along a network of runs, can move away from the area and then work their way back to drive the animals towards the traps by shooting and clubbing the ground. Young boys generally count rabbits among their first trap victims, and hungry trappers out of luck with other animals have generally been able to fill their stewpot with the assistance of a wire noose set on a rabbit trail. The British poacher, before the days of myxomatosis, would have had empty pockets on many nights had he not been able to rely upon catching a rabbit.

Deadfall Traps
After the pitfall traps, deadfalls would have been one of the next kinds of trap to be made by early man. He probably started by hurling stones at animals from a cliff-top or a high tree, and it would require only slightly more subtle thinking to realise that a stone could be made to kill an animal when activated by the animal itself.

The stone deadfall trap has been used successfully for many thousands of years by peoples in all lands, its main application having been to kill small mammals up to squirrel size. For animals beyond this size, the weight of stone necessary would defy sensitive balancing, which is the key to success. In their simplest form, stone deadfalls are merely propped up a few inches with a short but strong twig. Bait is scattered around the twig, which is adjusted so finely that a slight touch will bring the stone crashing down. Alternatively, a cord can be attached to the twig and pulled by a concealed observer.

A rather more elaborate triggering device employs the 'figure 4' construction. Fig 46 shows the set-up for this, which requires only three pieces of wood suitably shaped and notched. The horizontal bar of the '4' carries the bait, which is either fastened around the bar or hung from its end. Like all deadfalls this trap is non-selective and is as likely to catch a bird as a mammal. One can, however, seek to entice certain animals by using the baits most attractive to them.

Fig 46   'Figure 4' trap with stone deadfall

It would not have been long before the stone deadfall principle was extended to other kinds of weights and a wide range of triggering devices. Eskimoes, for example, have used ice-blocks instead of stones.

An easy alternative for primitive forest-dwelling peoples would be to use a block of wood—part of a branch for small mammals, or a portion of a tree-trunk for larger ones. A. R. Harding in his book *Deadfalls and Snares* published in the USA in 1907 describes this as a pole deadfall, and suggests that by choosing poles between 4in and 6in thick the catch can be varied from skunks to opossums in North America. In Britain, the range might be from stoats to mink. Fig 47 shows a home-made pole deadfall. The cage, made from twigs and flat stones, would be about 12in square. The sides consist of stakes, 30in long and driven 14in into the ground, so as to prop up the stones, and the roof is formed of sticks laid across the sides.

Four stouter sticks make up the deadfall guides at the mouth of the cage, as shown, and a half-sawn log is placed, cut surface upper-most, between these. If the ground is hard the log can be omitted, but

Fig 47   Pole deadfall trap

on soft ground it ensures a better kill. The pole deadfall is propped at an angle by means of a prop-stick and prevented from slewing by notching the end on the ground and holding it in place with a stick driven into the ground. The trigger and bait-stick is fastened to the prop where this rests under the pole. The end on the ground inside the cage has a chicken or some other fleshy meat fastened to it. Animals coming to the trap will reach inside for the bait and, by pulling this, release the pole which strikes them across their backs.

Animal Catches
The opossum, or 'possum as he is usually called, is the only indigenous marsupial (or pouched mammal) in North America, although Australia can boast many examples from this primitive group in her fauna. One of the features of the group, apart from the obvious pouch housing the mammary glands for suckling, is the small and under-developed brain, so that the opossum, which is no exception, is rather slow and stupid. Were it not for its great tenacity for life and an apparently hardy physique, it would no doubt, like so many other marsupials, have succumbed to pressure from its more advanced mammalian relatives. Even so, its slowness combined with a certain greed makes it susceptible to deadfall traps of the kind just described; which, in view of the value of its pelt, is fortunate for fur trappers.

The common North American skunk is unmistakable, the only animal in that part of the world to have so conspicuous a white stripe along the back of its black coat. It also has another and less pleasant characteristic, unlikely to be forgotten by anyone without experience who has tried to kill a skunk caught in a trap and suffered the full force of a discharge from the animal's battery of anal musk glands. The scent is ejected as a mist-like spray for a distance of eight to ten feet, although downhill it could be carried a much greater distance. So long as the animal has its tail down it is relatively safe, but when in defence it will lower its head, erect its tail and fan the tail hairs. Faced with this, one can only be advised to retreat and it is worth remembering that a skunk's defence is not confined to a single salvo from its glands. However, skunks are reluctant to discharge their scent, and if not crowded they will soon adopt a less menacing posture. The best way of killing a skunk, to avoid the effect of its musk, is to drown it, grasping it by the neck and hindquarters and keeping the tail down. The skunk can be caught in a deadfall snare suitably baited with a frog, small dead rodent, or even a fowl.

The mink belongs to the same family as the skunk and the common stoat and weasel in Britain are near relatives. The stoat, like its cousin, the ermine, changes it coat colour in winter, becoming snow-white except for the black tip to its tail in all but the southern counties.

Mink are found near rivers, lakes and dams, where their burrowing activities can be a nuisance, breaking down riverbanks and also dam walls. Water bailiffs, too, have no love for them, complaining that they kill off prime fish, especially salmon and trout. Natives of North America, mink are now spreading in many parts of Britain, the animals having been introduced originally for fur-farming and subsequently escaping sporadically in many districts. Mink can be trapped using a deadfall but, in practice, a cage trap using fish bait is more likely to be successful, especially if it is previously left baited and unset for a day or two to give the animal confidence.

All the mustelids, the family to which these animals belong, tend to be omnivorous, so that finding an attractive bait is not too difficult. In many cases a tunnel alone is intriguing enough to induce them to enter, so that a steel trap placed inside is likely to produce a catch. Stoats and weasels are residents of copses and woodlands from which they move out to feed in open country, but never too far away from cover for a hurried retreat when danger threatens. They are frequently accused of raiding poultry yards and are notorious in the eyes of gamekeepers for their attacks on his gamebirds. Hens are, therefore, a likely bait in traps, but often a knowledge of their habitual paths enables effective use to be made of steel or the new spring traps without using bait. Stoats and weasels are trapped as vermin and are not protected in Britain.

Trail-set Deadfalls
Trail-set deadfalls have been designed to operate by dropping a weight suspended from a tree branch overhanging a natural run. Fig 48 shows an example of one of these. A rock, or log, held in a harness of cord is pulled over a tree-limb overhanging a trail until the weight is about a foot above the ground. The free end of the cord comes down to the base of the tree and is fastened to a short length of wood having a side-branch, as shown (or a nail could be driven through instead). This projection is then engaged lightly in a notch cut into the trunk of the tree. The trigger is baited and any pull on the bait releases the weight, which descends on the animal. Fig 48 also shows an alternative triggering arrangement which relies upon a trip-cord across the run instead of a bait. A particularly deadly version, designed for bears, uses a harpoon buried in a log in place of a stone or plain log.

The ordinary stone or log deadfall is used as a trail-set trap for larger mammals, such as deer, antelope, badgers and porcupines, which follow regular trails. The significant difference when trapping

Fig 48   Trail-set deadfall trap. Two alternative triggers

for any one of these lies in knowing the bait which is uniquely appropriate (see Chapter Nine, on Baits). The deadfall must be so suspended that it will drop on to the creature's neck or back which should be broken by the falling weight. The damage would probably be less severe if the stone caught an animal about its rump, where there is more fat and muscle padding the backbone. Knowing the animal's body length is therefore important in determining the distance to be allowed between the bait stick where the animal's head will be, and the point where the deadfall weight must land.

Portable Deadfalls
Apart from the many variations of the deadfall designed for construction in the field, there have also been numerous forms of portable traps which employ this principle. Some of these have been made and sold commercially since, at least, medieval times. C. Roth, in his account of medieval mouse traps, mentions two wooden ones constructed to the same sort of general pattern as that seen on the window shutter of St Joseph's workshop in the Mérode Altarpiece. The two listed by Roth were from manuscripts dating around AD 1450, while the Mérode Altarpiece is thought to be a little older, *circa* 1430.

The basic construction was that of a wooden tray measuring about 8in by 4in. One or two uprights of dowel rod form would extend from the base, and if there were two they were usually joined by a wooden bar across their tops. The weight was a heavy block of wood shaped to fit inside the tray and drilled to slide up and down the dowels. A piece of cord, fastened to the centre of the block by a staple, passed through a hole in the cross piece and down to a trigger mechanism on the side of the tray which was usually linked to a bait paddle inside the tray. Movement of the paddle released the trigger and brought the weight crashing down on to the animal seeking the bait. The type seen in Fig 49 is an example of one commonly in use during the last century, and is now in the collection of Derby Museum.

An example of a mouse trap on the same principle but of slightly different design is the 'Mortis' trap, designed and patented by Richard Adcock during the last century. Fig 50 shows the difference is that the dowel slide is fastened to the weight and slides up and down a hole in the three-sided frame built between the ends of the tray.

The other deadfall trap found on the St Joseph panel of the

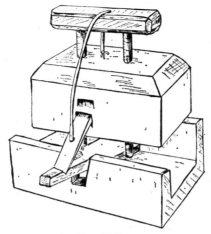

Fig 49   Deadfall mouse trap

Master of Flemalle's painting operates on yet another principle, namely, the use of a clapper tautened by a twisted cord spring so as to place pressure on a wooden board held at an angle by a baited prop. Removal of the prop brings the wooden board down as pressure on the clapper is released.

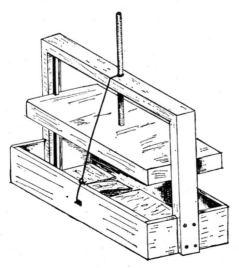

Fig 50   The 'Mortis' trap

The box deadfall has one advantage over other types and that is its double role as a deadfall and tunnel trap. A box, about 1ft long, 6in high and 4in wide, is built from $\frac{1}{2}$in timber but without ends. The weight is a block of wood 1in thick, running the whole length of the box and wide enough to use the sides of the box as guides. Both the sides of the block and the box must be well polished to ensure a smooth sliding action of the surfaces against each other. The block has a waxed cord stapled to the centre of its top surface and running through a hole in the centre of the roof of the box. The cord is long enough to stretch to a trigger on the outside of the box when the weight is raised as high as it will go. The floor of the box is provided with a square hole, 3in long and 3in wide, into which is fitted a treadle platform of tin plate. Wire pivots soldered to the platform base fit into the sides of the hole and project through on one side for attachment of the trigger lever. The action of the trigger can be seen from Fig 51. The platform is suitably baited and the trap placed in a run frequented by mice. If field mice are being caught, the tunnel can be camouflaged with grass and twigs, but care must be taken to ensure that the triggering mechanism is not fouled by vegetation.

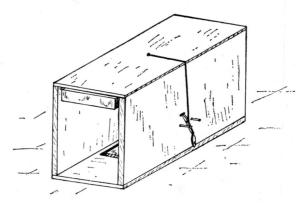

Fig 51   Box deadfall trap

The Board-Flap Trap

A slightly different action is employed in the board-flap trap, which is also intended for mice. It consists of two boards, each 1in thick and 12in square, hinged together on one side as shown in Fig 52. The base has a piece of stout wire fastened midway between the two sides and 1in from the front edge, and carefully formed to provide an arc through which the upper board can slide when a hole is made in it

Fig 52   Board-flap trap

exactly corresponding to the position of the wire on the lower board. Another hole is drilled 3in from the hinged edge of the upper board and made wider on the lower surface than on the upper. The lower board has a hole drilled, of about 1½in diameter, to correspond with the hole in the upper board when the two are brought together. The hole in the upper board takes a bait wire 1½in long and having an eye formed on the outside of the upper surface. The hole in the lower board is to receive the bait when the trap is triggered, and so prevent the mass of bait allowing the mouse to escape. A spindle of split cane, 9in long, is fitted through the eye of the bait wire and lightly caught under a tin-tack fastened at the opposite end of the upper board. The spindle, when in position, receives the upper end of the guide wire and keeps the upper board raised. Movement of the bait wire releases the spindle from the tack head and so allows the upper board to slide down the wire guide.

Snares

Just as pitfall and deadfall traps cannot be designed to catch mammals exclusively, so snares set to catch a particular mammal are as likely to capture another kind or even a bird.

Snares are almost as old in origin as the pitfall and deadfall, and there is good evidence to confirm that they were used by Palaeolithic man. The material from which they have been made has depended upon where they were used and the resources available. Sinews have always been favourites among primitive hunting peoples—the products of the catch being made to provide for future supplies. The long sinews of wild oxen or deer, when softened with grease, would make admirable draw-cords.

Entwined horsehair has also been used for thousands of years, and several strands twisted together have some of the strength and properties of wire. The hair is taken from the horse's tail and one author, who no doubt spoke from practical and possibly painful experience, recommended that the horse chosen should be a good-tempered one. If a long hair is doubled about its middle and then twisted from about a third of an inch beyond the bend, the loose ends can be threaded through the loop formed and fastened to an anchoring stake.

Modern nooses are made of wire, preferably twisted brass wire, and the loop made by clipping the loose end to the main part or fastening it to a brass eyelet. A modern snare is often used 'stopped'; that is to say, the travel of the loop along the main body of the wire is limited. In this manner a snare can be set to catch an animal but will not cause severe chafing of the skin.

Another way of providing a more humane snare is to use a swivel where the snare wire is fastened to the anchoring stake. This prevents an animal twisting the snare during attempts to escape and either severely chafing its skin or pulling free the anchor stake in the process.

Those who are experienced with snares, used either alone or linked with some spring device, consider them to be among the most efficient and humane types of traps for animals. Certainly they have the further advantage of portability, and a skilled trapper can frequently manufacture them from whatever he finds to hand in the field.

The Poacher's Weapon

Above all, the snare has become by far the most favoured weapon of the poacher. It is easily concealed about the person and, deftly hidden in undergrowth of grassland and forest, snares have probably been responsible for more free dinners than any other ruse employed. Nor are poachers to be found only among the underprivileged members of society, for among their ranks can be numbered landed gentry eager to take advantage of a neighbour's laxity, professional men welcoming the thrill of the game as a relaxation from exacting daily work and—it must be admitted—the occasional gamekeeper glad enough to supplement his normal fare.

Some of the techniques used by poachers reveal the large amount of fieldcraft mastered by the better ones. Richard Jefferies, author of *The Amateur Poacher* and *The Gamekeeper at Home*, records how 'wires', the countryman's expression for a snare, are preferred by poachers to shooting, because, apart from their silence, there is seldom any blood to stain the pockets. He also explains how farm labourers-turned-poachers will make use of dry land drains in order to conceal wires.

The important point to remember about snares is that success depends upon restricting their use to animals of regular habits. Animals which seldom follow set routes from their holes, burrows or lodges will only be caught in a snare by pure chance. Since it does not depend upon a bait for its action and is not a means in itself of attracting animals, a snare must be set in places known to be frequented by animals and its effectiveness will, therefore, largely depend upon the extent of the trapper's knowledge of animal lore.

Snares are ideal for catching rabbits and have also been used quite effectively for catching pheasants and guineafowl. All these animals have long necks from which a tightened noose has little chance of being pulled free. Animals of regular habits but with short or 'podgy' necks are far less suitable victims for snares, unless the snares have been designed to catch an animal by its foot, as in the Aldrich snare for catching bears.

The snares we are considering here are the simple, straightforward kind, which can be employed in all manner of sizes and made from many different materials. The snares seen in the illustration on p 86 are both examples of home-made snares used by primitive peoples in underdeveloped countries. There is a fair degree of skilful employment of local materials in the trap used by Eskimoes, mostly for catching squirrels and Arctic hares. The noose is made from a sinew, probably reindeer, and the trap is interesting in using a novel 'slip-knot'. One end of the noose is fastened to a hole in the end of the shaft of a hollow long-bone; the other end is drawn through the bone cavity after removal of the marrow. The free end of the noose is now secured to a peg and, in turn, an anchoring cord is attached.

The snares shown in the lower picture form a line of twenty-seven nooses, and are used in the Upper Shan States of Burma, particularly under jungle conditions. Each snare is a very cleverly contrived article consisting of a sharpened anchor peg, daggerlike, with a hilt to which is bound a fine springy cane. The tip of the cane has bound to it the functional noose, and the strings linking the separate snares, hilt-to-hilt, are spaced at intervals of no more than 12in, so that the whole forms an effective barrier in jungle undergrowth. The springiness of the canes allows a gradual arrestment of entrapped animals.

The method of using these snares is to set them out in an area where ground-living animals, such as small game birds, are known to abound. Tribesmen would then form a circle enclosing an area behind the line of traps and, at a given signal, drive the animals towards the traps by shouting and beating the ground.

Similar traps are designed for small animals, such as rabbits, stoats and weasels, in Britain, but stronger ones are made for bigger animals like foxes and badgers. These snares are of all-steel construction with double-action swivels which prevent tangling by rotation at the noose side and also at the steel wire lashing side. They are available from S. Young & Sons, Ltd, but there has recently been a fair amount of public condemnation of the use of snares for taking foxes and more will be said of this later.

Snares for Larger Animals

For very large animals, snares designed to secure the creature by a foot have been found efficient, though often inhumane. A. S. Mossman and B. G. R. Reynolds, writing in the *Journal of Mammalogy* in 1962, have described a number of mammal traps used in Africa and included among these is a foot trap for antelope (Fig 53). This makes use of a trip stick placed across an antelope trail. When the animal stumbles on the stick, its foot will go automatically into the noose which, being attached to a sapling acting as a spring, causes the beast to be swung up above the trail. This is a common adaptation to a simple noose and has the advantage of keeping the trapped animal clear of scavengers.

The Aldrich Trap

A more modern and well-designed foot snare, intended for catching grizzly and other bears, is the Aldrich trap. This is made in the United States where there are a number of regulations restricting the methods of trapping bears. Some states, such as Maine, ban steel

Fig 53   Antelope foot trap

traps entirely, while others, like New Hampshire, restrict their use to pens having 3ft high guardrails and marked by notices carrying the words 'Bear Trap'. There is little basic difference between the latest types of bear traps and the mantraps used a century ago, so that any legislation which either bans bear traps or requires warning to be given of their siting has the merit of being humane.

The Aldrich trap is spring-activated and needs to be placed near a pen containing baits. The spring has two arms and, between these, long double prongs anchor the trap to the ground as well as securing one arm of the spring. The other arm is pressed down and the tripping mechanism primed by catching the trigger. Above the prongs there is a hook and the swivel eye is fastened through it. The cable of the noose is passed over a hook on the throwing arm of the spring.

The noose is so placed that two-thirds of it is beyond the trigger and one-third behind; so adapting it to a bear's foot movement in which the claws of the foot are pressed on to the ground first, followed by the weight of the heel. The trigger is set not less than $1\frac{1}{2}$in above the ground and small forked sticks support the loop of the snare so that its height is 4in in front and only 3in behind the trigger. A strip of soft leather or rubber is threaded on to the loop to act as a stop, grass is thrown over the snare to camouflage it, and the swivel is anchored to a substantial tree (Fig 54).

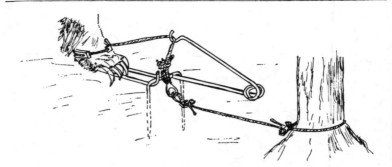

Fig 54   The Aldrich bear trap

Behind the Aldrich trap, a pen of logs is built with the bait well secured. On the other side of the snare and leading to it, there must be a series of not less than three stepping places to guide the bear to the trap. These step-sites are made by leaving gaps among interlaced brushwood to provide limited open ground which the bear looks for, and are arranged to lead the bear in such a way that a particular foot, left or right, is placed in the noose. If the left foot is to be placed in the noose, the spring is set on the left, and vice versa, the objective in either case being to ensure that the spring throws away from the bear.

The North Carolina Hanging Snare
The more traditional sapling-spring snare traps are designed to take animals by the neck or body. One used many years ago in North America, and now adopted by the US Army for survival training, is the North Carolina hanging snare.

Fig 55 shows the details of this snare which is designed to catch small deer, raccoon, opossum and fox in such a way that, like the Aldrich, the catch is twitched into the air out of reach of small ground predators. There are many variations based upon this pattern, particularly in the form of the triggering device and the siting of the noose.

The bait-set snare, already mentioned among bird traps, is designed more for mammals, and the chief requirement is a broad-based tree, preferably with surface roots leaving an angular recess in which to lodge the trap. In the 'V' between roots a small pen is made from stout twigs as shown in Fig 56, to a height of about 8in. Above the

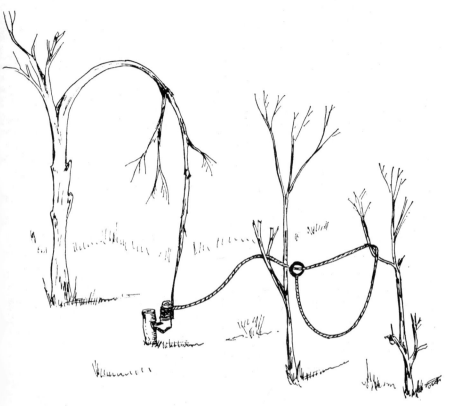

Fig 55   Carolina hanging snare

pen, two pegs are driven horizontally into the trunk of the tree, in
line with the twigs below. The bait board has a long nail driven
through and this catches under the pegs. The cord of the noose is
attached to the nail and carried on above to tie on a sapling driven
into the ground on one side and bent over to create a spring. The
noose itself is placed carefully at the entrance to the pen. Suitable
bait, depending upon the animal sought, is attached to the bait
board. It might be a fish or frog if the trap site is a riverside one and
mink is being trapped. Unfortunately, a snare of this kind cannot be
selective and there is always the risk that an otter might be taken,
which, in Britain, would be quite contrary to conservation practice.

E. W. Pfizenmayer, in his book *Siberian Man and Mammoth,*

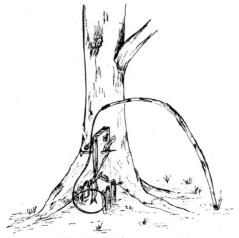

Fig 56   Bait-set snare

mentions having seen a snare made by Yakut tribesmen in the Verk-hoyansk district of Siberia. Though fundamentally the same as the North Carolina version of hanging snare, this one, designed to catch mountain hares, uses an interesting trigger. The spring is formed from a long pole held across a tripod formed from long stakes pushed into the ground, so that two-thirds of its length is behind the tripod. The trigger is linked with the tip of the one-third of the pole in front of the tripod (Fig 57).

Fig 57   Pole snare

The trigger itself is a small piece of wood rounded at one end and wedge-shaped at the other, with a groove cut across the centre of the wedge. The cord of the snare is allowed to rest on the groove of the trigger and is fastened to the tip of the pole. It is then secured by a horsehair string attached to an anchored peg below and looped over the trigger at the point of the notch. When a hare struggles in the noose, the loop slips off the trigger, so releasing the noose cord, and the weight of pole behind the tripod jerks snare and hare into the air.

Cluster Snares
For taking deer in California, cluster snares have been developed by Ashcraft and Reese for setting on regularly-used migration tracks.

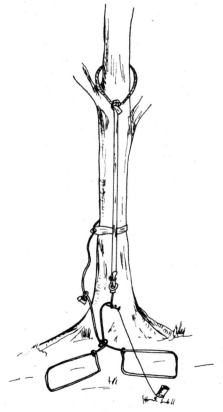

Fig 58   Cluster snares

Attached to a tree or post, they are activated by a string trigger when struck by deer, and the result is to pull up the snares which entangle one or more of the animal's legs. The method of this action can be interpreted from Fig 58, where it will be seen that the snares are secured by one cord held in a rubber band made from car tyre inner-tube fastened around a tree trunk. The other cord is linked to the trip-string and also to a long band of rubber. This rubber is secured to a higher branch and is under tension. When the trigger string is pulled away, the tension in the rubber is released and in springing up it pulls the nooses with it. A novel feature of this trap is that a small cowbell is attached to the noose cord anchored to the tree. When the deer struggles, the bell rings and attracts the trapper concealed nearby. The deer cannot be hurt, as the rubber band anchoring the cord prevents excessive tightening of the noose, and the purpose of this trap is to capture deer for tagging and subsequent release in field research experiments.

The deer concerned are wapiti, a name believed to have come from the Shawnee Indians, and they are now confined to the western part of North America, particularly in the Rocky Mountain area and the western states. The largest herds are in the Yellowstone National Park. These animals, akin to the red deer of Europe, are the biggest deer in North America, and spend their summers feeding on the mountains, spreading out over a considerable distance. During the winter, they descend from the heavy snowfall regions to spend a period sheltering in the lowlands.

The Portable Snare
The portable snare is an improved version of the poacher's snare, one of the oldest constructions for general field use. The advantages of the modification are that the snare does not need to be concealed and can be used anywhere there is a suitable springy branch or sapling; also it has so few components that as many as fifty can be carried by one person. The essential materials for construction are three pieces of wood, shaped as seen in Fig 59, a length of cord and wire snares, home-made or preferably commercial ones. The diagram indicates how the separate units are fitted together, but it may not be apparent that the bait stick is in reality a lever. It is hinged, by means of a nail or piece of stout wire, inside a mortise joint. The upright is secured by wire to the base of the spring sapling as shown, and it will be more secure if notches are cut into the corners of the upright around

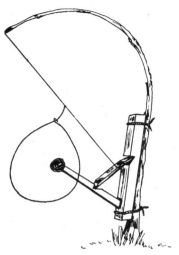

Fig 59   Portable snare

which the wire is wound. The trap is intended to catch mainly rabbits or small vermin, such as stoats and weasels, but again it must be emphasised that it is likely to be a killer and is non-selective—it could as easily take a favourite terrier or cat as a wild creature.

Finally, a double box snare combines the use of snares as well as providing a portable pen into which small mammals can be attracted. It has been adapted for use above or below ground. When used above ground, it requires a complete wooden tunnel, but when placed in mole runs the top only is used as a platform, with hoops of hazelwood, or similar material, holding it in place. The full box version, suitable for small vermin, rats and mink, and also grey squirrels, is shown in Fig 60. Basic requirements are a four-sided wooden box, to serve as a tunnel, with holes drilled in the centre and about an inch from each end of the top to take the trigger string and more cords respectively. The rest of the construction is exactly as described for the box fish trap on p 119, except that a single oblique hole on one side is drilled to anchor the spring stick. Dislodging the bait stick inside brings about a rapid release of the spring and consequent tightening of the nooses.

A double box snare of this kind could be used to take any animals which are sufficiently curious to investigate a tunnel, and weasels are

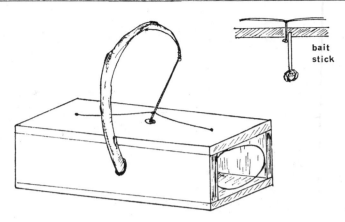

bait
stick

Fig 60   Double box snare

notorious in this respect, as also are most members of the mustelid family. The trap could be placed in thickets, among the undergrowth, where it is known that suitable animals are likely to be caught. Efficient camouflaging with leafy branches will make the trap appear less strange to animals and obscure it from human trap thieves. The trap could also be used in snow if covered over to provide camouflage. If it were intended to use such a trap for taking rats, it would be worthwhile placing a suitable bait in the centre of the floor.

Spring Traps
Any trap employing a spring is entitled to be included in this section, and spring-activated snares were described in the previous section only because it was felt that the snare was the more important feature of them.

The term 'spring trap' is sometimes used to refer to the kind more properly described as steel traps, the gin-trap variety. The spring here was mostly of the flat-spring type, whereas more modern traps introduced to replace the inhumane gins depend upon coil springs. The breakbacks for rats and mice also use coil springs.

With all traps using metal springs it is essential that the springs are suitably tempered. This means that in the course of production the spring metal must be successively hardened and cooled until it has acquired the right amount of elasticity without having become so brittle that the spring snaps under extreme tension. The Newhouse traps have always had a good reputation in this respect, but many otherwise admirably designed traps have been failures owing to soft or brittle springs which gave up after one or two settings. Traps left with springs set for long periods test the spring tempering severely, so that a defect soon becomes apparent. With all traps incorporating springs, it is inadvisable to leave them set when not in use.

Mole Trapping
Let us take as the first example of a spring trap one which is so like the double box snare described in an earlier section that it might be wondered why it should be included here. The only good reason is that it was the prototype from which have developed commercially-produced forms with metal springs.

We are here concerned with the home-made mole trap depicted in the frontispiece, which shows a model of two of these traps in a simulated field situation. The trap consists of a flat board with two hazel hoops, one at each end, bent into half-circles and glued into holes already drilled. The insides of the hazel hoops, which are flat from splitting a twig, are grooved to hold nooses of twisted horsehair arranged exactly as in the box snare previously described. The only difference in the mole trap is that, instead of a bait stick, the knotted trigger-cord is wedged with a Y-shaped twig, small enough to avoid catching on the floor of the mole run, but large enough to prevent a mole from by-passing it.

The difficulty with these traps is not in constructing them, but in placing them in the right position. They must go into a run currently in use as indicated by fresh hillocks of soil being thrown up, and they should fit freely in the burrow without restricting the movement of the parts. Many accounts of using these traps recommend that surface soil disturbed in digging should be made good after placing the trap but, in practice, when using this or any other sub-surface mole trap, the writer has found it an advantage to allow a small air-gap through the surface and into the run. Moles do not like a draught in their tunnel system and will soon attempt to seal an opening, which means that they may well come to the trap within a short time of it being set.

Moles are perhaps the most subterranean of mammals, for they are seldom seen on the surface, except in traps or after their tunnels have become flooded. Their underground territory is a labyrinth of major and minor chambers interconnected by runways. Usually there is a central chamber which serves as a nest and this is sometimes built under a stone wall. Tunnels radiate from the central chamber and because the mole creates these by pushing away earth, using its forefeet and powerful snout for digging, some method of disposing of the surplus soil has to be found. The mole uses the rather clever expedient of pushing up vertical tunnels, at intervals, from those running parallel to the ground surface. The accumulated soil is thrust through the surface, so establishing the characteristic mounds or ridges found in mole-infested pastures and woodlands. The nest chamber is deep in the ground and it is unlikely that young moles leave this until they are almost fully grown, which is, perhaps, the reason why young moles are seldom if ever taken in traps.

It is sometimes possible to detect a mole's activity underground from the disturbance on the surface. The earth vibrates and heaves as the small creatures push their way along only a few inches down. On these occasions it has been a practice among gardeners to apply a shovel smartly at the point of disturbance, in order to stun the mole momentarily. A quick jab into the ground can then often throw the animal out.

Barrel and Half-barrel Traps

From the above trap has come a range of more sophisticated types, one of which is the full-barrel trap, known as the 'Perfection' and made by Scott of Edinburgh a few years ago. It is now generally considered obsolete, but was favoured strongly by Scottish professional mole-catchers before World War II. It functioned like a double box snare, except that the box was barrel-shaped. The snares, when set, fitted into grooves in the inner surface of the barrel, and the spring, a long wire one with a coil at its end, was fastened to the barrel.

The full-barrel trap had one special advantage over other kinds in that it fully enclosed the snares. This meant that the openings and spaces in which the snares were going to do their work could not be fouled by settling earth (illustration, p 103).

There are also half-barrel traps. As the name implies, these do not have the full cylinder but a half-cylinder—the top section with fittings for trigger cord and nooses. These half-barrels are usually of a light-weight metal construction, galvanised iron sheeting being popular. A modified but now obsolete version of all-metal construction was set by pressing metal loops instead of snares through the end slots in the metal plate used in place of the board in the home-made one.

The central catch on the top of the spring went through the central slot of the plate and was held by the trigger. A further improvement, and one still available, is seen in the illustration on p 103. It is the Duffus trap and is shown with one end set and the other unset. Wire nooses are pressed through slots in the metal half-barrel, but the springs are separate for each noose and consist of double coil units. There are also independent triggers for each noose. The aim of all these traps is to take moles regardless of their direction of approach, and in this last trap it is conceivably possible for a mole to be taken at each end, providing the vibration from release of the first noose did not also trigger off the second. These traps are extremely light in weight—a mere 5oz each.

Many mole-trappers prefer scissors-type, or tongs-type traps to use the alternative names. In a typical example seen in Fig 61 (a), two

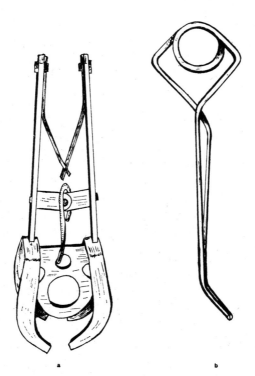

a   b

Fig 61   (a) Tongs-type mole trap; (b) Arouze scissor-type mole trap

iron jaws have metal bars from the arch tops. The bars are linked by a central hinge to give the scissor action, and tension is applied by flat springs riveted to their tops and pressing together between the bar arms. A hook over the hinge supports a tongue which keeps the jaws apart and acts as a trigger. Placed in a mole run with the arms projecting through the soil surface, it only requires a mole to blunder against the tongue and dislodge it for the jaws to spring instantly together, so gripping the animal. The protruding arms indicate to a trapper when the trap has been sprung, so that if this is not apparent there is no need to disturb the setting.

The simplest mole trap is the Arouze, made in France, allegedly by French prisoners at one time, and constructed from a single piece of wire bent into the form of sugar tongs (Fig 61 (b)). A metal tongue keeps the arms apart in the burrow.

'Guillotine' Traps

The last kind of mole trap to be described is what the writer calls the guillotine trap, and it was extremely popular in the days before the fashion for moleskin trousers and waistcoats demanded perfect pelts. From the illustration on p 86, it will be seen that there is a framework of flat metal bars, pronged at the bottom. Across the top is a bar through which passes a metal rod. Inside the frame the rod is joined to a flat plate bearing long steel spikes. The rod is surrounded by a coiled spring and the plate can be pushed up against the increasing tension of the spring. It requires a fair effort to get it into a position where it cannot slip back, because it lodges against a notch in the hinged metal bar fastened to the top of the frame. This bar is, in turn, secured by another hinged catch on one side, just above a prong, the catch also serving as the trigger. It is still possible to buy this trap in the United States, where it is sold under the Victor label by the Animal Trap Co of America.

In use, the trap is placed in an opened burrow and held in place by pressing the prongs through the floor. When the trigger is pushed by a mole, the tension in the spring is released and shoots the spiked plate downwards. It will be readily appreciated that a moleskin suffering this treatment would resemble a sieve.

From guillotines for moles, we pass to guillotines for mice, although the mouse version approximates more closely to the action expected from the name. These traps were in popular use during the Victorian era and probably preceded the now more widely employed breakback traps. They could be single-catch or multi-catch, but the basic element of each was a block of wood. The example illustrated on p 104 is a single-hole version with a slightly fashioned block. Four-hole versions were made with a hole and the appropriate metalwork on each of four sides of a square-topped block of wood.

The action was simple. Bait was fastened to a lever hinged above the back of the hole. Another lever, acting as a catch for the first, was hinged at the front of the hole, but also supported the guillotine when this was raised to maximum height against the tension of the angled spring seen on the left of the block. On the right of the block was a metal guide to ensure that the guillotine would drop vertically, and across the front of the hole, at the bottom, there was a metal bar serving as a block against which the guillotine could press the victim. A mouse would put its head into the hole to get the bait and in agitating the lever release the guillotine.

So much for the downward chop. Another style of mouse trap had an upward chop, functioning similarly to the metal loops in the all-metal half-barrel mole traps already described. An example of a three-hole version is shown on p 104, but there were also four-hole types and it is conceivable that there were others with fewer or more numerous holes. The action is readily apparent—the upward movement of a wire loop under action of a released spring. The method of triggering may not be so immediately clear and depends upon two factors, the persistence of small mammals to get at food and the gnawing habit of rodents. The wire loop is held down against the spring tension by a loop of string. This is secured under the block, passed through the wood over the wire loop arm, down through the block again and round to the front of the block to be fastened on a nail head projecting out a short way. In being threaded through the block, two strands appear in the hole and effectively bar a mouse from reaching bait originally placed at the back. In its efforts to get at the bait, the mouse gnaws through the string and thereby releases the wire loop. Such traps were popular in Europe and the United States during the last century and essentially similar types have been manufactured until comparatively recently.

Breakback Traps

We now come to the well-known and universally used breakback traps. Exactly when these became available is not certain, but it is likely to have been sometime before the 1850s as no indication of this break-through in design is hinted at in patent records. A prototype might have been of the kind loaned to the writer by S. Young & Sons Ltd. It is certainly a breakback trap, but its size—about 7in by 4in—suggests that it was intended for rats. The mechanism is a little different from the modern version in that the snap wire does not fold back in an arc of 180°. When set, it has a catch-wire linking the snap and the bait-trigger wire. That it had been well used was obvious from the impression of the snap worn on to the baseboard.

Modern types are normally available in small sizes for mice, with a baseboard approximately 3in by 1½in, and in larger sizes, approximately twice as big, for rats. They are also made for manual or automatic setting. The automatic, or self-setting, types are safer in the hands of older or short-sighted people and useful when working in a poor light. They are not capable of fine, or two-way, setting, which provides a more efficient trapping mechanism. Traditionally, they are made of wood and wire, but there are all-metal varieties which are sometimes stronger and less likely to suffer from the mechanism being pulled out of the base after a little use. The writer has found the Victor two-way mouse traps superior as catchers, despite their relatively short life in protracted field-collecting trips.

There are several deviations from the orthodox pattern and one of interest is a folding trap. This is strongly made, quite efficient and, of course, extremely portable. Seen in Fig 62, this trap is made of iron and wire, the horseshoe-shaped base having its upper surface hollowed out to receive the snap wire when folded. When set, the snap

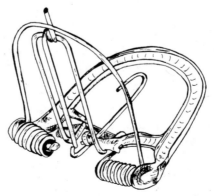

Fig 62   Folding breakback mouse trap

wire is held at right angles to the base by a lever at the top, and this, in turn, is caught by a bait wire at the bottom. When the bait wire is agitated, the snap wire is released to clap over the animal.

Obviously, none of these traps is selective, and though unlikely to catch other than rats or mice when used indoors, if placed in the open they can catch voles, shrews and small birds equally as well as mice.

There is a lot more to the use of these traps than merely baiting and leaving them in a convenient spot on the ground; and other aspects of trap lore, if carefully observed, will not only increase the chances of success but, where a number of traps are being employed, increase the trap-to-catch ratio.

In field conditions, traps can be placed on recognisable runways in in grass or under bushes and hedgerows. Fresh scats will indicate a currently used run. Where large-scale trapping is being undertaken, some marking system is needed to enable traps to be found easily. This should not be so conspicuous as to attract the attention of all and sundry, and here a knowledge of gipsy signs, such as a broken twig or knotted grass, can be useful. A record of positions and numbers should also be made in a field notebook.

The fineness of setting must be adjusted to the animal to be trapped, so that traps laid for shrews will need to be much more delicately adjusted than those intended for field mice or voles. In most instances, too, it is better to place breakback traps across a track rather than in line with it. The reasons for this are that, if approached from the side, the bait pin will be dragged or pushed out of position more easily, and also that the snap wire will have a smaller arc to travel to catch an animal at the side of the trap than for one at the end; in other words, there is less time for an animal to escape before the wire snaps over it.

As with all traps, breakbacks should be handled infrequently and then, if possible, with gloved hands, since animals are very sensitive to the smell of human contact. New traps should be 'seasoned' by burying them in soil and grass for a while to remove smells of metal and other manufactured materials. Pre-baiting can also be a useful operation, and by this is meant that the traps are left unset with bait attached until this appears to be taken regularly, when they are primed. Traps for use outdoors will last longer if their metal parts are coated with wax.

Rats are often suspicious of well-used traps with blood on them, but the suggestion that a well-used but otherwise clean trap also arouses their distrust is probably ill-founded and more likely to be due to the persistence of human smell from too much handling. Traps soiled with blood should be boiled until clean, and then heat-dried to prevent rusting of the metal parts.

Steel Traps

These, too, are spring traps, but call for special treatment and consideration. In Britain, they have always been known as 'gin traps' or simply 'gins', the term 'gin' having been applied historically to any mechanical device or, even more abstrusely, to any device that did not require human manipulation to make it work. A staked fishing device, as we have seen earlier, was referred to as an 'engine' and it is this word of which 'gin' is an abbreviation.

In the United States and many other countries these traps are referred to collectively as 'steel traps', because they are all-metal, though not necessarily restricted to steel. South African trappers use the Afrikaans expression 'slagysters', 'slag' meaning 'to kill' and 'yster' meaning 'iron'.

The origin of steel traps is uncertain, but they are probably many centuries old. It has even been suggested that the first gins were man traps, and that it was these which inspired the use of smaller versions for vermin. Certainly, man traps were used in the steel-trap form as early as the eighteenth century, though steel traps existed well before this. Man traps were terrible inventions with which men of means sought to protect themselves and their property from their less fortunate fellows. They were best known as the silent guardians of estates against poachers, and there are horrific stories of the mangled results when unwary gipsies or vagabonds fell foul of them.

Clever and ardent poachers had ways and means of detecting them; using long wooden probes, for example, but it didn't do to take chances for they were carefully hidden in coverts and set so as to take a man's leg at the knee and smash it. Even if the leg were not broken, which would be a rare occurrence, the injury might well become gangrenous, for the traps would be dirty and rusty although probably well oiled around the moving parts.

A typical example of a man trap is like a larger version of a fox gin of the kind seen in the picture on p 138, about 4ft 6in long, with jaws 18in in diameter. This type and the box version depicted on p 137 were used in World War I between the trenches, for though by

Page 189   Tunnel traps: (*above left*) the Fuller trap; (*above right*) the Lloyd trap; (*below*) the Sawyer trap

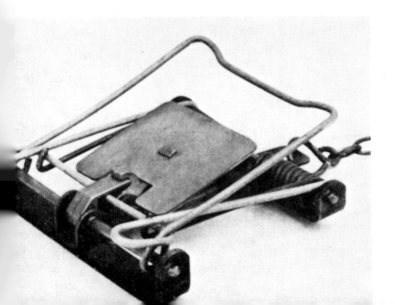

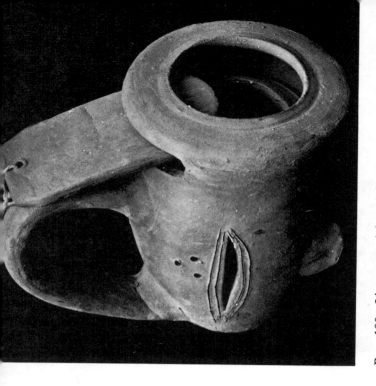

Page 190   Live traps: (*above left*) Victorian cage live trap for
mice; (*below left*) Arouze-type wire cage mouse trap;
(*above right*) a pottery mouse trap as used at
Djerba, Tunisia

then they were illegal in Britain, warfare takes no heed of peacetime legislation. The box version is particularly vicious. When set, the row of spikes in the mouth point downwards, and below them are two full-length toothed steel plates, also turned downwards. The trap would be buried so that its mouth would be just below soil level and suitably camouflaged. A victim stumbling into it would press a trigger lever which would cause the toothed plates and the spikes to swing upwards. Little imagination is required to visualise the agony of the entrapped man.

Civil use of man traps in Britain was prohibited by an Act of 1827 which also forbade the use of spring guns. These were another form of anti-poaching device and were fired by the tension of a cord being altered when a trespasser, negotiating a path across which it was stretched, tripped over it.

Estate owners and fruit farmers displayed notice-boards to warn off would-be poachers and a typical notice illustrated on p 137 is displayed in the Guildhall branch of Leicester Museums.

Gin or steel traps were produced at first by country blacksmiths, often to special order. When mass-production methods were introduced into industry, steel traps were ideal objects for manufacture, either as the sole product of a small firm or as a side-line for a larger one. We have already seen how such production methods were stimulated by the expansion of the fur trade in North America and, to a lesser extent, by the needs of colonists from Europe faced with predators of all kinds in the tropical countries they were exploiting during the late eighteenth and early nineteenth centuries.

In North America, there is a long and well-documented history of the steel trap, more especially related to beaver trapping by the mountain men. The first evidence is to be found in inventory lists preserved in various archives in the United States. One list relating to the properties of Thomas Tusler dates back to 1650, and there are early seventeenth-century ones for Captain Daniel Taylor. On these lists 'steele trapes' appear and are recorded separately from noose traps. Carl P. Russell, author of *Firearms, Traps and Tools of the Mountain Men*, thinks that the steel traps would be of the English rat trap (gin trap) type. From this period onwards, there is much evidence of orders for locally-made steel traps by such organisations as the Hudson Bay Company, John Astor's organisation, the North West Company of Canada, the Louis Missouri Fur Company and the American Fur Company. The agents of these business enterprises were often fastidious in ordering traps, insisting upon high-quality material and precision working of the instruments.

The United States Office of Indian Trade had a considerable business in traps, which were supplied to the tribes, sometimes in exchange for skins, sometimes for cash, and occasionally as peace offerings when signing treaties. The traps were made by various individuals, but often, though the workmanship was good, the makers had had no field experience and their traps did not function properly. So often was this the case that in 1822 the Office of Indian Trade started to import some of its traps from Britain.

Most of the earliest steel traps used in North America were based on the pattern of the Mascall trap and had a round or oval base-plate. This pattern was common throughout Europe during the seventeenth century and examples are known from Russia and France.

Later, the pattern changed and concentrated on the flat base-plate with jaw pillars mounted at either end. This was a development of the English gin trap with flat base-plate continuous as a fixed mounting for the steel spring(s) as seen in the fox trap on p 138. The final stage in development came when the springs became independent of the base-plate and were merely hinged around the jaws by means of 'eyes'. One reason for adopting this pattern was that it enabled the springs to be folded against the jaws and the chain to be wrapped around the whole unit, thus producing a much more portable structure. Various examples of steel traps used in the North American beaver trade are shown in Fig 63.

At the end of the nineteenth century there were only a few beavers left in the United States and trappers were looking for something else likely to prove profitable. So it was that attention was turned on the muskrat, but conventional traps, even small ones, were not suitable because when they gripped a foot, usually a forefoot, this was so delicate and sensitive that it quickly became numb. And when numbness set in and the animal was freed from pain, its struggles would intensify so that soon the leg bones would break followed quickly by a parting of the skin, and the animal, minus a foot, would escape.

The answer to this from the trapper's point of view was the production of traps having double gripping jaws. In addition to orthodox jaws, these new traps had a secondary pair located about an inch below them and when the trap was sprung the closing jaws gripped a wider section of the muskrat's foot. Newhouse traps with single

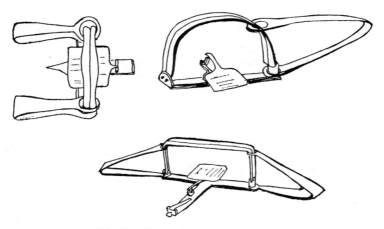

Fig 63   Examples of beaver traps

springs, Nos 81½, 91 and 91½, were produced to take both muskrat and mink.

Jump and Coil-Spring Traps
Two further developments of steel traps were the introduction of the jump trap, based upon early Austrian and French patterns (Fig 64), and coil-spring traps. One English type of coil-spring gin trap resembled some of the modern American versions, though others made in the States have horizontal instead of vertical springs (Fig 65).

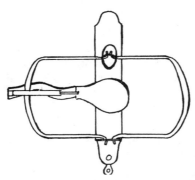

Fig 64   Jump trap

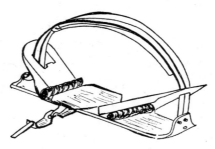

Fig 65   Horizontal coil-spring steel trap as used in the United States of
America

Jump traps manufactured by Blake & Lamb (now the Hawkins
Company) in the United States were so contrived that animals
stepping on to the pan were held by jaws designed to close around
the upper parts of the limb where they could grip stronger bones
than are found in many animals' feet. The No 1½ was designed for
mink and the No 1 for muskrat, and no doubt their light weight also
helped to make them popular with trappers.

In many respects, but especially as a catcher, the steel trap proved
superior to any other kind. Though inhumane, if the prime consideration was a good return for a minimum of effort, together with long
trap life, then these traps probably had no equals. And now that
they have been outlawed in England and Wales, and are to become
illegal in Scotland in 1973, gamekeepers and estate owners are complaining about the alleged inefficiency of the new traps designed to
replace the gins. Partly, this is simply traditional prejudice against
using something new and unfamiliar, but it is also true that trials
with the new traps, while substantiating their claim to be more
humane, have been less demonstrative of their efficiency as catchers.

The form and appearance of steel or gin traps do not vary very
much from one manufacturer to another, and some typical examples
are seen on p 138. All three are of orthodox pattern, using flat steel
springs.

The rabbit trap, also suitable for rats and small vermin such as
stoats, weasels, squirrels and opossums, is the pattern preferred by
experienced trappers. It has a rounded spring, as opposed to the
angled spring with slides seen in the fox trap, and is used universally
in the Newhouse series of traps. The disadvantages of the angled
spring are that it does not retain its strength for long, and that,

unless securely fastened, the sliding catch can easily slip over the spring and so prevent the jaws from closing properly.

In the bear trap, it will be noticed that the double springs are at right angles to the line of the jaws. This is sometimes the most convenient arrangement but, if necessary, they can be brought into line with the jaws simply by rotating them, so that they resemble the springs in the fox trap.

Henry Lane Ltd have also made a steel trap with a heavy-gauge wire and coil spring and a single coil at the rounded end to give additional tension. An adaptation, the No 22 Dorset fox trap, is still made and is sold in Scotland and Ireland.

Most manufacturers built these traps to the same patterns but in varying qualities, the better grades being of heavier-gauge steel and often having brass catches. The grade selected would probably be related to the purpose for which a trap was to be used and, to illustrate this point, Lane's manufactured a Gilpa steel trap in an ordinary grade and a better quality Dorset grade. If the trap was required for continuous rabbit trapping, the better quality version would be the obvious first choice, if cost were not a consideration, though Mark Hovell, who also recommended these traps for catching rats in his book *Rats and How to Destroy Them*, considered the extra quality of the Dorset trap to be unnecessary, especially if it was to be used within buildings.

Trap Teeth and Jaws
There was often variation in the pattern of teeth used. A blunt version might have two rows of wavy-edged teeth, especially in larger traps, such as in the bear trap illustrated or, again, the teeth might be spiked, as in the fox trap, or the man trap illustrated earlier. The majority of English-made gin traps have teeth as seen in the flat spring and coil spring versions of the rabbit trap. When the jaws closed, the square-ended teeth interlocked with the rounded indentations.

Newhouse traps differ in having toothless or flat-edged jaws. This is because they were primarily developed to catch fur-bearing animals and toothed jaws can cause a great deal of mutilation to a skin, as well as indescribable suffering to any animal in their grip. Rubber-covered jaws have also been tried and have certainly reduced the amount of pelt damage, but one is very sceptical of the claim that they do so little damage to an animal that it can be captured alive and released unharmed. If an animal is caught by a steel trap about its neck or middle it must inevitably suffer internal injury from compression. Caught by a foot, and even though not in pain, many wild creatures, rodents particularly and also foxes, will bite through the limb in order to escape. In the United States, a number of states have either banned the use of toothed jaws in steel traps, or restricted the spread of the jaws, as in Massachusetts where the limit is 5½in.

In traps of this kind, sizes are based upon the length of the jaw. Thus a 4in trap, suitable for rats or chipmunks, has 4in long jaws and, when set, the jaw space is a 4in square. The smallest size the writer has seen is a 1½in trap designed a long time ago for mice. Among the biggest are the 16in bear traps.

Steel traps are also often identified by a number, but as this is a trade description varying from one manufacturer to another it can lead to confusion. For example, a Newhouse No 6 is the 16in bear trap, while one manufactured originally as a No 6 by W. & G. Sidebotham was a 4in or 5in rabbit trap.

Steel-Trap Techniques

In the practical field application of steel traps for animal capture much depends upon the skill and experience of the trapper. Success could be measured in various ways, and among these would obviously be the catch-to-trap ratio, that is the proportion of the number of catches over a given period of time to the number of traps set. An even sterner test of skill would be the proportion of the catch represented by the animals actually being sought, for although steel traps are fundamentally non-selective an experienced trapper can set them in such a way that they are more likely to take one particular animal than any other. Location, fineness of setting, camouflage and type of bait used are other important factors in the calculation of potential success.

The trap, however, is only the basic requirement, and the trapper needs a number of accessories. If he is going to dig the trap in he will need a spade or trowel. Special trappers' spades are made, but the types used by commandos of the armed forces are particularly suitable and sometimes available from government surplus supply stores. A spade needs to be light in weight, short-handled and have a pointed blade for use in hard ground when necessary. Anchoring stakes or pegs are also required. Wooden pegs can be used but steel pegs, for obvious reasons, are preferable, and peg sizes must be related to trap sizes and the animals in mind. For very large animals, such as bears or big cats, it would be necessary to use a tree-trunk for anchorage. A sieve is also a valuable piece of equipment for use with steel traps, its purpose being to produce fine soil, free from stones which might block the mechanism, when covering over a dug-in trap. Chains and a swivel joint on the trap are other important accessories not always supplied as built-in features.

Finally, the baits used can make a great deal of difference to the range of animals that can be taken, and indeed to taking them at all. Details of baits for all purposes will be found in a later chapter, but for steel traps they will fall into three groups. These are fresh baits— freshly-killed animals, fresh fruit or cereals; fetid baits—disembowelled carcasses buried for a week or so before use; and scent baits, often called lures in the USA—extracted from scent glands of fur-bearers, also musks and strongly smelling oils, especially fish oil and oil of aniseed.

The Care of Steel Traps

A good trapper will pay attention to the mechanical efficiency of his trap and its cleanliness. New traps should be boiled in water containing a little caustic potash to remove their unfamiliar smell of newness and to get rid of any oil and grease on parts other than the moving joints of jaws and catches. The boiled traps are then hung out to dry and when a light coating of rust has formed they are stained. This involves simmering them in a staining solution, such as water containing the mashed hulls of walnuts, or crystals of logwood, until they are black. They are then taken from the staining bath with hands covered in clean gloves and again hung out to dry. All traps should be thus treated after each trapping operation to ensure that they carry no human smell or any traces of blood from previous kills.

Mechanical efficiency can be assured by attention to the adjustment of the shank of the tread pan and to the catch, or dog. The jaws, too, must move freely at the hinges where they link with the spring.

Apart from the siting of a trap—the term 'set' is often used to describe the situation in which it is placed—the setting or priming of a trap is all-important. For this, two sticks, each about a thumb's thickness and 12in long, are necessary, and they should be whittled at one end to give a flattened surface on each side for about 3in. A stick is held in each hand and the spring, or springs, depressed. One person can manage a single-spring trap but it may require two for a double-spring version, since foot pressure is necessary to flatten the springs and one foot should be kept on the ground. The catch which holds one jaw down is thrown back before depressing the spring. Once foot pressure is sufficient to allow free movement of the jaws, the one to be held down is turned outwards, using the flat end of one of the sticks, and the catch is thrown over it. The catch may need to be pressed down while the pan or treadle is raised by the flat end of the other stick. This is passed *under* the free jaw until the notch on the pan is caught by the catch over the jaw to be fixed. The free jaw is then lowered until level with the fixed jaw. The object of placing the second stick under the free jaw is to avoid getting it jammed should the jaws accidentally snap to.

A well-known professional trapper has recommended this procedure for dealing with double-spring traps. He places the ball of each foot on the spring either side of the trap, reaching down meanwhile to grab a jaw in either hand. Pressing down with each foot, he then pulls up with his hands so that simultaneously the springs lower and the jaws open. With the springs down, it is relatively easy to keep them there while one boot is edged over to keep the jaws apart by covering a quarter of each. With his hands free, he is then able to work the dog (trigger) under the pan and then gradually ease up. With the dog under the pan catch, boot pressure on one spring is released while a hand is slipped under the loose jaw to hold the pan in position until the relaxing tension leaves the trap in a set position. He claims to be able to set a No 4½ wolf trap in his living-room by this method without scratching the floor.

Obviously, the priming of steel traps should be undertaken with a great deal of care, as they can be extremely dangerous in the hands of unskilled or careless operators. When carried, they should be held by the lower part of the springs, and hands should never be placed within the area bounded by the opened jaws. Gloves should be used when carrying set traps and, if possible, different pairs should be used for handling clean and dirty traps, other than those used for water-animals.

Siting Steel Traps

We now come to methods of siting steel traps. When used in the field there are many situations possible, but those found to have most success are the trail set, bait set, dirt-hole set, burrow set, box set and cubby and coop set. The choice will depend upon the animal to be trapped and the habitat situation available.

The trail set, sometimes referred to as a blind set, is used to capture animals of fixed habit which frequent particular and obvious tracks. The traps are unbaited and can be used singly or in groups. A shallow hole, or holes if multiple traps are used, must be dug on the trail and the shape of the hole should correspond with that of the trap. Its depth should be such that when the primed trap is in position it is about ¼in below the surrounding surface. With a small trap requiring only a stake to secure it, the peg can be placed alongside and will also be about ¼in below the surface. Large traps, such as those used for capturing foxes, require what Americans refer to as a 'clog', and which is really a log of wood grooved around the circumference in the centre region so as to secure the chain from the trap. To the log can be fastened a grappling hook or trap drag, like a miniature anchor, intended to prevent the trap being hauled away after being sprung. A trap drag can easily be made by knocking two or three 4in nails through a piece of lead piping. The piping is then hammered flat and the nails curved upwards towards the point where a wire fastening is attached. The appearance of a trap in this situation is seen in Fig 66.

Placed in the hole dug for it, the trap is first covered in the pan region, with a piece of paper or cloth, put into position with a stick. Its purpose is to prevent soil filtering into the moving parts and blocking them. The hole is then filled with sieved soil until the level

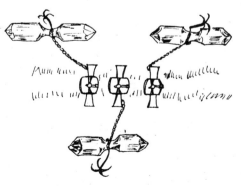

Fig 66   Trail-set for steel traps

reaches that of the surrounds. Finally, the whole area should be carefully brushed over to give as natural an appearance as possible.

The effectiveness of the trap, which is meant to be sprung by the animal placing its foot on the pan, can be increased by placing one or two sticks on the track on either side of the trap. This induces an animal, especially a fox and creatures of a similar kind, to step precisely in the direction of the trap and eventually to tread firmly on the point where the pan is hidden.

A bait-set trap is not, in the case of steel traps, one which has bait on the pan, and steel traps, which are intended to secure an animal by its foot, should never be used in this way. Putting bait on the pan would encourage an animal to put its head down rather than its foot.

A steel trap set in conjunction with the placing of bait is sunk into the ground as with a trail-set trap. One way of using bait, especially if it is fresh animal bait, is to hang it on a bent sapling directly above the trap pan. This will encourage an animal to jump up and down in an effort to drag the bait away, so that sooner or later it is bound to tread on the pan. To encourage repeated jumping, the height of the bait should be so adjusted as to be just out of the reach of the kind of animal to be trapped. This method is used with some success in parts of Africa and India, especially with traps set for jackals and hunting dogs. It is also a method which has been used by the natives of Siberia for catching Arctic foxes.

There is another method of attracting an animal to bait set near a trap, although not necessarily hung over one, which is useful when sight is more significant than smell for a predator. The trick is to tie a feather or bird's wing to a stick or bush close to the position of the bait. The feathers flapping in the breeze will attract the animal's attention, when it is more likely to see the bait and ultimately tread on the concealed trap.

The Idstone trap was one which was designed to use four gin traps in conjunction with fresh bait, such as a recently-shot pigeon, and its purpose was to catch ground vermin, like stoats and weasels. The construction can be seen in Fig 67 where (A) represents a cover over a hole about 15in deep, (a) is a separate trap door in the cover, (b) the gin traps and (c) a tethering post. Inlets to the trap hole are afforded by use of land drains leading from the surface to the bottom of the pit, which is about 3ft square inside. The trap is pre-baited with the gins unset for a night or two, fresh bait being put in through the trap door. When the trap is receiving regular visitors, the gins are set.

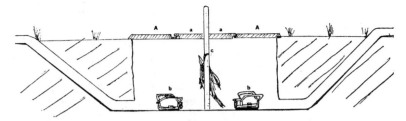

Fig 67   The Idstone trap

Small mustelids have a keen sense of smell and so would be easily attracted by a bait such as freshly-killed birds from which the skin has been ripped open and allowed to spill blood. They are also inquisitive creatures and often use land drains as a normal routeway on their day-to-day travels, sometimes holing-up in them when pursued by dogs or ferrets. So earthenware drains leading to a trap would not arouse their suspicion. The presence of food would also attract a number of stoats and weasels, which would return repeatedly to an apparently safe source of supply. It is for this reason that the Idstone trap is pre-baited, because when the traps are eventually set there is a chance that all those inside the hole would take victims. An advantage of this trap is that it is reasonably selective, since it will only trap animals which move underground and the size of the entrances will restrict the kind of creatures able to reach the hole.

A dirt-hole set is used near a bank or mound, and to greater advantage if a lead-in of bushes or scrub can limit the direction of approach. The dirt hole is slanted into the bank at an angle to the surface for a depth of about 8in and to give a base about 3in in diameter. In front of the hole, and about 12in from it, a triangular hole is dug to take a trap, which should be of the double-spring kind having the springs set at angles of about 45 degrees to the jaws and facing towards the dirt hole. The trap is dug-in in the usual way, fetid bait is thrown into the dirt hole and soil added to surface level. Fox urine sprinkled on nearby grass will increase the chance of attracting foxes, or the urine or glandular scents of other animals will attract those of a similar species.

Placing surface traps near the burrows of animals such as rabbits is not recommended, but careful positioning of gins in rabbit burrows has been found effective, providing they are buried and the ground surface restored as naturally as possible. No baits are necessary.

A box set is used where it is difficult or undesirable to bury traps, as, for example, when traps have to be placed in areas frequented by domestic animals or children. The box is simply a tunnel, too small for domestic animals to get under; or preferably a floorless type, upturned, and with holes small enough to admit stoats or weasels at either end. Inside, two steel traps are set on the ground surface, just below the holes. Between the holes, fresh bait can be placed as an attractant.

For catching rats, Mark Hovell patented what he described as the 'Terrier' Signal Run trap (Fig 68). This was simply a box-set with a

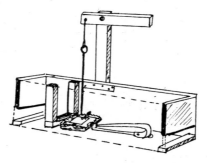

Fig 68   The 'Terrier' Signal Run trap, invented by Mark Hovell

single 5in gin trap inside. The box was 2ft long, 9in high and 7in wide, and the entrance at each end was 3½in high. The buttresses inside force rats to move over the trap pan. The signal cord is attached to the fixed jaw of the trap and keeps the signal lever horizontal when the trap is set. If the trap is sprung, the fixed jaw is raised and the signal arm drops—a convenient way of knowing that the trap requires inspection.

These traps can be set in a variety of situations where rats are found, more particularly in barns and warehouses. Placed on known rat runs, usually close to walls or on overhead beams, they are especially useful, because the signal can be seen by an observer on the ground. If used on a beam they would have to be suitably anchored by tying with a rope.

Cubby or coop sets operate in a similar fashion to the dirt-hole set, and can be used where there are no banks or mounds, but where stones or twigs are lying around. The coop is made as naturally as possible so as to provide a complete shelter with an opening only at one end. Bait is placed in the back of the shelter, and the trap dug in at the opening.

Such sets are also useful for taking water-loving mammals such as mink and muskrats. Though mink are wary animals they can be taken using a No $1\frac{1}{2}$ steel trap in a cubby set of flat stones, so constructed that the entrance is in shallow water and the bait, of fish oil or mink musk, is used in the back of the set. If the cubby is placed in shallow water and the trap is secured to a stake by an adequate length of anchoring chain the muskrat will move into deeper water and there it will drown. Alternatively, a body grip trap could be used.

Where steel traps are used in controlling rats, especially inside buildings, they are frequently left on the surface, and can be quite successful if left unbaited on a well-worn routeway providing they are free from human smell. Care, however, should be taken to ensure that they face the line of the run at an angle not greater than 45°. If they are placed at 90° to the run line, when rats spring the trap the rising jaw nearest to them may well throw them clear to escape surprised, but undamaged.

Rats commonly run at levels above the ground, especially in barns and warehouses with shelving or horizontal beams. Traps can be mounted on these structures and secured by their chains to a nearby wall.

Although 3in and 4in steel traps were made especially for catching rats, Mark Hovell found them to be inferior to 5in rabbit gins. He learned through long experience in battling against rats that a 5in trap would kill a rat by gripping it around the head and body, whereas a 4in trap would only hold by gripping a leg. Not only might a rat gnaw its own leg free, but other rats might assist when discovering one of their kind held captive. The small so-called 'rat gins' also had sharp-toothed jaws which could easily sever a limb.

This is not to contradict the previous statement that steel traps were designed to capture by seizing a limb. The original purpose of the steel trap was, indeed, to hold a man by his leg, or to hold a rabbit so that it was good for marketing fur and flesh. Rat-catching, on the other hand, was not envisaged in their original design, though, used as suggested, they have proved quite successful in this field of trapping.

Reactions of Trap Prisoners

Because steel traps often capture an animal without killing it, there is some need to know in advance the likely reactions of trap prisoners. Stoats, for example, have been known to sham dead, only to become very much alive and extremely vicious when handled. Gamekeepers, aware of this, always dispatch a stoat before touching it. A polecat caught live in a trap will behave like a wildcat, pulling the trap in all directions and snapping viciously. Pine martens, on the other hand, though frightened when held in a gin trap, are nevertheless shy and quiet. There is a record of one marten which, when caught in a gin, bit the anchoring brass wire into $\frac{1}{2}$in pieces. Although the trap was made free in this way, the sheer weight of it was too much for the animal to drag away.

Trappers putting out large numbers of steel traps must visit their trap lines regularly, and in any case not less than once a day. These traps are recognised as being inhumane, so that it is essential to give as much consideration as possible to the relief of animal suffering. In all fairness to professional fur-trappers, they are, with a few exceptions, humane people and make every effort to end the suffering of animals as quickly as possible. They also need to secure skins in as prime a condition as practicable, and those of long captive or dead animals would, at best, be of low grade and more often than not useless.

CHAPTER EIGHT

Mammal Traps: 2

Humane Spring Traps

In Britain, the outlawing of gin traps has been accompanied by a government order requiring new types of spring traps to be submitted for official approval, and this has prompted inventors to make a careful study of those mechanisms which will not only catch animals but will also kill outright and humanely.

This is not to suggest that other countries have not given similar thought to humane methods of trapping. Cage traps for live capture, for example, though probably introduced in Britain, have been extensively developed in the United States by trappers and manufacturers anxious to provide humane catchers, and so good are they that some are now imported into Britain.

Mention has already been made in an earlier chapter of the Verbail Chain Loop trap, invented by the late Vernon Bailey of the US Biological Survey. A combination of spring trap and snare, it was the outcome of Bailey's increasing concern to find a method of capturing animals alive and less painfully than with conventional steel traps. He also saw a possible use for it in scientific research, where animals could be marked or examined and then released, and also in fur-trapping where it could save young and unprime animals.

Recent research by workers of the Fish and Wildlife Service of the US Department of the Interior, however, suggests that the Verbail trap, invented between the two world wars, was not as efficient as it was claimed to be. Comparing it with steel traps under exactly similar field conditions, it appeared that the Verbail trap was liable to cause severe chafing of limbs. It is believed to be no longer in production, but one can none the less admire the motives of the designer, who also invented the beaver trap used by the US Biological Survey and won an award from the American Humane Association for its humane functioning.

Humane societies in the United States did a lot of campaigning between the two great wars in an attempt to get steel traps outlawed. Though a total ban was not achieved, at least some provisions concerning their use were enforced in a number of states. Traps used for taking water animals had either to be so set that the animals taken would be drowned, or the trap had to kill instantly. One trap to emerge as a result of this legislation was a muskrat trap manufactured by the Pennsylvanian firm of Gibbs. In reality, it was two traps in one, the inner trap being similar to a No 1 with a jaw spread of just under 4in. It was coil-spring-operated and set in normal fashion, but once set it had two other large wire jaws extending outwards. One of these would be stationary, but the second needed to be pulled back, using considerable force, until parallel with the set inner trap. A wire pin was then fastened over the set spring and under the jaws of the first trap. When an animal such as a muskrat treads the pan the inner jaws snap together and hold the foot, and this releases the pin securing the outer jaws which then close around the animal's body with enough force to kill it.

On the European continent, humane trapping has been practised for many years, particularly in France, Germany, Holland and Denmark. In these countries the tunnel traps, now being used increasingly in Britain, have been strong favourites for giving a good return of catches.

Following the banning of gin traps in Britain, the new replacements were all spring traps. Many designs were submitted to the Ministry of Agriculture, Fisheries and Food, but so far only six have been approved by the Humane Traps Panel. These are the Fenn, Imbra, Juby, Sawyer, Fuller and Lloyd traps. When traps such as these are approved, the approval is not unconditional but stipulates the type of animals for which each trap may be used and the situations in which they can be set. Breakback mouse and rat traps and underground mole traps are exempt from the Approval Order.

All the new traps so far produced have been concerned with the needs of gamekeepers who want to destroy ground vermin, such as stoats, weasels, grey squirrels, rats and mice, and farmers who want to get rid of rabbits. There has not, as yet, been a spring trap produced which is suitable for taking foxes in the way that the gin trap could do. It is this last deficiency which has so irritated Scottish landowners faced with the banning of gin traps from 1973.

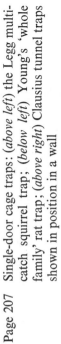

Page 207 Single-door cage traps: (*above left*) the Legg multi-catch squirrel trap; (*below left*) Young's 'whole family' rat trap; (*above right*) Clausius tunnel traps shown in position in a wall

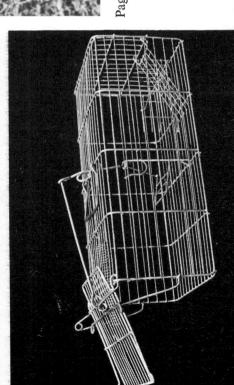

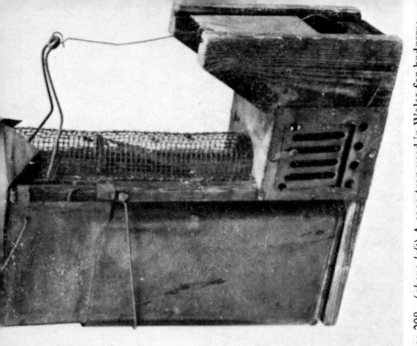

Page 208 (*above left*) A cage trap used in Wales for badgers; (*below left*) a giraffe wheel trap as used in the Nile region of North Africa; (*above right*) a German self-setting mouse trap

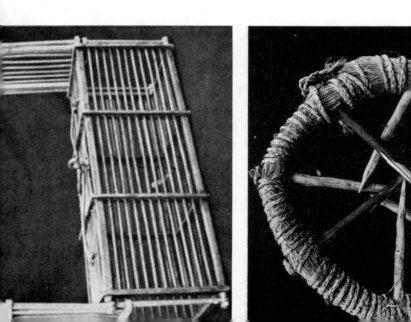

The Fenn Trap

One of the first and now probably the most popular of the new spring traps is the Fenn. It has undergone three modifications from the prototype developed by Mr A. A. Fenn of Alcester, in Warwickshire, and the Approval Order specifies that it may be used either to kill or take grey squirrels, stoats, weasels, rats, mice and other small ground vermin, when set in artificial tunnels constructed for the purpose, or to kill or take rats or mice when set on their runs in the open. It is not considered suitable for rabbits, but has taken young ones.

Following early reluctance by keepers to adopt it, it underwent extensive field trials, not only by the Ministry of Agriculture, Fisheries and Food but also by the staff of the Eley Game Advisory Station, formerly ICI Game Services and now the Game Conservancy. These field trials showed it to be highly efficient in its most recently modified form, the Mark III. Earlier versions had had structural weaknesses which made them unpopular with keepers.

A report issued in 1961 described a 100-days field trial with twenty-five of these traps. During this period 130 head of vermin were taken, the bag being made up of sixty-four young rabbits, twenty-seven rats, twenty-five weasels, eleven hedgehogs, two stoats and one grey squirrel. The keeper carrying out the trial admitted that though he was reluctant to give up the foolproof gin, he would be happy to use the Fenn. The report suggested that the Fenn should not be regarded as the last word in humane traps, and indeed expressed the hope that even better traps might be expected in the future.

The picture on p 155 shows a Fenn trap being placed in a tunnel and a detail of the trap itself. There is a similarity in form to that of a gin trap, both jaws are under the control of the coil springs. Keepers have found difficulty in setting the jaws apart, but use of the thumb grip seen in the illustration makes this task much more simple. The release of the catch when the pan is depressed causes both jaws to spring together.

The Imbra Trap

The Imbra trap is manufactured by Tetra Engineering Co Ltd of London and was one of the first of the new British traps approved for taking adult rabbits. The Approval Order makes the condition that the trap shall be used only for taking or killing rabbits when set in rabbit holes, or for taking other small vermin, such as weasels, stoats,

grey squirrels, rats and mice when set in tunnels artificially constructed for this purpose. In fact, they are large traps and as there is
some difficulty in using them in conventional tunnels, the technique
of using two-piece tunnels has been introduced. The illustration on
p 156 shows a grey squirrel taken in an Imbra trap placed in such a
tunnel, though here the normal masking of sticks, bark or grass
turfs around the tunnel has been removed.

In Fig 69 there are three illustrations showing the method of

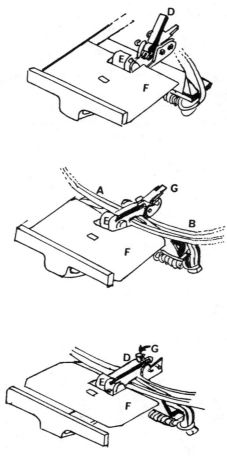

Fig 69   The Imbra trap

setting the trap. A and B represent the lower sections of the arms seen in action in the picture on p 156. A is a single thickness of metal, while B, though single at the top, has a slot at the bottom in which A slides up and down. In this way, a kind of scissor action is involved. Flap D is lifted and arms A and B are depressed to open as fully as possible. Flap D is then made to engage the release trigger E on pan F. For handling the trap and transporting it safely, the safety catch G is locked into the slot on the flap D. It must be remembered, however, that the trap cannot be sprung until the safety catch is released.

The Juby Trap

The Juby trap is superficially rather like the Imbra and has jaws or arms which cross over with a scissor action. It is manufactured by Gilbertson & Page, Ltd, under licence from the Ministry of Agriculture, Fisheries and Food.

Both traps have a safety catch, a great advantage over the gin trap which was always lethal when being moved about after setting. The Imbra and Juby traps differ in the spring action controlling them. In the Imbra, a simple coil spring is attached between the bottom ends of the arms, so that when these are opened fully, the spring is under great stretching tension. The Juby trap has two coil springs joined by bows, one bow from the adjacent ends (see picture, p 156) and the other bow from the extreme ends. The bow from the extreme ends provides axles on each side for the bottoms of the arms to rotate on. When the arms are to be opened fully, they can only reach this position if the bow joining the adjacent ends of the springs is depressed. The catch is then slipped over the arms to engage the trigger on the pan.

When used for catching rabbits, both the Imbra and Juby traps are placed in the mouth of a burrow having an overhang. They are bedded into the burrow with the pan parallel with the floor, and lightly covered with sieved soil. The horns of the jaws must be covered so that the trap, when finally set, is invisible. The pans must be placed so that the rabbit's front paws will spring it, and there must be sufficient clearance above to allow free movement of the arms.

The Sawyer and Lloyd Traps

The Sawyer and Lloyd traps have in common with the Fenn a

restriction to taking or killing stoats, weasels, grey squirrels, rats and mice in tunnels constructed especially for the purpose, or, for taking or killing rats and mice on the runs in the open. The Sawyer and Fenn are similar in appearance and action, both depending upon tension from coiled springs being exerted equally upon the two jaws. There is a slight difference in the arrangement between springs and jaws; in the Fenn the release mechanism is at the spring end of the trap, while in the Sawyer it is at the opposite end. The Sawyer was designed by Mr F. E. Sawyer of Wiltshire and is manufactured by Capjon Pressing Co, also of Wiltshire (picture, p 189).

The Lloyd trap, manufactured under the authority of the National Research Development Corporation, is rather different from the traps previously described and looks much more like a gin trap (picture, p 189). The illustration shows how the spring follows the pattern of the gin, especially of the wire-spring Dorset version mentioned earlier. One difference, of course, is that the jaws are of plain metal rod and untoothed. Also, when set, the jaws are not parallel with the ground surface but at right angles to it. This is because the setting catch is not applied over the outer edge of one jaw. Instead, the base of the fixed jaw has a bar running across and it is over this that the catch is placed. Beyond the base bar in the fixed jaw, and in a similar position on the free one, the jaw is bent to an angle of about 90°. Actually, it is a little less than 90° on the free jaw, and the rod is bent inwards so that this jaw is slightly smaller and will move inside the fixed one when the trap is sprung. The animal caught is enveloped by the jaws.

The Fuller Trap

The Fuller trap is unique in having been designed exclusively to take squirrels and is intended for use in gardens where these animals have become pests, rather than for forest use. Manufactured by Fuller Industries at Horsham, in Sussex, the trap looks like a box, and indeed it could be considered as a box trap with its own built-in spring action (picture, 189).

Apart from the methods by which these traps function, they have in common an advantage over the gin trap in that they are all less likely to injure or kill animals other than those for which they are intended. Having said this, it is important to qualify the statement by emphasising that they will only be humane if used in exactly the way authorised. In support of this view are the findings of a field trial of

Sawyer traps recorded in the Eley Game Advisory Station Annual Review for 1968/9. The trap worked well on the whole, but one partridge was taken alive and a cow was caught by the tongue. The report maintained that had the traps been placed sufficiently far back in the tunnels these accidents would never have happened.

With these new traps, as with gin traps, it is most important that they are maintained in good order, since they will only function when in first-class mechanical condition. Cleaning after use should be a routine measure, and as instinctive an action by a keeper as cleaning a shotgun. When not in use, it is advisable that the jaws are sprung on to a piece of stick or thick rubber, rather than be allowed to spring together empty. This is particularly important with Fenn, Sawyer and Lloyd traps. If traps are to be left in position for long periods, any not taking vermin should be reset once or twice a week in order to remove any debris which has accumulated around them. This applies especially to traps set on the surface inside tunnels, where leaves can easily be blown during autumn.

Keepers are now using these new vermin traps in large numbers to protect estates during a rearing season for game-birds, and some surprising results have been reported. A recent letter to *The Field* reported the surprise of a gamekeeper on finding two stoats caught by one tunnel trap. His astonishment was even greater a few months later when he found not two but three stoats in one trap and all dead.

There would seem to be no doubt that these humane spring traps are heralding a new era of trap usage and design. The Humane Trap Panel of the Ministry of Agriculture, Fisheries and Food has money available for inventors of suitable traps, especially for a designer who can produce a satisfactory humane fox trap, and we may well see a further range of humane traps becoming available in the near future.

Gopher and Beaver Traps

Before leaving spring traps, it is worth mentioning two which have been developed in the USA for two animals which pose particular problems. The first is a gopher trap, for taking pocket gophers. These are small burrowing mammals with fur-lined cheek pouches used exclusively for carrying food, which can consist of root vegetables, alfalfa leaves and roots, and tree-bark, especially in pine plantations. The second mammal is the beaver. Like the gopher, the beaver can cause trouble by burrowing and by damming streams and rivers.

The gopher traps are rather neat spring devices used in burrowing systems, where they are best set as shown in the accompanying diagram (Fig 70). A cone-shaped hole is dug where the gophers throw up fan-shaped mounds from their burrows. A trap is placed one either side of the hole and attached by anchoring cords to a stake on the edge of the hole at ground level. The traps are placed to point in opposite directions with the claws away from the openings. When the upright plate is pushed by a gopher, the claws are released to pin around the animal's body.

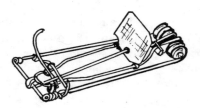

Fig 70   Trap for pocket gophers

It is necessary to clean out the burrows well when the traps are placed inside, not only to get rid of earth which could foul the traps, but also to avoid warning a gopher that its run has been interfered with. Because gophers are sensitive to light it is as well to cover the top of the hole with a sod of earth or a flat board. The burrowing systems of gophers are quite extensive and in some respects reminiscent of those of moles, but gophers are rodents—the only fossorial ones living in America. The gopher digs with its fore-claws but probably uses its incisor teeth as well when constructing the tunnels which can vary in depth from a few inches to more than a foot below the surface. Gopher hills are produced on the ground surface from debris pushed out of the burrow by the tunnelling animal. A plug of earth always seals the surface-penetrating end of a tunnel and it has been suggested that this is to keep out snakes. Nevertheless, gophers are readily taken by burrowing snakes, and although men find them difficult to grasp on the rare occasion when one pushes out of a burrow, the gopher is a frequent prey to hawks, owls and predatory mammals. A vegetarian which attacks bulb roots, it is no friend of the gardener and can be equally active throughout the day and night. Add to this an apparently high and frequent fertility, and one can understand why it is regarded as such a menace and the reason for extensive trapping in an attempt to control it—it would seem almost impossible to eradicate it.

A number of different kinds of traps are recommended for catching beavers, including steel traps, but the one now most frequently used in North America is the Conibear. Of recent design, it is intended for taking a variety of animals, but the No 330 is popularly preferred for beavers, when used in shallow water. Fig 71 shows the trap and some

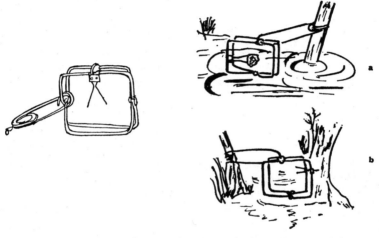

Fig 71   The Conibear trap, and two sets for use with a Conibear in catching beavers: (a) is a waterset; (b) is a trailset

of the popular sets favoured. It consists of two, four-sided metal jaws scissor-hinged as shown. One side of one jaw, when unset, has a forked trigger (this can be baited) and on the opposite side of the other jaw is the catch, or dog. The coil spring has two arms at an angle with the coil and ending in loops which encircle the two jaws. When the spring arms are compressed together, the jaws can be swung around so that the catch engages a slot on the hinge of the trigger. Release of the trigger causes a reversal of this action and the immediate death of the animal, which is caught about its neck or middle.

The Everitt Trap

A veteran spring trap is seen in the illustration on p 156. This is an Everitt trap and was designed to catch rats, combining the features of a gin trap and the guillotine-type of mouse trap described earlier. It can be used in exactly the same situations as a gin trap, but has some advantages over it. A gin trap, if not placed in a correct position, could be knocked aside by a large rat, or the snap of the trap jaws might fling the rat away from the trap. The Everitt trap, being constructed more like a tunnel, is approached more stealthily by a rat and when it is sprung it catches the rat about its middle, or at least around its neck and shoulders. Rats fare no better than other animals which are victims of steel traps, especially when these are not set correctly, and there have been many three-legged rats which have returned to their holes to tell their families of the terrible engines used by men.

The Wall Trap

Yet another veteran trap, the Wall trap, was used staked to the ground close to the wall of a building. It could be sprung by means of a trigger device and the arched jaw would fly up to pin the victim against the wall face. It was useful for ground vermin which made tracks alongside boundary walls or buildings.

   The basic features of this trap were very similar to those of a breakback trap, but it was much larger. A hoop of steel with a toothed edge was pulled back against the tension of a spring and clipped into place when set, as with the wire jaw of a breakback trap. The trap had to be securely fastened to the ground with metal pins and the bait secured to the bait lever. The wall served as the equivalent of the baseboard of the conventional rat or mouse trap, and as the trap was adapted to catch animals which hug walls tightly when travelling abroad, it was important that the trap was set on a well-frequented animal track. It could, of course, have just as easily caught a small cat pursuing the stoats, weasels, rabbits or rats for which it was intended.

Box and Cage Traps

From the evidence produced by Roth, we know that medieval mouse-catchers employed cage traps of a design which persisted right up to Victorian times (picture, p 190), and even as late as the early part of the present century wire-cage traps were extremely popular for catching mice alive. An example of one which was used in Amherst, USA, about 1840 is seen on p 190, and is so like the Arouze model made in Paris that the latter must surely have been exported to America along with steel traps of that name. It is also like the 'Wonder' rat trap made at one time in Britain, and the 'Monarch' at present in production by S. Young & Sons Ltd. These traps are alike in having double-funnel entrances, rather like some of the fish traps, except that it is usual for the second funnel to have a trap-door floor which drops under the weight of a mouse or rat. The trap-door is either sprung or counter-weighted to return it to the original position, leaving the animal stranded in the second compartment. Such traps are of the multi-catch variety and the haul can be re-moved by using the door at the end of the second section. A slightly larger trap designed for rats and small vermin, such as stoats, weasels and squirrels, is manufactured by Havahart. It has the same action as those already described, but is square in section. All these traps are normally baited, both on the drop trapdoor and imme-diately under it, in the second compartment.

Cage traps of this kind can be used in almost any situation. Rats and small vermin, such as the smaller mustelids, are not averse to entering fowl houses, so there is no reason to suppose that they would find a cage trap objectionable, providing that it contained some interesting bait. The only recommendation, as with all traps manufactured from metal, is to 'season' it to get rid of the smell of newness before putting it into use. As vermin may be out hunting at any time of the day or night, it is advisable to leave a trap contin-uously in position, but as they tend to be more active at night it may be advantageous to rebait the trap in the evening. If there are signs of vermin around and the trap has not been catching any, it will be worthwhile moving it to another position.

The second type of box trap for mammals is that which has a drop-door at the entrance, usually closed by a release mechanism operated from inside by a captive animal. This group can be divided into two sections; those which have only one door, and those with doors so placed at each end that when both are left open there is an apparent run-through. A run-through cage trap can encourage animals mistrustful of apparently end-blocked boxes.

One of the most interesting box traps the writer has come across, even though it may be a little crude functionally, is a pottery mouse trap from the Isle of Djerba, in Tunis, North Africa. As can be seen in the illustration on p 190, the trap door is supported by a piece of string stretched over the carrying handle. The string goes through a hole in the rear of the trap, to fasten inside, and is coated with fat. If the mouse likes the fat and chews the string sufficiently, the trap door will fall and the mouse will be caught. The intriguing features of this trap are the nicely thrown pottery body, with afterwork providing a handle, internal guides for the trap door and foot to keep the body firmly on the ground. The purpose of the piercing on the sides is not clear, unless the long slits are meant to provide access for a sharp knife, with which to dispatch the occupant.

Modern cage traps of the single-door type are variously made entirely of wood or wire, or a combination of both. The operating principle involves a sliding, hinged or cantilevered door for access, linked with a bait hook or treadle. As soon as an animal pulls at the bait, the door drops and it is caught. Some examples are shown in the illustrations on p 207. These traps vary from small ones designed for mice, rats and small vermin, to larger ones for catching foxes. There is probably no upper limit, and large cage traps have been used in Africa for catching antelope. The only factor to be observed must be the relationship between the strength and gauge of materials used and the size of animal to be trapped.

Legg Squirrel Traps

In Britain, a special series of traps are made for squirrels. This does not imply that some other traps will not catch squirrels, or that these special Legg traps will not catch anything else. The particular features of these traps collectively is versatility for any situation. The midget trap is ideal for catching an odd grey squirrel in a garden. The single-catch is useful in situations where it is unlikely to attract more than one at a time, and where a little more space than usual is desirable for the occupant, as in cases where a trap cannot be visited frequently. When there are large numbers of squirrels, the multi-catch is beneficial, the first occupant often serving as a decoy for subsequent visitors.

These traps have won approval by the Ministry of Agriculture, Fisheries and Food and the Forestry Commission in Britain; not least because in areas where red and grey squirrels overlap (unfortunately an increasingly rare situation), they allow for the release of the red ones, which are subjects of priority conservation in Britain.

The midget and multi-catch traps are alike in having a simple push-up, self-return door, while the single-catch has the usual sliding door released by agitation of a bait lever.

It is recommended that the traps are placed in open situations devoid of undergrowth, but preferably with a carpet of leaves. Bait is scattered all round the trap, but especially near the door and inside. The door is pinned up for a few days until bait is being taken regularly from inside the trap.

When referring to squirrels here we are really considering the grey variety. A native of America and introduced into Britain during the nineteenth century, it is regarded as a pest in both countries, although possibly better tolerated in its native country than in Britain where it has spread to all districts and taken over many of the areas which were once the strongholds of its red relation. Squirrels of both hues are alike in the kind of damage they can do, but the grey form is especially disliked for its habit of peeling the bark from young deciduous trees and eating their young shoots and buds. They also enter market gardens destroying quantities of peas and beans, annoy fruit farmers by spoiling their fruit and, even worse, get on the wrong side of gamekeepers by taking the eggs of pheasants and partridges and sometimes their young.

As with most animals which are to be trapped, it is important to know something of their habits. Grey squirrels are generally associated with collections of trees—copses, young plantations, small woods and forests—and if seen at any distance from trees they will have been away travelling on some forgaging expedition. Yet, despite their association with trees, they spend a lot of time on the ground, and when pursued will rather escape to a convenient rabbit burrow than climb a tree. None the less, they make permanent nests, or dreys, in trees and these are often the best indication of a squirrel's base. Oak and beech are their favourite nesting trees but many other deciduous trees are used and conifers will be inhabited if necessary.

Grey squirrels are active mainly in daylight hours, the greatest activity being shown just after daybreak and just before dusk, but except in public parks, where they soon become very tame, they tend to hide themselves away and it is necessary to 'freeze' in a wood for several minutes after entering in order to see them come out into the open.

The Whole-Family-Catch Rat Trap

Similar in principle to the combined features of both single and multi-catch traps is the whole-family-catch rat trap sold by S. Young & Sons Ltd. As will be seen from the illustration on p 207, it has a single door activated by a lever from a bait hook and, at the opposite end, a flap-up, self-return door. The flap-door is too small to admit an adult rat and the idea behind the trap is to entice a female rat to enter the main door, take the bait, and be caught. If she has young, there is a fair chance that her calls will attract the family. Unable to get in through the main door, they will gain access through the flap-door, hence the trap's appropriate name. Such modern traps as these, with their automatically closing doors, are a useful advance over the original box trap which had a door propped open by a stick which had to be jerked away by means of a cord held by a hidden observer.

Most cage traps can be camouflaged with tree branches and grass, which also provide warmth for captives until such time as they are released, but there are two, best described as hutch traps, where this insulation, at least, is not quite so necessary. These are the Martin box trap, made in Scotland, and the Longworth small mammal trap.

The Martin and Longworth Traps

The Martin trap is designed to catch medium-sized mammals of the vermin variety. Its advantage is that, unlike spring traps, it provides for selection; so that if such rarities as polecats or pine martens were caught in Britain, they could be released. Although operating with a bait treadle in the same way as most cage traps, the Martin has half of its length made up as a wooden box. Inside this can be placed dried grass or other suitable bedding, together with food and water to keep a prisoner in good condition until released. Despite its appearance, it is not a heavy trap.

The Longworth trap (Fig 72), made by the Longworth Scientific Instrument Co Ltd, of Abingdon in Berkshire, is the outcome of a need for a suitable trap for use in scientific field surveys of small mammals, where it is essential to release the animal after measuring or tagging. It was designed by D. H. Chitty and D. A. Kempson of the Bureau of Animal Population, Oxford.

It is a two-part unit consisting of the trap section proper and a

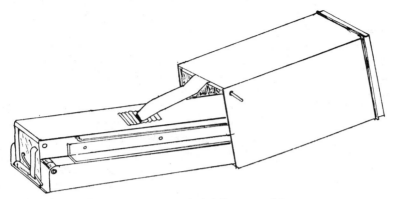

Fig 72   The Longworth small mammal box trap

nest-box. When carried around, the trap fits conveniently inside the nest section; in use, the two are linked together in one line. The trap is lightweight, being of aluminium construction, and has an overall length of 10in when the two units are locked together. The trap section is 2⅜in wide and 2⅛in high, while the nest-box is slightly larger, 3⅜in high and 2⅝in wide.

The whole structure is the product of both scientific and engineering planning. The locking mechanism for the two units provides a rigid combination unlikely to come apart under field conditions; indeed, the writer has found traps which had been kicked away by cattle, still intact and the occupant unharmed. The trap has a hinged flap-door operated by a trip wire at the opposite end. The trip is linked by spring-steel wire to the door and the whole is capable both of varying adjustment for fineness of setting and for pre-baiting. The details of adjustment and setting are too complicated to explain in the absence of the trap itself, but full instructions are supplied with each order. Methods for handling a catch from these traps is given by Southern in the *Handbook of British Mammals*.

The Longworth trap works extremely well and catches shrews, voles and field mice. The nest-box must, however, be provided with suitable bedding, such as straw, dried grass or dried leaves, and not, as some misguided operators have tried, with cotton wool which is totally wrong for small mammals whose feet and legs become en-tangled in the fine strands. Strands of raw sheep wool, on the other hand, picked off barbed-wire fences or thornbushes, make admirable bedding, since the natural oils in the wool provide maximum insulation from the cold.

Mention of insulation leads to what the writer considers to be the most serious drawback of this trap. Being all-metal, the interior of the nest-box is liable to heavy condensation during cold nights, and this internal dampness could be lethal to some small mammals. In addition, the outside suffers from collection of dew. As the sun rises this evaporates, and the effect on small animals like shrews of thus reducing the internal temperature to that of an ice-box becomes all too apparent. It is possible, however, to counter these deficiencies in some measure. The inside of the nest-box can be painted with a non-toxic insulating resin, such as 'Pallidux' (obtainable from Liquid Plastics Ltd, Preston, Lancashire)—a material used for lining fish-ponds and tanks—which is fairly rodent-proof when set. The nest-box as a whole can also be provided with an insulating jacket of some material such as hardboard, fibreboard or expanded poly-styrene, though of course this means additional bulk to carry. The basic cost of these traps is fairly high, about £1·50 ($4·00) each, and one feels that the manufacturer might well investigate other materials for the nest-box section, which does not require the same kind of fine mechanical adjustment as the trap unit.

Longworth traps were invented for scientific use and although they can be used either individually or in small numbers spread out sporadically, they were primarily intended for use in field experiments relating to problems of small mammal population and distribution. For this purpose they are used in large numbers, perhaps a hundred or more at a time, laid out on a grid system so as to provide a trapping pattern capable of repetition, for purposes of comparison, from one area to another. They will catch shrews, mice and voles equally well when baited with grain, but one needs to allow time for pre-baiting if a reasonably representative sample of a population is to be caught.

Home-made Mammal Traps

Two home-made small-mammal traps which have proved themselves under field conditions are a bamboo trap used in Trinidad and a plastic tube trap designed by Ernest B. Brown. The bamboo trap is an adaptation of one used originally for catching land crabs, and is now found effective for the Indian mongoose, *Herpestes auropunctatus*, wherever this has been introduced in tropical countries.

Details of its construction are shown in Fig 73, where it will be seen that the basic structure of the trap body is made up of bamboo taken between the nodes of a stem (the 'joints'). A piece 2ft between nodes is taken and should include one node as a seal for an end. The piece selected should be about 3½in diameter. The trigger assembly pieces can also be carved from bamboo, the only other requirement then being an elastic band made from a piece of old inner tube.

Fig 73   Bamboo mongoose trap

The trapdoor is 5in long and 3in wide, rounded to fit the contour of the inside of the bamboo at the bottom and notched to take the rubber band at the top. The door fits into a 3¼in hole made in the top of the bamboo at a point 3in from the open end. It is motivated by a bow formed from a flat piece of bamboo fitted into a slot made behind the door hole and having the rubber band fixed as shown.

One inch from the opposite end of the trap, a 1in square hole is cut in line with the door hole, and into this is fitted the shaped trigger. From a notch on the trigger to a notch on the rear face of the door, three-quarters of the way down from its top, is stretched a 'flying stick'. The trigger is coated with a suitable bait at the bottom and, when agitated, releases the flying stick, which in turn releases the door.

Mongooses are attracted to anything which offers a place into which they can crawl and secrete themselves. They tend to live underground or in earth banks, where the presence of a colony can be recognised by the many holes on the surface. A bamboo trap sited in such an area would not need to be hidden as the curiosity of the animals will be sufficient to ensure a catch.

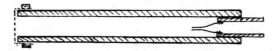

Fig 74   Section of a plastic tube trap

The plastic tube pipe-trap is a basic design which can be varied to accommodate mammals of different sizes, but is probably best suited to small mammals of shrew and vole size. The construction is simple. The body of the trap is formed from 1¼in polyvinyl-chloride water piping with 1½in inside diameter. Into one end is inserted the trap element, formed from 1½in outside diameter aluminium tube and two stainless steel strips of flexible shim stock measuring 3in by 1in and 3/1,000in thick. The strips are notched to fit inside the aluminium tube, riveted to its sides, and bent so as to spring slightly against each other. The trap element is wedged inside the trap body.

At the opposite end, the seal is constructed from a 2½in diameter piece of wire gauze of ⅛in mesh, held in place by plastic tubing with an internal diameter of 1¾in. Suitable bait (see chapter on Baits) is put into the sealed end of the trap and when animals push through the flexi-steel tongues to get it, the tongues act like a one-way valve.

The Clausius Trap

On the European continent, the term 'box trap' implies a type now being adopted for vermin control in Britain. Known as the Clausius trap, it is used extensively in France, Belgium, Holland, Germany and Denmark. It is sometimes known as the 'see-saw trap' since it consists of a wooden box frame and a rocking see-saw treadle inside. It is about 24 in long, 4in wide, 5in high at the closed end, and 4in square at the open end. Thus the top slopes. Inside, a platform, stretching the whole length except for an inch at each end, is pivoted, the pivot being so placed that, when set, the platform is slightly longer at the open end and hence tipped down in that direction. Under the platform at the open end, there is hinged a three-sided wire frame, the free ends of which are pointed. The closed end of the trap can be either of glass, perspex or ½in wire mesh (picture, p 207).

The trap can be baited at the closed end. Visiting animals will walk along the platform, but when they have passed over the pivot point the platform tips down. At the open end, the wire frame drops and the spiked ends dig into the trap floor. Thus the platform cannot reverse its position, even if the prisoner tries to back-up along the trap.

These traps can be used singly in the field, and have been found successful for weasels when sited in straw ricks, stacks of wood, along walls and beside streams. They have also been placed on the centre of a plank serving as a bridge over a stream, and if the plank is no wider than the box trap animals are likely to use the box as a passage way. In this situation, a glass-ended box is preferable. Again, they have been found to catch very well when placed at the foot of a stone wall from which lower stones have been removed, as on dry-stone walling boundaries. Two traps are placed side by side through the thickness of the wall, but with open ends on opposite sides.

When catching stoats and weasels, the traps should be left in position for a time after a catch, because these animals live in family groups. If there has been no further catch for about a week they should be moved elsewhere.

Run-Through Box Traps

The second group of box or cage traps is the run-through, or double-ended variety, a type of trap which is particularly useful when animals are timid and unlikely to enter an apparently closed box. If such creatures can see daylight and a clearway through the other end, they will be more inclined to enter. Animals in this category include mink, bobcats, small antelope and pine martens.

There have been many designs for this kind of trap. An early one was the 'Terrier' Death Run Trap designed by Mark Hovell to catch rats. In many respects, it looks like the Havahart productions so popular in the States and used all over the world, the main difference being that the trigger mechanism of the 'Terrier' was mounted over the top of the cage, whereas in the Havahart models it is on the side. The manufacturers of the 'Terrier' were Duke, Waring, Crisp & Co, at whose Soho wire works, in London, were also made the 'Wonder' cage rat trap and the 'Pullinger' mouse trap during the period between the two world wars.

Havahart Traps

The Havahart range of cage traps probably includes some of the best examples of this type obtainable, and their value is enhanced by the wide range of sizes available, from a 10in by 3in by 3in for mice to 42in by 11in by 13in for wildcats, large raccoons and nutria. The

No 2 trap, measuring 24in by 7in by 7in, is illustrated on p 85 in the set position. In these traps the doors are hinged at the edges of the flat metal roof so that they slope down at each end when sprung. Since they are also of metal sheeting, a captive animal is sheltered from rain, in a manner not seen in many of the all-wire-mesh traps. There are also wire frames hinged at each end of the trap, and these drop down to lock the doors when the trap is sprung. The triggers are continuations of the door hinges and interconnect with a lever from the bait treadle inside the cage. However, if a closed-ended trap is needed, it is quite easy to move one of the trigger levers out of the way and simply operate one open door. The metal framing and strengthening struts, together with the heavy galvanised finish, make these traps extremely durable and long lasting. Incidentally, the Havahart range includes a special fox trap with a live-bait compartment at one end.

As the object of a run-through trap is to allow a shy animal to enter without suspicion, the trap should be fixed so that it does not operate for a day or two and it should be pre-baited. It is also possible with this kind of trap for animals caught in, say a town garden, to be transported to an open area elsewhere and there released unharmed.

If a cage trap is to be operated near an animal's hole, one end should be left closed and rocks or logs arranged around it to prevent an emerging animal from progressing farther from its hole without entering the trap. If there is more than one hole, the others must also be blocked. Muskrats can be caught with a No 2 Havahart trap set among logs and bushes alongside the water where the animals are working.

For catching mink there is a special Havahart trap, the No 6, which can be set under water. It has doors which will drop easily when the trap is submerged, and also has a baithook instead of the usual pan, on which fish bait can be speared. It is intended for siting at a point where tributaries enter a main stream, but should be protected from floodwaters by placing it among rocks or brushwood. If it is placed in position a month before trapping is to begin, fastened so that it cannot be sprung, and pre-baited for a fortnight before trapping starts, the chances of the immediate success will be all the greater.

The No O Havahart trap, intended for small mammals, can be used instead of the Longworth trap; in fact, in tropical areas where exposure in an open cage structure may not be so vital as in temperate areas, it could be more successful owing to its run-through feature.

The counterpart of the Havahart trap in Britain is the wire box trap sold by S. Young & Sons Ltd. It is not made in as wide a range of sizes as the Havahart, the smallest being 24in by 6 in square and the largest 48in by 15in square. The doors at each end are snapped shut, when released, by built-in springs. This can be a disadvantage when the springs become worn, as it might then be possible for heavy animals to force their way out again if the locks do not operate. The traps have open wire tops, and thus captured animals can be exposed to rain without adequate shelter. The trigger mechanism, operated like that of the Havahart trap from the bait treadle inside, is over the top of the cage. This would seem less satisfactory than having it at the side, as it is more liable to be tripped by falling debris from overhead trees, or become jammed when the trap is being camouflaged. The galvanised metal bottoms of these traps can also be cold for captured animals, as well as collecting water in rainy weather and urine from the captives.

Traps for Badgers

The illustration on p 208 shows an interesting trap used at one time in North Wales for catching badgers. Its particular feature is the tremendously strong construction, necessary since the badger is a powerful animal and would not be long contained in a sheet-metal and wire trap. The whole trap was constructed of $\frac{1}{4}$in wrought-iron rods and $\frac{3}{8}$in square-section wrought-iron framing. The double doors moved up and down on iron guides which looped over at the top to provide carrying handles. It needs a strong man to carry the trap alone, and it would certainly require one at each end to manage the trap complete with a badger. The trigger and door release mechanism was nicely adapted to the sliding action of the doors, the trigger being operated conventionally from an internal bait hook. Movement of this released a containing hook for the door-release levers, which were pivoted on the bars of the trap top and caught under the raised doors. In many respects this badger trap resembles the antelope traps used in Africa for the smaller species such as duiker and steinbok.

Badgers are mainly nocturnal creatures and rather shy, but they do occasionally move about in the daytime. They produce 'sets', which usually consist of a series of entrance and escape holes associated with their underground burrows, and their presence in a district can

be confirmed by the discovery of scratching trees, where the bark
has been scraped for a distance of several feet up the trunk. The
animals live in semi-woodland districts, but also hunt over meadow-
land. They are often accused, probably wrongly, of being poultry
thieves, killers of gamebirds and wreckers of fences. They may be
guilty of the last, although they will frequently burrow under a fence
rather than push through it, but this also brings them into disrepute
because the hole they make under a fence also allows foxes to penetrate it. Farmers seeking a culprit for lost poultry will sometimes
find feathers in a badger's hole, but such untidiness is not in character
for a badger, which is rather meticulous about the outside appearance
of its house and even chooses a latrine site some distance away. If
bones and feathers are found at the entrance to a set, the thief, more
than likely, is a fox—an untidy and rather dirty animal—who has
borrowed a badger's home. In fact, instances have been recorded
where a fox has moved in on a badger, which has promptly departed
in disgust.

Badgers are not easy animals to trap, because they are shy and
wary, but a trap of the kind described, used as a run-through type at
a time when natural food is scarce, could be successful. Badgers,
although carnivorous animals by definition, will, as so many carnivores have to do, tackle all kinds of food, insects and snails often
making up a fair proportion of their diet. A badger will even dig up
bulbs and roots when animal food is scarce, and despite its apparent
shyness in the presence of man, it can be a fearless fighter if cornered.

Live-catch Box Traps

All cage traps suffer by comparison with spring traps in being less
easily portable, so that fewer can be carried on a trapping expedition.
Even so, they have much in their favour. They are live traps, and
now that we are rightly becoming more mindful of a need to show
humanity towards the dumb creatures of the world, such methods of
capturing animals are to be applauded.

Furthermore, although not selective (and what trap is except by
virtue of size?), they allow for selection after capture. If what you
have caught is not what you want, you let it go free again. Such a
facility is vital in the interests of wildlife conservation, and can be the
means of sparing domestic animals much harm and suffering. There
is no longer any excuse for a gamekeeper's wife who displays rugs of
tabby-cat skins.

Fur-trappers in the United States are now beginning to take to these box traps, which not only enable them to free immature or unprime fur-bearers but also keep prime catches in good condition and safe from predators. And as for scientific research, live-catch box traps have no rivals. Their only possible limitation is that one cannot easily discourage trap-prone animals, though the writer regards it as a personal compliment when an animal he has handled after it has been trapped comes back for more.

One run-through, live-catch, mole trap developed by scientists for research purposes was an adaptation of a type used traditionally in Holland. The Dutch trap was described by Haeck and a modification, allowing retention of moles overnight, by A. J. B. Rudge in an article in the *Journal of Zoology* in 1966.

The Dutch version was really an adaptation of a deadfall trap but, instead of the weight falling into a box or tray, it dropped on to a block through which was bored a 2in hole. The block had slits at each end through which could slide doors fixed to the ends of the deadfall weight. Thus, when a mole pushed a trigger inside the block tunnel, the weight descended and sealed off the tunnel ends.

The reason why Rudge modified the trap by adding a container as an extension of the tunnel was to allow the mole to enter a compartment containing hay as bedding for warmth, and a supply of worms for food. Without these, the mole would not survive for more than about four hours, whereas with suitable bedding and about 50gm of earthworms, moles were found to survive up to eighteen hours of confinement in a trap. Some were caught in the same trap twice or three times, which suggests that trap-shyness for this model is not a likely problem.

In use, the trap is buried in a mole run so that the hole in the block is continuous with the run. In field trials, the writer has found that allowing moles free access through the trap for a few days sometimes helps to increase the catches when the trigger mechanism is later made operational.

Care must be taken in setting these traps, as soil will easily foul the door entrances and prevent closure. Perspex doors of $\frac{1}{4}$in thickness proved better than wood or metal, as they did not warp and slid easily through the slits in the trap body. The extra compartment has a wire-mesh floor to allow urine to soak away and so keep the bedding dry in the nest.

Automatic Box Traps

The last group of box traps for mammals is made up of automatic repeating traps, involving a resetting mechanism or providing multi-catch facilities. All of these traps which the writer has come across are for mice, due, no doubt, as one manufacturer puts it, to the mouse's innate curiosity. Certainly they are intrepid creatures and will find their way into anything offering even the tiniest access.

Mostly, these traps can be used without bait, though some bait can be used outside the trap to attract mice to its vicinity. The Pullinger mouse trap, described in Chapter Three, falls into this category but, except as a museum item, is no longer available. Another vintage type is illustrated on p 208. It is an example of a German self-setting mouse trap and is probably the ultimate in traps which make animals work hard for their own destruction.

It is a three-part construction. Starting with the trap set, as shown in the illustration, the mouse can enter through the raised trapdoor. Once inside, it quickly moves on to a treadle which operates a lever allowing the trapdoor to fall and close the entrance. The mouse can be released at this stage, if it does not venture farther, by removal through the side grille-door. The hope, however, is that its curiosity will overcome any fear and lead it on. The second stage is up the wire-mesh vertical tunnel, at the top of which is a hole leading into the third section. This has a collapsing floor and, when the mouse drops through, the wire arms projecting outwards move up and raise the trapdoor until the lever prevents it dropping. The mouse, incidentally, falls to a watery grave in the removable can at the base of the third section. If the mouse is sufficiently curious, it will destroy itself and set the wheels in motion for a repeat performance by one of its relatives.

Havahart also market a nice little machine for catching mice. In true Western style, it is called the 'Ketch-All', and consists of a box made of galvanised steel plate with sliding lid. Inside are three compartments, of which the centre unit, cylindrical in shape, is occupied by a three-vaned rotating structure. This vaned device has a spring which can be wound by an outside key, like a clock spring. The floor of the central cylinder has a pressure plate sufficiently sensitive to react to pressure from a mouse standing on it. The rear compartment houses the mechanical components activating the veined paddle, and the front compartment is to house captured mice. The lure is the curiosity of the mouse. Once inside the central cylinder, having entered through either of the side apertures, a mouse operates the hair trigger and, in the words of the instruction leaflet, 'is spanked into the hopper'. The mechanism is self-resetting and, as it will operate fifteen times from one winding, it should, in theory, be able to catch fifteen mice before it needs resetting.

For weaker-minded trappers who cannot face up to disposing of fifteen live mice (assuming that, in the meantime, they have not turned cannibals), an accessory drowning device is available. To use this, the sliding top is withdrawn from the hopper section, and in its place a narrow slide is inserted to which is attached a hose leading into a Kilner-type jar filled with water. Again, in theory, mice get thirsty and curious and tumble into the jar, there to drown. This trap (Fig 75) is so placed as to allow a gap of not less than 2in between it and nearby walls.

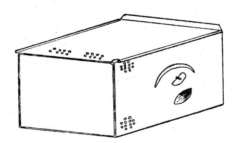

Fig 75   The Havahart 'Ketch-All' automatic mouse trap

S. Young & Sons Ltd also produce a multi-catch box mouse trap, constructed partly of wood and partly of perforated galvanised steel sheeting. From Fig 76, it will be apparent that this provides a hole at one end for mice to enter into a tube and funnel of perforated sheeting. Once they have entered the box from the funnel, they do not make the return journey. The limit in catch size here is presumably the capacity of the box, the first victim being expected to serve as a lure for others.

Miscellaneous Mammal Traps
Still using the principle of a funnel, a cane or bamboo trap for rats or lizards is known to be employed in Tanzania. It is made from ⅛in

Fig 76   Young's automatic mouse trap

strips of cane and is about 20in long and 2½in diameter at the open
end (Fig 77). The animals move into this trap for shade or from
inquisitiveness and, as it is flexible, the more the animal pushes in,
the firmer it is held, so that reversing becomes impossible.

Two more mammal traps from Africa are of the spiked-wheel
type. One used by the Shilluk people of the Upper Nile region is
about 6in in diameter and is intended for capturing gazelle. It is
made from a rim of dried grass bound with raffia-like material and
tied into it are spokes of sharp-pointed cane. In use, it is anchored by
means of a rope and stake near a drinking-place, so that animals
coming to the muddy edges of pools will step into it and be caught
by the leg.

The larger giraffe trap, illustrated on p 208, operates on exactly the
same principle. Also from the Upper Nile area, it is a product of the
Nuco people and, though similar in design, is more heavily constructed. Rope is used to bind the dried grass stems forming the rim,
and sharpened wooden staves form the rather fewer spokes. The
trap is about 12in in diameter and is meant to capture large antelope
as well as giraffes. Although these traps differ in constructional form,
the principle used is not unlike that of the treadle traps described
earlier.

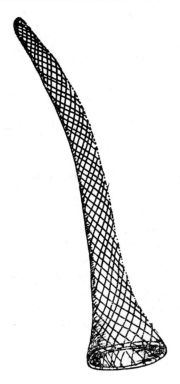

Fig 77   Rat and lizard trap

Altering the target from the limbs to the head, the principle is seen again in the spiked block trap shown in Fig 78. This device, which has been used all over the world, relies upon an animal putting its head through the spiked opening to get at bait in the back of the hole. Once its head is well pushed in, the spikes prevent any retraction. It can catch animals from mouse size upwards, according to the size of the block and aperture.

A different kind of trap for mammals is that known as the 'Wolf's Garden'. It has been used in Siberia by Yakut and Tungus tribesmen to destroy the wolves which attack their herds, and has also been used by the Karachais in the Caucasian area (Fig 79).

About 12ft in diameter, it consists of two concentric circles of log piles driven into the ground to a height of about 5ft 6in. The outer

Fig 78   Spiked-block trap

circle has a gap into which a door can fit. During the summer the
trap is left baited, but without a door, so that wolves become used to
the trap at a time when they are not a danger to domestic animals
owing to an abundance of wildlife.

In the autumn, the door is fitted to swing inwards. The trap is now
baited by putting a live puppy or young reindeer inside the inner
circle. When a wolf is tempted, it will push open the door to get at
the live bait and will move around the space between the two circles

Fig 79   The 'Wolf's Garden'

in the hope of gaining entrance to the second. When it reaches the door, it will close it to get past and, because it cannot turn in the narrow passageway, will be forced to run in circles without being able to escape. Others will enter and suffer the same fate, until the trap-owner comes to attend to them.

An Antelope Trap

The last mammal trap to be described is one devised by the Colorado Fish and Game Department, and adopted for use in South Africa for catching antelope. It is much the biggest mammal trap in use, comparable in size with a wildfowl decoy.

The general features of the trap can be seen in Fig 80, and it will be clear that an aircraft can be used to advantage in encouraging animals towards the 'crush', as the enclosure is called. This is preferable to using beaters and jeeps as, when these methods are employed to drive sensitive creatures towards a restricting funnel, many fatalities occur and the end result is often disappointing.

Fig 80   Antelope crush trap as used by the Colorado Fish and Game Department

The siting of an antelope trap is important and should be related to areas habitually used by antelope. The use of a familiar feature, such as an existing fence, will be an advantage, and the added fencing should be of nylon mesh netting 4ft high and attached to steel stakes. The side where the antelope will enter is not complete; the netting is fastened to the bottom of the stakes, but allowed to rest on the ground and so arranged that it can be lifted into place when antelope have been driven across. A siting such that the catch pen is in a hollow and not visible from the enclosed area is to be preferred. The crush and catch pen are made of heavier netting, not less than 7ft high and the pen is fitted with a swing gate controlled from an observation pit about 50yd away.

When the ground party have moved into the area and concealed themselves and their vehicles, the pilot of the aircraft (a helicopter is better than a light aeroplane) searches for a herd, communicating with the ground units by two-way radio. He discovers if the actual plane or its shadow is most effective in frightening the animals, and then moves them cautiously towards and into the trap. As it is necessary to hold them there while the ground unit lifts and secures the fence, a helicopter has obvious advantages over a fixed-wing aircraft.

When the fence is adjusted, the antelope are left for a day to quieten down. Then they are coerced into the crush by men on the ground and when all are inside the gate is closed from the observation hole. Again they are left to quieten, later being captured individually and transferred to vehicles for transporting. This procedure has been frequently used, especially in South Africa, for restocking farms and reserves with wildlife.

CHAPTER NINE

Baits

MOST human beings depend so much on their senses of hearing and vision that they do not readily appreciate the significance of the sense of smell to large numbers of lower animals, or the extent to which these rely upon it.

Though we do not use our noses nearly as efficiently as we could, we can train ourselves to do so, and sometimes this is best accomplished by suppressing more dominant senses. A blind or deaf person, deprived of a major sensory apparatus, makes more practical use of normally subordinate sense organs and either smells things more acutely or develops a fine and discriminating sense of touch. A chemist can train himself to analyse materials from their smells, while tea, coffee, or wine blenders depend upon the combined senses of taste and smell for the skills required to produce palatable combinations of single varieties.

Mammals have only monochromatic vision, that is they only perceive objects as black and white, and shades of grey. This is common, too, for many other back-boned animals. Some insects have colour sense; we know, for example, that bees use a limited range of colour vision to detect plants with flowers capable of yielding nectar. But we know also that bees and many other insects are sensitive to perfumes emitted by plants.

Armed with the knowledge that, to many animals, scent may be one of the most important, if not the most important of their senses, we are better able to appreciate the value of scented baits in trapping. Of course, not all baits are scented and we do rely on some animals also having keen sight, as when live animals are tethered near to a trap—the rabbit to attract a fox, a decoy bird to attract a hawk. Sometimes the live bait is used to stimulate other senses, such as when using a yelping puppy to attract a wolf.

We must also remember that there are animals with several senses co-dominant. Cats, for example, which depend more upon the co-dominance of sight and hearing than the sense of smell, may have one of these keener senses distracted when concentrating upon the use of the other. The head may be turned in order to bring an ear into direct line with a source of sound. With the eyes diverted from this line, vision will obviously be less than a hundred per cent in the direction from which sounds are coming. The factor which can re-direct vision is movement. A fluttering wing or a moving branch in a tree, however slight, will be spotted by the cat and its head will turn to concentrate the eyes on the source of movement. Movement may be equally important to other animals in identifying a prey. The falcon in the sky, for instance, has acute vision, but it is movement more than shape which reveals the mouse scurrying along the ground below.

Scent Baits

So what is a good bait? In all fairness, we must answer that it depends upon the animal we are attracting, and in this section it is proposed to concentrate mainly upon baits which are attractive to an animal's sense of smell. To meet this requirement, a bait must have one pre-dominant feature; it must either be volatile or at least there must be volatile ingredients in its make-up. A bait which contains vaporising substances will be moist, owing to either aqueous or oily content, and it is usually the oily baits which are most productive of nose-tickling vapours.

Such baits will only remain effective for as long as they exude tantalising vapours, and a trap exposed to hot sun soon becomes useless as the bait dries out and no longer attracts animals through their olfactory organs. For this reason, it is important that, when trapping in warm climatic conditions, traps should be sited in shady areas. This has a double advantage, for the animals will also seek shade.

Animal Repellents

Before further considering the properties of substances with which to attract an animal, it is worth noting some of the things which will repel them. And of all the possible repellents against which a trapper must protect his traps, human smell is the greatest. We may believe that our hands, for example, are dry, whereas, in fact, they are con-stantly exuding oily vapours which contaminate everything we touch. For this reason traps should never be handled by bare hands. Gloves should be worn or, at least, a clean cloth or clump of grass used to pick up and move traps, except when these are to be used in water.

It is true, of course, that animals which do not come into contact with human beings will not necessarily associate human smell with danger in the way that others continuously in contact with humans, and perhaps with reason to fear them, will do. But any smell which is foreign to the environment in which an animal lives will arouse suspicion if that animal is one which depends upon its sense of smell to give warning of impending danger.

Some animals such as rats, as we have already seen, find the smell of blood repulsive and will avoid traps which have injured previous catches and become contaminated with blood. Traps should always, therefore, be cleaned thoroughly after each catch in the manner already recommended for the cleaning of steel traps.

In the absence of other facilities for removing human and other smells, both from traps and an area in which they are set, smoke can be valuable—not tobacco smoke which is a foreign smell for most wild creatures, but the smoke of fired wood or dried grass. Animals generally fear fire and move rapidly away from it, as anyone who has been in the vicinity of a forest, bush or grass fire will be able to testify. On the other hand, animals are used to re-colonising burnt-out country, especially when the tender new grasses and plant shoots begin to appear.

Great care must, of course, be exercised when lighting any kind of fire in open country, where an uncontrolled outbreak could cause widespread damage, and every country lover should have made himself familiar with the fire-protection and fire-fighting rules in his area.

Bird Baits

Turning, for a moment, to other than scent baits, and the situations in which they can be employed, eyesight is of far greater significance in birds than a sense of smell. High-flying birds would find difficulty in detecting even strong odours emanating from ground level and terrestrial noises would seldom be audible. On the other hand, objects on the ground will remain visible to an animal with good vision no matter how high it is, providing there is no intervening cloud layer.

The expression 'good vision' needs some clarification, as some birds have a visual capacity which depends upon acuity—the ability to render an image which is sharp and has well-defined patterns. Such birds can spot a motionless prey from quite astonishing heights. Other birds react more readily to a moving target. Seed-eating birds will generally remain close to ground level, but acute vision and some sense of colour interpretation aids them in identifying even quite small seeds and berries.

These properties of the sight of birds are utilised in choosing suitable baits for bird trapping. Birds of prey can be drawn to a captive but moving decoy, and even a bird wing fluttering on a post or bush will attract them. Carrion-feeders will quickly spot a corpse pegged out on the ground, and a scattering of seeds will soon be found by birds of the bush and hedgerow.

A personal experience will illustrate how effective seed can be as a bait to help capture birds. A pigeon managed to find its way into the museum in which the writer works and rested upon a ledge high up in a central dome. There is a balcony some 12ft below the bottom edge of the dome and it was decided to attempt to catch the bird by baiting a cage trap here. The trap was baited inside and out with a seed mixture and during the whole operation of placing the trap and bait the pigeon watched most intently. Within ten minutes of leaving the trap set, the pigeon was seen on the balcony feeding. It worked its way steadily towards, and eventually inside, the trap, after which it stepped on to the bait pan and so shut itself inside.

Some birds, owls are good examples, frequently suffer mobbing by small birds, and the trapper can capitalise this situation by placing a stuffed owl near to a trap, or series of traps. A more up-to-date method of attracting birds is to reproduce bird song, using a tape-recorder. Placed inside a cage trap, this can collect many birds, especially those of gregarious habit.

These baiting devices are all subjective in their action, whereas making use of an animal's curiosity could be considered as an abstract bait. Weasels are instinctively drawn to tunnels, so that traps placed inside artificial or natural tunnels will be more successful than those set in the open. The same goes for mice, voles and squirrels. Again, stoats and weasels are quite unable to resist exploring piles of stones, so that traps set inside these will give better results than if sited in places of less interest to the animals.

Finally, among the so-called non-scent baits we can include water and salt, which have particular value in special situations. Water will attract all kinds of animals under conditions of drought, and salt has an especial appeal for animals living inland from the sea. We generally consider water to be odourless and tasteless, but anyone who has experienced a rain shower in the tropics after months of torrid heat will have reason to doubt these properties of water as defined in chemistry textbooks.

General Scent Baits

Returning to scent baits, it is usual to consider these under three categories. Firstly there are general scents which prove interesting for no apparent reason, but which seem to attract animals none the less. The second group are food baits, known to animals because they are regular articles of diet, or especially interesting because they are exotic. Lastly, there are scent baits which have sexual significance or are employed by animals to mark their own territories.

General scent baits include such materials as oil of rhodium, oil of anise, caraway, sweet oil and musk. These can be used to attract animals of many kinds, but specific types of animals can often be enticed to otherwise non-selective traps by means of baits which have a particular interest for one animal family rather than another. The family Canidae, for example, which includes domestic dogs, foxes, coyotes, jackals and wolves, will respond to valerian, which is a product of plant species of *Valeriana*. Members of the cat family, Felidae, including domestic cats, wildcats, lions, tigers, leopards, civet cats, serval cats and lynx, are attracted towards catnip coming from species of the plant *Nepeta*. All the bears, Ursidae, find oil of anise, from species of the plant *Pimpinella*, irresistible.

Food Baits

Among food baits can be grouped almost all the foods included in human diet, preferably in an uncooked, or unprepared, condition. Cereals such as oats, barley, wheat and maize can be soaked in water, as this not only makes them soft and therefore more natural—animals living on cereals would frequently get them in the wild from living plants—but also increases the chance of grain scent being exuded.

Fresh fruits are useful for many animals, especially frugivorous and herbivorous kinds, and will attract birds, as well as many rodents, squirrels and lagomorphs (rabbits and hares). Grey squirrels in

Britain are often found raiding vegetable plots in gardens, and also orchards. They are very fond of garden peas and beans, both of which they pod with their forepaws and then eat the seeds. They have also been accused of taking the softer orchard fruits, such as cherries and plums, from which they eat not only the pulpy flesh, but also the seeds after cracking the hard shells. One fruit which seems to attract a great many animals is the apple; among those which have been caught by its use as a bait are flying squirrels, muskrats, opossums, various finches, starlings, and pigeons. In Africa monkeys often raid orchards and cultivated fields and can be caught out of the fruiting season with a bait of imported bananas, a fruit which can also be used for capturing nutria.

Meat is, of course, the most important bait for carnivores. It needs to be fresh for most animals in this group, who will not be interested when it has become dry and high, but there are a few who will be attracted to bait which has gone a stage beyond being merely dry, and become fetid. This applies to most dogs, including foxes. Meat in any shape will attract carnivores, but carrion-feeders, such as jackals, crows and vultures, are more interested in a whole carcass than a joint.

Natural Baits

The last group of baits could be described as natural baits, since they are either the products of animals used directly, or concoctions which incorporate these substances. It is often possible to use a live animal as a sexual bait, especially if a female is available and more especially if it is a female mammal in season. The products of the scent glands of animals have also been used for a very long time to lure others. Such scents will sometimes attract only animals of the same type, whereas other scents will have a much wider appeal.

Beaver castor, or castoreum, for instance, is invaluable for attracting other beavers. The castors are scent glands located on either side of the anal opening and can be dissected out quite easily from a dead beaver, though care must be taken to avoid removing other glands lower down which will have no effect. The true castors are dried and then ground into a powder which is mixed with glycerine. It can be applied to areas around the trap site or, if a cage trap is being used, it can be smeared on the bait pedal. The scent of mongooses, polecats and skunks can be used similarly.

Other animals, particularly members of the dog family and mongooses, mark out their territory with urine. Sometimes faeces are used as well. These substances can be used as a bait because animals of the same kind will be interested in re-marking the soiled areas with their own excreta. Scent marking is a behavioural feature in animals which is still not fully understood, despite recent more intensified research into its function. No doubt it is a social activity and could be a means of marking territory, as has been suggested by Schenkel for the wolf. Lorenz thought that scent was deposited by dogs to warn off intruders; Wynne-Edwards, on the other hand, considered that scent marking was associated with the population density of specific animals, providing individuals with information concerning rivals and enabling dogs to know of bitches on heat. Anyone who has kept a bitch will know that if she is carried some distance away from her home and carried back, there will be no trouble from the attentions of amorous visiting males.

The stimuli which induce members of the dog family to disperse scent by urinating, defaecating or body rubbing are first, the presence of familiar permanent objects in their environment, such as wooden posts, stones and, of course lamp-posts; and secondly, the existence of objects having unusual odours. Traps must come into this last category and preferably the scent bait should be so applied that the animal is induced to tread near a point where a steel trap is buried, or to enter a cage trap.

In using baits of any kind, pre-baiting is a most useful procedure and, when trapping is being undertaken on a large scale in a given area, makes for increasing toleration of the traps as time goes on. In pest destruction, commercial trapping and scientific research, the increased yield in catch-to-trap ratio from pre-baiting more than compensates for the time involved in waiting during the preliminary stage.

Some Baiting Tips

Another general tip applies to baits which are being used in conjunction with deadfall traps. Such baits should always be compressible and preferably in paste form, otherwise they may prevent the weight falling its full distance and, in the case of small animals, may leave enough space for the catch to make good its escape.

Where bait is being used on or in a trap, it serves to induce the animal into springing the trap and must, therefore, be fastened securely to the trigger or pedal. With some baits it is best to tie them to the trap trigger, or pieces of meat can be threaded on to suitable cord which is then secured to the trap. A similar method has been found very effective when using breakback traps to catch field rodents. In this case maize seeds (sweet corn is the best variety) are soaked overnight and are then soft enough to be threaded on to cotton, using a sewing needle. If three or four threaded seeds are tied to a bait lever, this will prevent the bait being taken by small mammals from the trap without springing it. The animal is also more likely to pull in all directions and so sooner or later release the wire jaw.

With many animals, birds and rodents particularly, a bait lead-in can be very useful. This is simply a scattering of the bait—animal scent such as urine, or food bait such as grain—in the vicinity of the trap. The animal is thus induced to 'feed' or 'smell its way' into the trap site, and the more it concentrates on feeding or smelling the less vigilant it will become.

There are so many possibilities in selecting baits that it is as well to test response by experiment. In a given trapping situation, a variety of baits can be tried out over a period of time under similar conditions and it should soon become apparent which are the ones favoured by the potential catch.

For many years it has been possible to purchase ready-made, portable and long-lasting baits from proprietary manufacturers. In Britain, S. Young & Sons, Ltd, market two preparations—'Young's Irresistible Bait' and 'Young's Draw Game'. In the United States and Canada, baits and lures are marketed by a number of trapping agencies and supply houses. Allcock Manufacturing Co, the manufacturers of Havahart traps, also distribute Hawbaker's baits, which come in handy sizes to provide for between twenty-five and 100 sets and are specifics for rodents, rabbits, squirrels, muskrats, skunks, foxes and many other animals.

Specific Baits

Specific baits are those which can be used for particular animals, and the ones listed here have all been recommended by various trappers. There is no guarantee, however, that a bait which one particular trapper has found to be successful, will work equally well for someone else. Trappers, like cooks with recipes for cakes, find that baits which are effective with one can be a complete flop with another, and the only sure way to discover which of the following are most suitable for one's purpose is by trial and error.

Shellfish and Fish

Common baits which are likely to work in fish traps include pieces of strongly smelling fish, especially herring. Stale bread can be useful for minnows and pike, and worms may well be valuable in a small-mesh fish trap. Fishermen have used small crabs and frogs in fish traps with success, and eels have been caught using the entrails of sheep, rabbits, or chickens.

Snakes

Apart from basket traps used by primitive tribes, it is possible to use small-mesh cage-traps and these can be baited with whole eggs in their shells. Live mice or frogs can also be used, where these can be contained in a compartment isolated from the catching area of the trap.

Birds

Birds of prey will be attracted by live bait, such as young rabbits, pigeons and, in the case of owls and small hawks, by live mice. They will also respond to fresh meat, but it must really be fresh.

Carrion-feeding birds can be drawn to any recently killed animal, also to eggs, stale bread, grain or chaff.

Game birds, including pheasants, partridges and guinea fowl, will respond to composite baits. A formula recommended is: 1 quart raisins, 1 pint each of wheatseed, white peas and small maize seeds and a few sunflower seeds. These are mixed and scattered in and around traps being used.

Pigeons can be taken with use of New Zealand maple peas, whole maize and wheat seeds in the ratio of 4:2:1.

Starlings will take grain and bread, but are very fond of raisins.

Sparrows go for coarsely ground (kibbled) wheat, soaked bread and chicken feed, also any kitchen scraps.

Mice

A general rodent bait can be made in a large quantity for extensive trapping according to this formula: 2lb melted beef suet; 2lb peanut butter; 2lb ground raisins; 2lb oatmeal; 1lb paraffin wax. The ingredients should be ground and mixed, and the product can be stored in old plastic squeeze-bottles having removable tops, and squeezed out as required.

Mice can be drawn by oats, biscuit crumbs, flour, whole wheat, and canary seed (*Phalaris canariensis*). The popular bait for mice—cheese—is not necessarily better than any others, its general use having no doubt been prompted by mice attacking stored cheeses.

Voles will also respond to cheese, but any cereals will attract them, especially crushed oats.

Rats

Because of the ever-persisting war against rats, a great deal of effort has gone into devising baits for them, with or without poison mixed in with it.

Hovell recommended the following formula: 1lb flour; 3oz treacle (molasses); 3oz grated cheese; 1lb breadcrumbs.

Another formula is: 1pt oatmeal; 1oz sugar; 4 drops oil of rhodium; 3 drops each of aniseed and caraway oils; and a little powdered musk.

Some experts have suggested that perfumes such as rhodium, aniseed and caraway oils, as well as musk, have more value in repelling human smell than specifically attracting rats or any other animals.

Other possible baits for rats, all recommended by trappers at one time or another, are raw or cooked meat, fish, bacon, carrot, tomato, melon, apple, dripping, rolled oats, fresh bread (stale bread is passed by), sunflower seeds, parsnip and celery. These baits will attract many other rodents, including muskrats and pocket gophers.

Herbivorous Animals

Rabbits, hares and small deer, also sometimes squirrels, will visit traps baited with lettuce, cabbage, and fruits such as tomatoes, melon rind and apples. Root vegetables, such as carrots, can be effective and one suggestion for making live traps attractive is to spray them inside with cider.

Carnivores

The fox has been attracted by selections from a varied list of baits. The most favoured ones are probably fox urine, some of the scent oils, such as those of anise and rhodium, and use of live baits, especially young rabbits or small fowls. Live-bait animals are kept in cages arranged in such a way that a fox must pass through a double-door type of live trap in order to attempt to reach the bait.

A fetid bait for foxes, coyotes and jackals can be made by chopping up fish, placing it in a tin with a pierced lid (to allow gases to escape), and keeping it for about a month before use.

Another lure recommended as suitable for this same group of animals is made as follows:

Combine 1 part each of fox urine, gall and anal gland extract of fox, coyote or jackal, as appropriate. To each 3oz of the mixture add 1oz of glycerine and 1 grain of corrosive sublimate.

S. Young & Son Ltd, in Britain, sell a ready-made bait known as 'Young's Fox Lure'.

Mustelids and their relatives, including skunks, martens, polecats, mink, stoats and weasels, will be drawn to traps baited with chicken entrails, pieces of fish, extracts of appropriate scent glands, and canned dog or cat foods. Fish is generally considered best for mink, and sardines or herrings are especially suitable.

CHAPTER TEN

The Ethics of Trapping

CATCHING animals by means of traps is a method of hunting and, like all other forms of this human activity, it is liable to be interpreted or misinterpreted in many different ways.

Protagonists of animal trapping argue as to the efficiency of particular types of traps and the advantages of one trapping method as against another. Pest eradicators judge traps and trapping methods against other control measures such as shooting, pesticides and the destruction of habitats. Scientists who use traps in research are concerned with their thoroughness in sampling populations and selecting one kind of animal in preference to others.

The opponents of trapping argue against its use almost exclusively on the grounds of inhumane capture of animals, coupled with a doubt concerning the economics of a process which they consider unselective and liable to yield a small return for much effort.

From these conflicting opinions, which are often reinforced with vested interests, it is difficult to elicit facts and truths. Nor is the quandary lessened by a lack of constructive, planned investigation. Rather is it confused by the use of traditional techniques unfounded upon any basis of scientific reasoning. The best trappers, who know their animals and the country in which they live, have learned to adapt their trapping techniques to changes in season, changes in environmental topography and changes in the response of animals which mature in an area subjected to heavy trapping programmes. It is not a skill to be acquired without the tutelage of an experienced master.

Effects upon Wildlife

Despite this lack of factual evidence either for or against the use of animal traps, there is some information which can help to influence public opinion. And here the first thing to consider is what effect trapping has had upon wildlife. Is there evidence of wild animals having been eliminated as a result of trapping, either intentionally or unintentionally?

Three animals which have suffered from the effects of trapping in Britain during the last hundred years are the wildcat, the polecat and the pine marten. They have been persecuted by man for centuries, either for their pelts, useful as a commercial commodity, or because of their alleged attacks on game. The persecution increased during the eighteenth and nineteenth centuries and at various periods was encouraged by the offer of bounties or 'tail money'. J. Ritchie, in his book *Beasts and Birds as Farm Pests*, reported 901 wildcats, martens and polecats killed between 1831 and 1834 on the Duchess of Sutherland's estates.

By 1907, all three animals had become extinct in England and the polecat in Scotland. The wildcat and marten have managed to hang on by a thread in the far north of Scotland, and the polecat and marten have survived in the more remote and less populated areas of Wales. It is true that methods other than trapping have been used— shooting and poisoning—but these animals, by nature, fall foul of traps more easily then they succumb to guns. Poisoning has never been as popular as trapping because it offers even less opportunity for catch selection.

Between 1930 and 1954 deliberate trapping of polecats in West Wales almost eliminated them from that area. This was during a period of intensive rabbiting. The polecats were trapped before each rabbit-trapping operation, to protect the trapped rabbits from molestation, and some were caught in the rabbit gins as well. Myxomatosis then put an end to the need for controlling rabbits as agricultural pests and also knocked the bottom out of the market for flesh and skins.

Pest and Population Control

There is, of course, another side to this story. For years prior to the myxomatosis scourge, farmers had been battling against ever-increasing numbers of rabbits in Britain, and an average of no less than 40 millions a year were slaughtered between 1950 and 1953. As a result of the Ground Game Act of 1880, farmers had been made responsible for employing rabbit-catchers; but both farmers and catchers, as well as commercial trappers hiring land from the farmers, looked to the rabbit for part of their annual income and so

did not for some time regard it as a pest to be eradicated completely. Under the Pests Act of 1954, British farmers were empowered
to reduce rabbit-breeding areas as well as the animals; but at the
same time a section of the Act made it illegal from 1 August 1958 to
use traps other than spring traps approved by the Ministry of Agriculture, Fisheries & Food.

Whether or not trapping is the best method for controlling pests
is difficult to establish, and of course, a great deal depends upon the
pests involved. Many people favour shooting for rabbits, ground
predators and bird pests, and this is reasonable providing first-class
shots are used and one can afford the time to wait until subterranean animals decide to surface. Traps do have the advantage of
waiting for their catch to come along. The argument that they are
non-selective compared with shooting is not wholly valid as, in the
hands of a skilled trapper, a high degree of selectivity is possible with
many kinds of traps, even the killers. Conversely, the writer has
recently had both a fox and a polecat brought to him, both shot and
both mistaken, or so he was told, in the half-light of dawn, for rabbits.

The writer's own preference would be to achieve any necessary
population control of birds and mammals by means either of traps
or shooting, as opposed to the use of poisons. A good rifle-shot, live
trap or a humane-killing trap can be a 99 per cent guarantee against
cruelty, whereas poisons are indiscriminate in their effects and it is
virtually impossible to guarantee a lethal dose. And the side effects of
sub-lethal doses can be horrible, especially in the case of avian
poisons used in baits, since both birds and mammals can be affected
and predators and carrion-feeders are liable to suffer secondary
poisoning. Use of poisoned baits under licence is still permitted in
Britain by the Bird Protection Act of 1954.

The use of mammal traps of the approved spring variety has been
subject to legal control in Britain since 1958, and a number of
American states have also introduced legislation aimed at humani-
tarian control over trapping. In Britain, the Spring Traps Order not
only regulates the traps that can be used and the animals which can
be taken by them, but also requires trappers to inspect each trap
once during every period between sunrise and sunset if it is likely to
catch a rabbit.

At the time of writing, a lengthy and furious exchange of letters
has been taking place in *The Field* on the subject of snaring foxes.
The letter which sparked off the series reported findings of foxes

which had been held by snares for several days. Some of the finds were apparently still alive but emaciated and injured from their struggles; those which were dead had not died quietly—or painlessly. The correspondence produced a substantial amount of evidence confirming that incidents of these kinds were not isolated events. Yet in defence of those using snares in this way, if indeed a defence is possible, counter accusations were levelled against the methods of fox-hunting societies.

Mole-trapping is another source of controversial discussion. In favour of eradicating moles are gardeners, parks directors and sportsground supervisors, as well as farmers resenting their undermining of land under crops. George Bolam, the author of *Wild Life in Wales*, held largely opposite opinions and, while conceding their nuisance to arable farmers, considered that mole tunnels served as useful drainage channels. The farm pests eaten by moles were, he thought, fair compensation for the minor irritation of having hillocks in pastures, and even the hillocks themselves had potential as a good top dressing for grass when disturbed by grazing sheep.

Again, mole-trapping—the old mole-trapper was called an 'oont-catcher'—can be far more humane than gassing, the effect of which is not necessarily limited to moles.

The Voice of the People

In trapping, or for that matter in any other form of animal control, it is usually public agitation which results in legislation being eventually brought to bear on inhumane or unethical practices. In Britain, the commission set to explore the incidence of cruelty to wild animals was very largely the product of continued representation from bodies such as the Royal Society for the Protection of Birds (RSPB), the Royal Society for the Prevention of Cruelty to Animals (RSPCA) and Women's Institutes. Organisations like these need public support if their voice is to be sufficiently loud to attract the attention of government ministers and parliamentary representatives of all political colours.

Sometimes a public relations programme is valuable in drawing attention to alternatives to cruel practices. A recent example of this was an exhibition featured by the Zoological Society of Montreal which combined a display of the horrors connected with certain aspects of the fur trade and the humane alternative—the utilisation of art furs, now currently in vogue in North America.

The Fish and Wildlife Service of the US Department of the Interior has published a number of pamphlets providing a fair amount of information for intending trappers. While endeavouring to give accurate instructions for using and setting traps, there is also ample warning to heed state legislation which might outlaw certain traps and trapping procedures. There is also a general encouragement to utilise selective and humane methods. Such a service, with its high level of conservation motivation, is to be applauded and could with advantage be used as a model by the governments of many other countries. Yet there are always critics of government action and the airing of such criticism is an important privilege of a democratic society seeking to procure redress of grievances. Thus the United States Department of the Interior is reported to have given way to pressure from sheep and cattle ranchers and to have employed professional trappers to set out poisoned baits for coyotes.

The likelihood of achieving general agreement on whether or not animal trapping is morally permissible seems remote at present. A time may come when animal capture methods acceptable to all can be devised, but meanwhile the best we can do is to make every effort to use only those presently available methods known to be humane. There will always be objectors citing the bulkiness of cage traps as a deterrent to their use on large-scale operations, or the ineffectiveness of approved spring traps compared with the outlawed gin. But these are merely quibbles—excuses for an unwillingness to try something new, or to provide a labour force adequate for the handling of bigger traps.

Fortunately in Britain, in Europe and in North America government departments are now showing the way. They are proving that box traps and other humane machines can be very effective while still conserving wildlife through selective capture and painless killing. A new word has even crept into our trap nomenclature—the 'tender trap'. Almost certainly coined in the United States, it is now being used in Britain as a general term implying any humane catcher.

Drugs versus Traps

Any discussion of the ethical problems connected with trapping must include some mention of the utilisation of traps for scientific research. For some considerable time trapping has been the method favoured by scientists for capturing animals and it is only comparatively recently that the practice of using drugs as soporifics and tranquillisers has developed.

One recent example of the joint use of both traps and drugs concerned biologists working on the movements of Kodiak bears in Federal sanctuaries off the coast of Alaska. The object was to trap the beasts alive for tagging and the trappers used Newhouse No 150 steel bear traps, the understanding being that these should be kept under close surveillance to ensure that the minimum of injury or suffering was inflicted by such heavy traps. The traps were attached by chains to heavy logs so that the trails they left when they were pulled away by the captive bear would be easy to follow. When the bear was located it was 'tranquillised' by a thrust from a hypodermic needle on the end of a 20ft aluminium pole. This was followed by a rather more potent hand-administered injection which immobilised the bear while it was being weighed, tagged and fitted with an electronic 'beep' system.

There is, however, still a great deal of research to be done concerning specificity of drugs, dosage rates and methods of utilisation, and until these substances can be used with greater precision and certainty the scientist will probably continue to favour trapping techniques for a wide variety of ecological and distributional investigations. And in this field the traps need to be both humane and selective, scientific research on trapping methods having shown that low selection incidence, more than any other factor, leads to poor evaluation of trapping programmes. Experimental trapping directed towards greater selectivity has investigated baiting techniques (Chitty and Kempson, 1949; Stickel, 1948) and animal response to traps (Crowcroft and Jeffers, 1961; Davis and Emlen, 1955; and Young, Neess and Emlen, 1952).

CHAPTER ELEVEN

Trap Legislation

HUMAN endeavour has always been fraught by attempts to repress it. Social interaction creates pressures which regulate the activities of the constituent members of a society. From primitive organisations controlled by all-powerful despots there have evolved hierarchical systems with a ruling or governing class. The governing class has either been selected by the ruler to provide him with advice, if asked for, or, it has been freely elected by the community in the best democratic tradition.

The ruling class has then devised laws setting out a code of behaviour and discipline. Sometimes the laws have been necessary to conserve the natural resources upon which the community depends, as when a society depending upon wildlife as a source of food was culling them at a rate greater than could be compensated by natural breeding. An organised society with a wise governing unit would be likely to limit the hunting and so make its own future secure. It was in this way that our first game laws, which included regulations for trapping as one form of hunting, appeared.

Early Game Laws
Of course, not all the early game laws were enacted for the common good—many were simply to protect the privileges of particular sections of a community—but in the first instance the main purpose of hunting laws was to ensure survival of the society. The form such laws took would vary. Sometimes there would be imposed what we now call a bag size, that is a limit on the number of animals taken at any one time. Other hunting laws would provide for closed seasons, usually the breeding season, in order to allow animal numbers to recover after periods of hunting. Oddly enough, some laws forbidding hunting during breeding seasons were formulated not through any desire to conserve populations of animals, but because taboos among

some tribes forbade eating the flesh of pregnant animals. Fortunately, such taboos played their part in conservation just the same.

Conservation has also been achieved by restricting the hunting of female and young male animals, but it has always been difficult to discriminate when using traps that kill, and now that we are more conscious of the need for conservation perhaps the time has come to consider outlawing any trapping procedure which kills and is non-selective.

From time to time basic laws formulated for community survival have been supplemented by others motivated by the compassion and benevolence of an evolving civilisation. In the field of hunting, there has been pressure from protectionists to legislate against inhumane methods. Similarly, when survival of animal groups has been threatened, more particularly during the last fifty years, conservation laws have been introduced to prevent species extinction and so preserve animals for aesthetic rather than materialistic reasons.

The problem of introducing any legal system, however, is not in framing the laws, but in enforcing them. In small tribal units this problem is less likely to occur when the ruler is invested with un-questioned authority; the difficulties arise as political units grow and their members become more widely distributed. When this happens and the power of the ruler diminishes in direct proportion to his distance from the furthermost members of the society, he has either to police his territory or provide punishments of sufficient magnitude to deter would-be offenders. Eventually, both a body to enforce legislation and a code of punishment for transgressors are required. For legislation becomes pointless when there is not the power to enforce it, and even a meagre punishment which can be enforced is more effective than severe punishment which cannot.

Aims of Legislation

The types of legislation affecting the form and use of traps have concentrated on three main aspects. These are: conservation of wildlife, humane capture and pest control; but there have always been other laws designed to protect a person's estate from trespass, and trapping, especially as practised by poachers, frequently in-fringed the rights of private landowners.

Following the fall of the Roman Empire, the Gauls and Germans abandoned the game laws devised by the Romans, which had allowed a fair share of game to all members of society, and superseded them by Germanic and Frankish laws which restricted the right of hunting to the elite. Such laws, however, were difficult to enforce. Roman roads were allowed to deteriorate and so communications were poor. Cleared land once clad with forests became forested again and wildlife abounded. There was plenty for all, though few could take advantage of it legally; so in the absence of effective authority common men took what they wanted illegally. Poaching became rife.

All over Europe, kings instituted forest laws which were harsh and cruel. Hunting was only permitted under licence. Offenders were imprisoned, beaten and stoned. In Britain, during the Dark Ages, because of the depredations of deer, wolves and wild boar, it was necessary for agriculturists to hunt and destroy them. Professional hunters, given great freedom and authority despite their often humble origins, were only curbed during a two-month close season in winter.

The Saxons appear to have relaxed hunting rules even further and encouraged the capture of deer, which they regarded as pests, by the simple expedient of using nets or paddock traps. But from the tenth century onwards, game laws again became severe, not only in the restriction they imposed upon common husbandmen's grazing rights, but also in the nature of the punishment inflicted upon offenders.

Medieval Game Laws
The greatest anomaly of the medieval game laws was the restriction of hunting to 'qualified persons'. Just what was necessary to qualify seems never to have been made very clear. Terms such as 'esquire' served only to confuse as they were never accurately defined, and though licences to hunt were required only for 'game' it was seldom clear which animals constituted 'game' and which did not. Anyone, however, could hunt the fox, and this concession may well account for the continuing popularity of this sport which, by tradition, never suffered the same restrictions as shooting.

Despite their undefined nature and great unpopularity, the game laws were retained for centuries, their continuing existence in Britain being largely due to the nature of the country's government. Parliamentary representation was almost completely in the hands of rural gentry, for whom statutes of this type had obvious advantages. Poachers who were caught suffered severely at the hands of magistrates and it was during this period that man traps came into widespread use on estates. Gamekeepers, often intimidated by gangs of poachers, were hard-pressed to protect their masters' game and estates, so that mechanical aids were looked upon as rightful armoury to deter trespassers.

Penalties for Poachers

As keepers were naturally more vigilant during daylight hours, poachers took to working at night, and in an attempt to counter this an Act of 1770 made night-poaching an offence. The punishment was six months' imprisonment for first offenders, but a second offence could bring a year's imprisonment and a whipping. In France and other European countries, the laws were even more severe than in England and yet, ironically, the extent of poaching was even greater.

As the conservation of game became increasingly difficult, pheasant rearing was made a domestic practice, and the first hatchery using wild eggs was started at Blenheim Palace in 1787. Subsequently, domestic eggs were produced and some even imported, but this was an expensive process and made the producers even more zealous in their efforts at game conservation. To protect their stocks, a new Act of 1800 made poaching by two or more individuals together subject to even greater punishment than for a single offender. The choice of punishment was a whipping and hard labour for a year, or service under impress in the navy or army.

Soon, however, the legislation to protect game had become so confused and the wrath of ordinary people so great that legal reform became a priority. For the first time, the game laws were partially revised in 1827 by prohibition of the use of man traps and spring guns. Further sensible reform occurred a year later in the form of the Night Poaching Act. By this law, both game and rabbits were protected at night. The distinction was made that trespassing in search of rabbits was not illegal (prosecution could only take place if a trespasser was caught with a dead rabbit on his person), but trespassing in search of game, if the trespasser was in possession of gun, snares or other instruments, was punishable. Game was defined as hares, partridges, pheasants, grouse, black game, bustards, heath and moor game. Punishment varied from three months' hard labour for a first offence to three years' hard labour or seven years' transportation for poaching at night in an armed band of three or more men.

The final repeal of the old game laws took place in 1831 with the introduction of a new Game Act. This allowed anyone in possession

of an authorising certificate to kill and sell game. Punishments of
imprisonment or transportation were retained for night poaching, but
daytime poaching, that is trespassing to take by killing game but not
rabbits, was liable to a fine of £5. Searching by trespass for rabbits
and game in daytime was liable to a fine of £2. An Act of 1848 removed the need for a certificate to take hares.

In 1862, there came a Poaching Prevention Act which included
snipe, quail, landrail and woodcock under the definition of 'game',
and permitted magistrates to confiscate the nets, guns and snares of
convicted poachers. It also allowed keepers and police officials to co-
operate so that poachers, driven on to a public highway by a gamekeeper, could then be searched and arrested by police.

Rabbits and Hares
Farmers received a concession in 1884 when the Ground Game Act
made it legal for farmers and other owners of land to take by killing
hares and rabbits within their own boundaries. The farmer did not
need to be the owner of the land, and could be merely an occupier.
In the words of the Act, he had a right to take rabbits and hares 'as
incident to and inseparable from his occupation of land, of taking
and killing ground game thereon'. Section 6 restricted the use of
spring traps to the confines of rabbit holes for occupiers of land, but
left landowners free to trap in the open.

A slight reversal of the 1848 Act took place in 1892 when the
Hares Preservation Act was published. This protected hares from
March to July, and was an important step in government legislation
of recent times because it showed appreciation by higher authorities
of the need for conservation. In 1911 an Animal Protection Act came
into force, and Section 10 was significant for the instruction that 'No
spring trap shall be placed so as to catch a hare or rabbit'.

No doubt owing to a shortage of manpower on the land during
World War I, the number of vermin, particularly rats and mice, increased enormously, and to counter this threat the Rats and Mice
(Destruction) Act of 1919 made it mandatory for occupiers of land to
destroy rats and mice on their property. Following this period, a
great deal of research and much inventive skill was devoted to the
problem of rat destruction, especially by means of traps.

Varnish traps were made illegal by the 1925 Act for Protection of
Birds—a period when legislation was particularly concerned with,
on the one hand, prohibiting inhumane methods of killing or cap-

turing wildlife, and on the other, with the destruction of pests. In 1932, the Destruction of Foreign Animals Act made legal provision for an attempt to control animals such as the grey squirrel, and was subsequently reinforced by an additional order, the Grey Squirrels (Prohibition of Importation and Keeping) Order of 1937. Further efforts to curb the spread of grey squirrels were made in 1957 when 'tail money' rewards of a shilling, and later two shillings were approved.

The Prevention of Damage by Rabbits Act of 1939 closed the loophole of the 1884 Act by making it illegal for any person to use a trap in the open for catching a rabbit. The term 'hole', when employed to define a site where traps could be placed, has been limited by court ruling to 'that area within the overhang of a rabbit hole', and excludes the 'scrape' or entrance to the hole. This ruling still applies to approved spring traps in Britain at the present time.

During World War II, the 1939 Act was relaxed and permits could be obtained to trap in the open—5,964 were issued in England and Wales. An attempt was made to suspend this provision permanently by a clause in the 1947 Agriculture Bill, but public opinion had now been alerted to the cruelty of gin traps in the open and the clause was rejected. In the following year, Scotland, where the provisions of the 1939 Act had not previously applied, was brought into line with England and Wales by Section 50 of the Agriculture (Scotland) Act.

The Pests Act of 1954

The most important legislation affecting wildlife in Britain stemmed from a committee set up by warrant in 1949 to report on cruelty to wild animals. Their report was published in June 1951, and was responsible for decisions which became law in the 1954 Pests Act. Section 8 of this Act made it an offence in England and Wales to use a spring trap, other than an approved one, after 31 July 1958, and the same Act made use of the gin trap illegal.

Following recommendations by a committee set up to investigate traps and give approval to those considered to kill humanely, the first Spring Traps Approval Order, under the Pest Act, was published in 1957. From time to time since then amendments have been published authorising the use of further, newly-approved, humane spring traps.

Again, because of peculiar difficulties in finding alternatives for the gin in Scotland, its abolition there was delayed, but the Agriculture

(Spring Traps) (Scotland) Act of 1969 has named 1 April 1973 as the effective date. In fact, the 1954 Act already applies there in respect of all animals except foxes and otters, and these alone may continue to be taken by gin traps up to 1973.

The 1958 Small Ground Vermin Traps Order has specified break-back traps for rats and mice, and spring traps set in their runs for catching moles, as the only two exemptions to the 1957 Spring Traps Order requiring approval of spring traps. Traps are also mentioned in the 1954 Bird Protection Act, under Section 5 of which it is illegal for anyone to set in position any 'springe, trap or gin' which is of such a nature and is so placed as to be calculated to cause bodily injury to any wild bird coming into contact with it.

In May of 1958, an Advisory Council for Rabbit Clearance was set up, and it is to this body that a Humane Traps Panel is attached, in place of the former Humane Traps Advisory Committee. In future, all traps submitted for approval in Britain will have to be passed by the panel before their use can be authorised.

North American Legislation
Legislation in other countries has taken different forms to that outlined for Britain, and in some instances a history of wildlife extinction has, in recent times, induced authorities to inaugurate methods of control on a far wider scale.

In North America, for instance, human activity has been responsible for the loss of a number of animals. The buffalo was only narrowly saved and the passenger pigeon has gone for ever. And this has happened despite a long history of legislation affecting wild animals, especially in the United States.

A special feature of US legislation in this field has been the transfer of authority from the Federal Government to individual states. Except for laws governing migratory birds and seals, both of which the central government consider to be extra-state in activity, it is considered more sensible that each state should control its own wildlife populations.

As may be imagined, this has produced a variety of different laws for given animals according to the area concerned, and trappers moving from one state to another need to be on their toes to avoid infringing local regulations affecting their professional work. Many states have also become licensing authorities, selling permits to hunt and trap wildlife, and in the main the resultant revenue is used to finance wildlife protection—a costly business in the USA. However, with income from an estimated 50,000,000 hunters, the country can luckily afford to put a lot of effort into the organisation and enforcement of legislation affecting wild animals.

Although wildlife legislation in the United States is largely a state business, the Federal Government has contributed handsomely to the research needed to formulate sensible and valuable laws. Its Biological Survey and Fish and Wildlife Service have made some most important investigations into conservation measures and have discovered much that has been found useful elsewhere in the world.

North American Bounty Laws
In the history of North America, legislation affecting trapping and trappers has been introduced for a variety of reasons. At first, most laws concerning wildlife were introduced with the object of controlling its spread or limiting depredation of the lands being cultivated by pioneer settlers; in other words, to deal with animals considered harmful. William Penn is thought to have been the first person to hire men as government trappers to kill wolves, but in general the official method of dealing with harmful animals was, and in many cases still is, the bounty system. Some of the early bounty laws can be traced far back into history; an example might be the Northwest Territory Codes for 1795 and 1799, the earlier of which had been copied from the Pennsylvanian Code. Among the rewards offered were two dollars for adult wolves, one dollar for wolf whelps, twenty-five cents for adult foxes and twelve and a half cents for young foxes and wildcats. A head had to be presented to a justice of the peace with a statement under oath concerning who had taken the animal, and also that it had been taken in inhabited territory. As a safeguard against the head being re-submitted the justice had to cut off its ears and tongue before making out an order for payment on the county treasury. In 1799, the rates were lowered and a distance limit of six miles only from the settlements was allowed for taking animals under the bounty system.

Territorial division took place over a number of years as states were established. Iowa attained territorial identity in 1838. Governor R. P. Lowe, at the first session of the territorial legislature in 1840, signed 'An Act to encourage the destruction of wolves'. On an optional basis, counties could offer between fifty cents and three dollars for wolves older than six months, the amount to be at the discretion of the commissioners. But even fifty cents was too expensive for some counties, which chose to opt out of the bounty scheme, until in 1844 legislation required all counties to pay wolf bounties.

From these beginnings the payment of bounties waxed and waned from year to year and from one territory to another, depending upon the size of treasury purses, the extent of the predator problem and the abuse of the system by trappers and hunters. The general effect was that, eventually, nearly all large wolves from Canada to Mexico were exterminated. On the other hand, foxes have adjusted to man's actions so well that the payment of bounties for them nowadays makes little difference to their numbers.

At certain stages, professional trappers aware of a decreasing livelihood, especially as wolves diminished in numbers, sought to perpetuate the species by selective killing to reduce the older males, but retaining bitches and young males. These and other abuses, such as extra-territorial trapping, have always thwarted the best aims of legislation concerning bounty payments, but such payments have continued because they make sense to ordinary people as a remedy for a social evil. The expense involved and the futility of paying bounties can be illustrated by a report from the state of Michigan in 1957. This indicated that over the ten years prior to 1957 there had been an average annual payment of $142,000 for fox bounties, without any apparent reduction in fox numbers. By 1965, the annual payment for all bounties was a record $254,090, and this at a time when Wisconsin and Minnesota were seeking to eliminate bounties altogether. On the other side of the fence, South Dakota, having suffered a pheasant depression in 1964, was seeking legislation to pay higher bounties for foxes.

There is such a mass of legislation concerned with wildlife and its management in the USA and Canada that it is not possible to provide a sensible chronological account of its development and the best one can do is to summarise those forms of control which have been given legal backing.

Close Season Legislation

Commenting on the state of US legislation in 1917, A. L. Beldon indicated that Pennsylvania had the worst record to date of any state in its failure to conserve game as an important asset; and that New England, western and southern states, though having given the matter some attention, could report no progress. By 1919, there were open seasons for bear between 15 October and 15 December and between 1 September and 31 December for raccoon in Pennsylvania. There was no open season for beaver, and in Delaware county foxes could not be trapped.

In 1917, Arizona, Kentucky and Oklahoma were still affording no legal protection for fur-bearers, but beaver were protected at all times in California, Colorado, Montana, New Mexico, and Washington, while in Utah there was full protection for the otter as well. In Florida, beaver and otter were protected from 1 February to 31 October, and bear were protected for a brief season in Mississippi. In that same year, 1917, the Federal government had introduced laws to protect all fur-bearers in Alaska, while the provincial governments of Canada had not only framed wise protective legislation, but were rigidly enforcing it.

Most states now have open and close seasons for animals. The lists of animals affected are often long, and frequently dominated by the fur-bearers, although deer, wild sheep and wild goats also figure, especially in Canadian lists. There are also laws to prevent the importation of potential pests, and to prohibit the removal of diseased animals from one area to another.

Comparison of recent state laws concerning closed seasons with those in force in 1919, shows that in Kentucky, for example, all animals could legally be trapped, in 1959–60, between 17 November and 15 January. In the same state in 1919, beaver, mink, raccoon, otter, opossum and skunk could be trapped only between 15 November and 31 December. In Louisiana during 1955–6, the season varied according to the animals involved, except for beaver for which there was a permanent closed season. Muskrat could be trapped between 1 December and 25 February, except in the parishes of Vermilion and Cameron; nutria between 1 January and 25 February, except in Vermilion, Cameron and Plaquemines parishes; mink from 15 November to 9 January, except in Vermilion and Plaquemines parishes, and all other legalised fur-bearers from 15 November to 15 February except in Vermilion and Plaquemines parishes. The three excepted parishes had their own seasons which varied a few days in either direction from those for the rest of the state. For 1919, Louisiana laws forbade all trapping of beaver and protected bear from 1 November to 15 February, but the same season was open for muskrat, mink, otter, raccoon, fox, opossum and skunk. The 1959–60 season was the first for thirty years when beaver had not enjoyed total protection. In 1965–6 there was a brief beaver-trapping season in Pennsylvania, lasting from 13 February to 14 March, but here beaver trapping had been allowed for a number of years.

Other Methods of Control
Some idea of the detail in which certain states have legislated to control trapping is afforded by the following examples of state laws. Legal trapping in Kentucky is possible providing a trapper: (i) obtains a written permit from the landowner on whose land traps are to be set; (ii) visits all traps and removes captures at least once in every twenty-four hours; (iii) supplies a written description of the trapline to the local conservation officer within twenty-four hours after the traps have been set; (iv) attaches to each trap a metal tag giving his name and address; (v) possesses a valid trapping licence, and (vi) only uses traps for which approval has been granted by the Commissioner of the Department of Fish and Wildlife Resources— only smooth-jawed traps are approved. Going back to 1919, the same state's legislation stipulated that traps should be set at least 18in inside a hole, cave or hollow log, but need only be visited once in thirty-six hours. Animals could, however, be killed at any time on a man's own premises in order to protect property.

The game laws affecting trappers in Pennsylvania in 1958 were summarised by the Deputy Attorney-General, John Sullivan. These prohibited the setting of traps closer than 5ft from an occupied hole or den, except for underwater sets. Muskrat and beavers could be taken only with steel or live traps and deadfalls. It was illegal to use a snare, a steel trap with toothed jaws or with a jaw spread of more than $6\frac{1}{2}$in. In confirmation of the last provision, it was held in Commonwealth v Bennett (175 Pa. Super 244), that the spread distance was meant to be 'overall', so that a spread of $6\frac{11}{16}$in was illegal. Trappers could not dig or smoke out a den or house of any kind except when occupied by a predator. Traps had to be visited once every thirty-six hours, except in the event of storm or sickness. A provision for counties designated by the Commission allowed the use of snares without springpoles for taking predators between 16 December and 31 March. Traps or deadfalls had to be marked with a tag or metal plate giving the owner's name and address, and had to be taken up or sprung at the end of a season. It was legal to use baited traps, and beaver and muskrat could be killed with firearms after being caught; also farmers finding wild animals other than beaver in fields under cultivation could dig out their dens. If wild animals, again except for beaver, were found destroying property, they could be killed, always providing they were not pursued beyond the boundaries of the property being damaged. Artificial lights carried by or on the person were permitted during the season when taking raccoons, skunks and opossums. Fur-bearers accidentally taken during a closed season, when trapping was legal for other animals, had to be reported to the Commission's director.

In Pennsylvania, there were regulations for beaver additional to those imposed for general trapping. They could only be taken by state residents possessing a resident's hunting licence, except farmers and their families who could trap without a licence on their own land but needed a licence for trapping elsewhere. Ten traps only were permitted. If more than the limit were caught, an excess had to be reported within twenty-four hours and taken for disposal by a Game Commission employee. Skins had to be presented to a salaried official of the Commission for examination and he would issue, at a cost of ten cents, a tag which would remain with the pelt until it was tanned. The Commission had power to close designated beaver colonies to trapping by posting them prominently, although a land-owner's permission was required for colonies on private land. Section 606 of the Game Law stated: 'It is unlawful to destroy or disturb or in any manner interfere with the dams and houses of beavers except upon special permit from the Commission.' Section 607 made trap robbing illegal, with special reference to the unlawful-ness of interference with traps set by the Commission's officers or agents, unless these had been set without prior permission on private land.

Fur-bearers becoming a nuisance would receive drastic treatment at the hands of the Commission, which was entitled to waive all protection.

As to penalties, in Pennsylvania a beaver or otter killed illegally could result in a trapper facing a $50 fine. Other animals killed un-lawfully could mean a $25 fine, while violation of other provisions might incur a $10 penalty.

Wildlife Conservation Measures
The Game Commission of Pennsylvania is empowered to fix seasons and set bag limits, or any other control necessary to ensure a proper balance of wildlife. The guidance comes from the legislature, and in

the event of the Commission failing to set seasons or bag limits then
a standard schedule, written by the legislature, goes into effect.
Which seems rather like trying to establish the balance of nature as
though it were as static as a jigsaw puzzle.

Bear trapping has been outlawed in a number of states and mention was made earlier of the guardrail required around a bear trap
set in New Hampshire. In 1969, in the state of Maine, a law was
passed outlawing the steel trap as being too cruel. Many other states
limit the jaw length—in Massachusetts the limit is 5½in—or prohibit
the use of traps with toothed jaws.

Details of state regulations concerning trapping can be obtained
from fish and game commissioners and directors of individual states;
a list of the names and addresses of these administrators is found in
the *Conservation Directory*, which can be ordered from the National
Wildlife Federation, 1412 16th Street, NW, Washington, DC 20036.

For some long time there has been mounting pressure in the United
States for the general banning of steel traps. But although interest in
humane killing and live-catching traps is increasing, the economics
of fur-trapping make a total ban on steel traps appear unlikely for a
number of years; unless the pressure in Britain and elsewhere to
produce humane traps can stimulate the invention of models as
acceptable to North Americans in the future as English steel traps
were in the past.

Meanwhile, United States legislation has taken a step in a different
direction, and one which has international implications. On 5
December 1969, President Nixon signed Public Law 91–135 which
became effective on 3 June 1970. This is a direct attempt to conserve
the wildlife resources of countries outside the United States by controlling the importation of species of fish, birds and mammals in
danger of worldwide extinction. Developing a list of such species is
the responsibility of the Secretary of the Interior, as is its periodic
review. This does not mean a blanket ban on importation, because
permits are obtainable for educational, scientific or propagation
purposes, and the ban is specifically restricted to animals in danger
throughout their range, not, for example, a group which may be in
danger in one country but in a satisfactory state elsewhere. The
implication for trapping, it is hoped, will be to discourage indiscriminate trapping of wildlife just because a market is known to
exist somewhere for the victims. To be really effective, however, this
kind of legislation needs to be taken up on an international basis.

The African Continent
In other parts of the world there have been sorry histories of diminishing animal populations and the complete extinction of a number of species. In South Africa, the loss of the quagga, the bluebuck and the Cape lion and the near disappearance of elephant from the Cape area, sounded a timely warning and stimulated the formation of nature conservation departments in all the provinces. Nature conservation legislation is now in force for protecting rare species, plants and animals, for introducing new stocks of once-common animals to areas depleted of them, and for classifying vermin and the methods which may be used to destroy them. In this way it is hoped to make amends for the ruthless extermination of so much that was rare and beautiful.

Elsewhere on that continent, the emergent African states, though resolutely opposed to South Africa's example in other spheres, have recognised her conservation practices as models on which to frame their own programmes. Now, in many areas, there are welcome indications of a general halt to a slaughter of wildlife which, though it had been barbaric for centuries, became intensified during the early decades of European infiltration.

Acknowledgements

THE completion of this book has been made possible through the generous assistance and advice of many people.

I am grateful for the assistance offered by my colleagues at the National Museum of Wales, in particular Mr Rollo Charles, Dr H. M. Savory, Mr G. Harrison, Mr Ffrancis Payne, Miss Hettie Edwards and Mrs R. Bridgman.

Mr Paul Jenkins was responsible for the line drawings in Figures 2, 6, 41 and 42.

Miss Cynthia Merrett kindly produced the typescript at short notice and with a precision that made the task of editing and proof-reading less arduous.

For information about specific traps, I have been fortunate in having assistance and advice from M. W. Bradley, D. K. Caldecott, Frederick Chambers, Lt-Col G. B. Donald, Jack Hampton, Phillip Glasier, Mrs Joyce Rushen, K. C. Walton, P. H. Whittaker and Prof R. D. Lockhart.

Traps for examination were kindly sent to me by the Allcock Manufacturing Co, B. E. Chaplin, the Earl of Cranbrook, A. Fenn Ltd, Gilbertson & Page Ltd, G. R. Hill, John Jacob, S. Young & Sons (Misterton) Ltd, the Librarian, Grantham, C. D. Boston, Director-General of the Imperial War Museum, Director of the John Judkyn Memorial, Stephen Locke.

The Division of Wildlife Services, US Department of the Interior, the Wildlife Management Institute, Washington, and the National Wildlife Federation, Washington, kindly supplied information about trapping legislation in the United States. Other information about trapping in North America came from Rossiter D. Olmstead, Fox B. Connor and John W. Kulish. Dr Douglas Hey supplied information about the trapping practice and legislation in South Africa.

For help with bibliographical research, I am grateful to Colin

Matheson, C. Chenevix Trench, Rossiter D. Olmstead and Fox B. Connor.

Most of the photographs came from the files of my own Department and are the work of Mr Erick Broadbent. Other photographs were generously supplied by the Forestry Commission, Leicester Museums and Phillip Glasier.

I am greatly indebted to my wife for her general help and encouragement throughout the period when I was writing and preparing illustrations, also for her assistance with the preparation of the index and in proof-reading.

Finally, I must acknowledge the kindness and encouragement of the publishers and in particular the meticulous editing undertaken by Mr T. Stanhope Sprigg.

Bibliography

Anati, E. *La Civilisation de Val Camonica* (Arthaud, 1960)

Anon. 'Anodes Protect Wire Crab Pots', *World Fishing* (1968), 17: (6): 57

Anon. 'BCFs New Lobster-Pot May Open Offshore Fishery', *Commercial Fisheries Review* (1968), 30 (6) 22–6

Anon. *Dictionnaire Archéologique des Techniques* (1963)

Anon. 'Enemies of Game' (ICI) Advisory Game Services Booklet, 17: 1961

Anon. 'Fur Catch in the United States', 1966. *Wildlife Leaflet, U.S. Dept. of Interior* (1967), 478

Ashcroft, G. & Reese, D. 'An Improved Device for Catching Deer,' *Calif. Fish & Game* (1957), 43: 193–9

Beldon, A. C. *The Fur Trade of America* (New York, 1917)

Bertin, Léon. *Eels: A Biological Study* (1951)

Bolam, George. *Wildlife in Wales* (1913)

Bretherton, R. F. 'Moth Traps and their Lamps: An Attempt at Comparative Analysis,' *Entomol. Gazette* (1954), V: 145–54

Brown, Ernest R. 'A Compact, Lightweight Live Trap for Small Mammals', *J of Mammalogy* (1969), 50: 1: 154–5

Burne, B. P. (et al). 'Collecting, Preparing and Preserving Insects', Canadian Dep. of Agric. (1955), Pub. No. 932

Carnegie, W. *Practical Trapping of Vermin and Birds* (1910)

Casto, William & Presnall, Clifford C. 'Comparison of Coyote Trapping and Methods', *J Wild Management* (1944), 8: 1: 65–70

Chitty, D. & Kempson, D. A. 'Prebaiting Small Mammals and a New Design of Live Trap,' *Ecology* (1949), 30: 536–42

Clarke, J. G. D. *Prehistoric Europe* (1952)

Clausen, Curtis P. *Entomophagus Insects* (New York, 1962)

Cornwall, I. W. *Prehistoric Animals and Their Hunters* (1968)

Crowcroft, P. & Jeffers. 'Variability in Behaviour of Wild Housemice (*Mus musculus* L.) towards Live Traps,' *Proc Zoo Soc Lond*, 137: 573–82 (1961)

Davis, D. E. & Emlen, J. T. 'Differential Trappability of Rats According to Age and Size,' *J Wild Management* (1956), 20: 326–7

Davis, F. M. 'Fishery Gear of England and Wales', *Fish Invest* (1937), Series II, V, No 4, 3rd Edition

270

Darwin, Charles. *Insectivorous Plants* (1875)

Dembeck, Hermann. *Animals and Men* (1966)

Edwards, E. & Mearney, R. A. 'American Parlour Trap Best,' *World Fishing* (1968), 17 (7) 32–3

Edwards, V. C. Wynne-. *Animal Dispersion in Relation to Social Behaviour* (1962)

Eley Game Services. Annual Reports 1962–9 (Fordingbridge)

Gallwey, Sir Ralph Payne-. *The Book of Duck Decoys* (1886)

Gibson, W. Hamilton. *Camp Life and the Tricks of Trapping* (New York, 1881)

Giles, R. H. *Wildlife Management Techniques*, 3rd Edtn (USA, 1969)

Graham, Michael. *Sea Fisheries* (1956)

Greenhall, Arthur M. 'A Bamboo Mongoose Trap' (US Fish and Wild Service Leaflet 453, 1963)

Greenslade, P. J. M. 'Pitfall Trapping as a Method of Studying Carabidae', *J Anim Ecol* (1964), 33: 301–10

Haeck, J. 'Een Val Voor Het Levend Vangen Van Mollen,' *Lutra* (1961), 3: 2: 24

Harding, A. R. *Deadfalls and Snares* (USA, 1907)

Harding, A. R. *Steel Traps* (USA, 1907)

Hardy, Sir A. *The Open Sea II* (1959)

Harris, J. R. *An Angler's Entomology* (1952)

Henderson, Junius & Craig, Elberta L. *Economic Mammalogy* (1932)

Herubel, M. *Sea Fisheries* (1912)

Hey, D. *A Nature Conservation Handbook* (Cape Town, 1968)

Hickin, N. E. *Caddis* (1952)

Hogarth, A. Moore. *The Rat* (1929)

Hollom, P. A. D. 'Trapping Methods for Bird Ringers,' (*BTO Field Guide No 1*, 1950)

Hovell, Mark. *Rats and How to Destroy Them* (1924)

ICI Game Services. Annual Reports 1956–61 (Game Research Station, Fordingbridge)

Imms, A. D. *A General Text Book of Entomology* (1948)

Jacob, John. 'The Mérode Mousetrap,' *Burlington Magazine* (1966), 760: CVIII 373–4

Jefferies, Richard. *The Amateur Poacher* (1905)

Jefferies, Richard. *The Gamekeeper at Home* (1890)

Jennison, George. *Animals for Show and Pleasure in Ancient Rome*, (Manchester 1937)

Jones, J. W. *The Salmon* (1959)

Karpe, Hermann Müller. *Handbuch der Vorgeschichte*. Band 1. *Attsteinzeit* (Berlin, 1966)

Kleiman, Devra. 'Scent Marking in the Canidae,' *Symp Zool Soc Lond* (1969), 18: 167–77

Laut, Agnes C. *The Fur Trade of America* (New York, 1921)

Lloyd, Francis E. *The Carnivorous Plants* (USA, 1942)

Lorenz, K. *Man Meets Dog* (1954)

McCracken, Harold, *How to Catch More Fur* (USA, 1945)

Markham, Gervase. *The Young Sportsman's Delight and Instructor* (1652)
Mascall, L. *A Book of Fishing with Hook and Line . . . Another of Sundrie Engines and Trappes to take Polecates, Buzzards, Rats* (1590)
Middleton, A. D. *The Grey Squirrel* (1931)
Mossman, A. S. & Reynolds, B. G. R. 'Some African Techniques for Capturing Mammals'. *J Mammalogy* (1962), 43: 2: 419–20
Munro, Robert. 'Notes on Some Curiously Constructed Wooden Objects Found in Peat Bogs in Various Parts of Europe, Supposed to have been Otter and Beaver Traps'. *Proc of Soc of Ant of Scot* (1891), Vol XXV, 73–89
Munro, Robert & Gillespie, Patrick. 'Further Notes on Ancient Wooden Traps—The So-called Otter and Beaver Traps. *Proc of Soc of Ant of Scot* (1919), Vol LIII, Fifth Series, Vol V 162–7
Netboy, Anthony. *The Atlantic Salmon* (1968)
Newhouse, S. *The Trappers Guide* (USA, 1867)
Obermaier, H. *Fossil Man in Spain* (Yale, 1924)
Oldroyd, H. *Collecting, Preserving and Studying Insects* (1958)
Pfizenmayer, E. W. *Siberian Man and Mammoth.* Trans M. D. Simpson (1939)
Provost, M. W. 'The Influence of Moonlight on Light-trap Catches of Mosquitos,' *Ann Ent Soc Am* (1959), 52: 261–71
Reid, R. W. 'Ancient Wooden Traps from the Moss of Auguharney, Aberdeenshire,' *Proc Soc Ant of Scot* (1922), LVI, Fifth Series, Vol VIII, 282–7
Ritchie, J. *Beasts and Birds as Farm Pests* (1931)
Robinson, H. S. & Robinson, P. J. M. 'Some Notes on the Observed Behaviour of Lepidoptera in Flight in the Vicinity of Light Sources, Together with a Description of a Light Trap Designed to Take Entomological Samples,' *Entomologists' Gazette* (1950), 1: 3–20
Roth, C. 'Medieval Illustrations of Mouse Traps,' *Bodleian Library Record* (1956), V (5), 244–51
Rudge, A. J. B. 'Catching and Keeping Live Moles,' *J Zoo Lond* (1966), 149, 42–5
Russell, Carl P. *Firearms, Traps and Tools of the Mountain Men* (New York, 1967)
Sanderson, Wilfred E. *Trapping with Havahart Traps* (USA, 1969)
Savory, T. H. *The Spider's Web* (1952)
Schenkel, R. 'Ausdruck-studien an Wölfen', *Behaviour* (1947), 1: 81–129
Service, M. W. 'The Use of Insect Suction Traps for Sampling Mosquitoes', *Trans Roy Soc Trop Med & Hyg* (1969), 63: 5: 656–63
Service, M. W. 'The Use of Traps in Sampling Mosquito Populations', *Ent Exp & Appl* (1969), 12: 403–12
Simmonds, P. C. *The Commercial Products of the Sea* (1883)
Smart, John. *British Museum Natural History Handbook for Collectors,* No 4a, *Insects* (1949)
Southern, H. N. *Handbook of British Mammals* (Oxford, 1964)
Stickel. 'Effect of Bait in Live Trapping *Peromyscus*,' *J Wild Management* (1948), 12: 211–12

Sullivan, John. 'The Pennsylvania Game Law and You—Traps and Trappers,' *Penn Game News* (1958) Dec: 34–7

Teale, Edwin Way. *North with the Spring* (1951)

Thompson, Ernest Seton. *Wolf Traps (How to Catch Wolves)* (USA, 1871)

Thompson, H. V. and Worden, A. N. *The Rabbit* (1956)

Thompson, J. L. Cloudsley. *Spiders, Scorpions, Centipedes and Mites* (1968)

Trench, Charles Chenevix. *The Poacher and the Squire* (1967)

Varley, M. E. *British Freshwater Fishes* (1967)

Wigglesworth, V. B. *Insect Physiology* (4th edtn, 1950)

Williams, C. B. 'The Rothamsted Light Trap,' *Proc Royal Ent Soc*, Series A (1948), 23: 80–6

Willughby, Francis. *The Ornithology of Francis Willughby* (1678)

Yonge, C. M. *The Sea Shore* (1949)

Young, H., Neese, J. & Emlen, J. T. 'Heterogeneity of Trap Response in a Population of House Mice,' *J Wild Management* (1952), 16: 169–80

Zupnick, Irving L. 'The Mystery of the Mérode Mousetrap,' *Burlington Magazine* (1966), 756, CVIII, 126–30

Index

Index

Page references in bold-face numerals denote illustrations

Aberdeen University Museum, 32
Aelian, Roman author, 41, 42
Africa, 17, 19, 26, 66, 108, 115, 172, 200, 218, 227, 232, 236, 267
Age, Bronze, 30, 36, 39
  Copper, 30
  Ice, 24
  Iron, 30
  Stone, 30, 36, 108
Agelena labrynthica, 80
Agriculture, Fisheries and Food, Ministry of, 21, 68, 69, 134, 206, 209, 211, 213, 218, 250
Alaska, 25, 59, 253, 263
Allcock Mfg Co, 70, 244
American Fur Co, 191
American Humane Assoc, 205
  Soc of Mammalogists, 20
Animal Trap Co of America, 65, 69, 184
Antelope, 16, 17, 41, 164, 172, 218, 225, 227
Ant-lion, 26, 79, 87, 88
  pit, **87**
Ants, 72, 76, 88
Araneus diadematus, 80
  sexpunctatus, 81
Argiopidae, 80
Aristeas, 18
Arizona, 263
Artwork, Primitive, 27, 30, 40
Ashley, Gen William H., 58
Asia, Fur markets in, 18
Astor, John Jacob, 58, 191
Atypus affinis, 78

Auquharney, Moss of, 32, 37
Aurochs, 41
Australia, 21, 74, 154, 160, 163
Austria, 50

Badger, 165, 172, 227
Bailey, Vernon, 69, 205
Baits, 14, 16, 20, 30, 37, 46, 47, 55, 56, 57, 60, 69, 90, 100, 101, 105, 118, 119, 124, 128, 130, 131, 142, 157, 160, 161, 163, 165, 166, 175, 197, 203, 237 ff
Baltic, Eel traps in, 116
Banding (ringing), 129, 132, 144
Banding, sticky, 99
Bartram, John, 72
Bassarisk, 59
Bavaria, 70
Bear, 25, 38, 41, 42, 63, 171, 241, 263, 266
  cave, 24
  grizzly, 18, 54
  Kodiak, 253
  trapping, 58
Beaumaris, Fish trap at, 110
Beaver, 18, 55, 56, 59, 192, 213, 214, 215, 242, 263, 264, 265
  trapping, 56
Beetles, 72, 97, 100
  carrion, 100
  dung, 100
Behaviour, animal, 19
Bertin, Léon, 116
Biological Survey, US, 205
Bird Protection Orders, 20

277

Birds, 17, 18, 22, 26, 27, 30, 68, 69,
    96, 162, 239, 240, 241, 244,
    245, 260, 266
  humming, 122
  migration, 19, 20, 260
  Royal Soc for Protection of, 127
  waders, 134
Bison, 27, 41
Blackbird, 130
Blackcat, 57
Blacksmith, 12, 50, 62, 63, 191
Blake & Lamb, 194
Board, Irish Sea Fisheries, 111
Bobcat, 59, 225
Bolam, George, 127, 251
Bolas, 24
Bordigues, 116
Bretherton, R. F., 95
Bristol Channel, Fish traps in, 113
Britain, 60, 68, 109, 112, 114, 116,
    121, 122, 132, 145, 146, 147,
    148, 160, 162, 164, 172, 175,
    192, 205, 206, 224, 244, 251,
    252, 256, 259, 260, 266
British Trust for Ornithology, 20
Brown, Patrick, 77
Buffalo, 18
Bugs, 100
  water, 97
Bullfinch, 125
Burgaw savannah, 72
Bushmen, 17
Bustard, 257
Butterwort, 12, 74
Buzzard, 127

Cabot, John, 18, 60
Caddis fly, 79, 84
Caesar, 41, 42
California, 177, 263
Cameron, USA, 263
Camouflage, 13, 16, 24, 25, 168,
    180
Canada, 53, 58, 112, 244, 262, 263
Cape Fear, 72
Capjon Pressing Co, 212
Carolina, North, 72
Carson, Kit, 55

Casto, William, 69
Castor, Beaver, 56, 242
Cat, 17, 22, 238, 241
  civet, 59, 241
  sabre tooth, 25
  serval, 241
  wild, 27, 40, 225, 241, 249, 261
Caveman, 11, 13, 27
Century, eighteenth, 131, 188, 191,
    249
  fifteenth, 17, 18, 43
  nineteenth, 19, 68, 191, 249
  seventeenth, 132, 192
  thirteenth, 42
Chamberlain, de, 49
Cheetah, 40
Chellean period, 26
Chesapeake Bay, 147
Chittendon, 55
Clarke, J. G. D., 26, 27, 157
Cleitarchus, 42
Clog, 199
Clonmacnois stone, 37, **38**
Cobweb, 78, 79
Cockroaches, 100
Cocoon, 84
Cod, 115
Collection of insects, 89
Colorado, 65, 263
Colthrop (*pedica dentata*), 41
Connecticut, Fur trade of, 59
Connor, Fox B., 70
Conservation, 17, 218, 228, 255,
    257, 258, 265, 266, 267
  Directory, 266
Cornwall, I. W., 24, 26
Coyote, 59, 69, 241, 247
Coypu, 21
Crabs, 108, 109, 111, 120
Crawfish, 108, 109
Creels, 28, 108, 109
  (creeves), 109
  English East Coast, 111
  Leakey folding, **109**, 111
Cremostogaster pilosa, 76
Crickets, 100
Crow, 124, 125, 126, 127, 135 ff,
    242

Crow, carrion, 126, **136, 139, 140**
    hooded, 126
Ctenizidae, 78

Darlingtonia californica, 75
Darwin, Charles, 72, 73, 75
Davis, F. M., 110
Decoy pond, 17, 149
Decoy, wildfowl, 17, 19, 145–9, **150**
Deer, 37, 43, 63, 164, 174, 177, 178, 246, 256, 263
    Red, 38, 178
    Roe, 38
Denmark, 37, 39, 206, 224
Department of the Interior, US, 59, 62–3, 205, 252
Diable fish trap, 115
Dog, 29, 241, 242, 243
    hunting, 200
Domesday Book, 111
Donald, G. B., 123
Dove, 124, 126
Drumacaladerry, 39
Duck, 135, 145 ff, 151
Duiker, 227
Duke, Waring, Crisp & Co, 68, 225

Earwigs, 100
Ecology, 91
Edwards, V. C. Wynne-, 243
Eels, 17, 115, 118
    migration, 115
    silver, 116
Egyptians, Ancient, 40
Elephant, 22, 25, 41, 42, 66, 157, 267
Elk, 18, 28, 42
Engagées, 54
Engines, fixed, 111, 113, 114, 121
England, 109, 249, 257, 259
Ephestia elutella, 99
Ermine, 18
Eskimoes, 30, 49, 157, 162, 171
Ethiopia, 42
Europe, 18, 25, 37, 115, 126, 191, 192, 206, 252, 256, 257
Exner, 91

Fairs, fur, 18
Falconry, 126
Field Studies Council, 20
Ffennell, Denzil, 96
Filets-Dragues, 115
Fish, 17, 27, 40, 69, 107 ff, 245, 266
Fish & Game Depts, US, 20
    Colorado, 235
Fisheries, Bureau of Commercial, 110
Fleas, 20, 99
Flémalle, Master of, 46
Flies, 75, 76, 101
Florida, 76, 263
Flypaper, 99
Forestry Commission, 218
Fox, 14, 27, 57, 68, 172, 174, 194, 199, 201, 206, 218, 228, 237, 241, 242, 244, 246, 247, 250, 251, 260, 261, 263
    Arctic, 58, 60, 157, 200
    Blue, 18
    Red, 59
France, 60, 116, 184, 192, 206, 224, 257
Frankfurt-on-Oder, 45
Freemen, 54
Friedrichsbruch, 36
Fuller Industries, 212
Fur, 18
Fur-bearers, 12, 48, 57, 63, 64, 69, 229, 263, 265
Fur Company, American, 58
Fur trade, 18, 48, 49, 60, 62, 64

Gallwey, Sir Ralph Payne-, 145
Game, Big, 60
Gamekeeper, 13, 22, 68, 69, 70, 127, 165, 171, 204, 206, 209, 213, 228, 257
Germany, 42, 43, 206
Gibbs, 206
Gibson, W. Hamilton, 117, 122, 147
Gilbertson & Page Ltd, 68, 125, 126, 211
Gillespie, Patrick, 37
Giraffes, 16, 26

Glasier, Phillip, 126
Gölen, Lake, 39
Gopher, pocket, 63, 70, 213, 214, 246
Grasshoppers, 100
Greece, Ancient, 18
Greenslade, P. J. M., 100
Grouse, 27, 257

Hammers, trapping, 69
Harding, A. R., 162
Hare, 26, 161, 176, 177, 241, 246, 257, 258
  Arctic, 171
Hawkins Co, 194
Hawley & Norton, 65
Heathcock, 128
Hepburn, J. S., 76
Herubel, M., 114
Hiestand, W. A., 93
Hogarth, A. Moore, 159
Holland, 17, 206, 224
Horse, 27, 29
Horsehair, 12, 14, 15, 151, 170
Hovell, Mark, 195, 202, 203, 225, 246
Hudson Bay Co, 49, 54, 191
Hudson River, 39
Humane capture, 16, 127, 170, 205, 250, 252, 253, 266
  Traps Panel, 206, 213, 260
Hydropsyche, 84
Hunters, 13, 17, 18, 254, 255, 256, 261
Hyena, 25

Ibex, 25
India, 17, 66, 200
Indians, 12, 18, 39, 48, 49, 54, 55, 57, 64, 128
  Iroquois, 63
  Shawnee, 178
Indian Trade, US Office of, 192
Insects, 71, 75, 76, 237
Insect eye, 91
Iowa, wolves in, 261
Ireland, 36, 37, 39, 110, 111, 116, 117, 146, 195

Italy, 36, 43, 44

Jackal, 200, 241, 242, 247
Jackdaw, 135, **136, 139, 140**, 151
Jacob, John, 46
Jacobs, S. N. A., 99
Jaguar, 17, 66
Jeffreys, Richard, 22, 171
Jennison, George, 41
Johnson, 106
Jones, F. Morton, 73, 76

Kentucky State laws, 263, 264
Kestrel, 127
Kholmogory, 18

Laibach, 36, 39
Lane Ltd, Henry, 195
Lavorieri, 116
Legislation, 56, 68, 127, 172, 173, 191, 194, 196, 206, 249, 250, 251, 254 ff
Leopard, 40, 241
Library, Bodleian, 44
Lime, bird, 42, 121, 122
Linnaeus, 72
Linyphiidae, 80
Lion, 17, 40, 41, 42, 66, 241
  Cape, 267
  Mountain, 70
Lobster, 108, 109, 110, 111, 120
  Norway, 110
Longworth Scientific Co, 220
Lorenz, K., 243
Louisiana, 59, 263
Louis Missouri Fur Co, 191
Lynx, 59, 241

McDonald, W. Y., 32
Madragues, 117
Magdalenian cave dwellers, 27
Magpie, 135
Maine, State of, 172, 266
Malaise, René, 101, 102
Mammals, 69, 76, 129, 153 ff, 237, 266
Mammal Society of Brit Isles, 20
Mammoth, 24, 25, 27, 157

Man, Cro-Magnon, 26
  Heidelberg, 26
  Neanderthal, 26
Marten, pine, 57, 204, 220, 225, 247, 249
Mascall, L., 50
Massachusetts, 196, 266
Mayfly, 97
Mediterranean, 114, 116, 117
Merkle, Rupert, 70
Mérode altarpiece, 46, 166
Mesolithic period, 28
Mice, 43, 44, 46, 66, 70, 184, 187, 206, 218, 222, 245, 246, 258, 260
Michigan, 59, 262
Mink, 12, 18, 21, 57, 162, 164, 175, 179, 203, 225, 247, 263
Minnesota State laws, 262
Minnow trap, 120
Mississippi State laws, 263
Moggridge, J. T., 77
Mole, 160, 181, 182, 229, 251
  Golden, 19
Mongoose, 222, 223, 242, 243
Monkey, 17, 42, 242
Montana, 59, 263
Moorhen, 125
Mosquito, 77, 106
Moszyński, 38
Moths, 20, 75, 98
Mottram, 132
Mousterian period, 26
Munro, Robert, 37
Museet, Nordiske, 39
Museum of Aberdeen University, Anthropological, 32
Museum, British, 41
Museum of Art, Metropolitan, 46
Museum of Wales, National, 46
Museum, Salzburg Natural History, 50
Musk, 56, 197
Muskrat, 13, 56, 57, 59, 192, 193, 203, 226, 242, 244, 246, 263, 264
Mygalomorpha, 78
Myrmeleon formicarius, 87
Myxomatosis, 249

Naquane, La Grande Roche de, 30
Nationalmuseet, Copenhagen, 28
Nature Conservancy, 20
Neolithic era, 28
Nephrops norvegicus, 110
Net, dredge, 115
Nets, 28, 36, 40, 41, 107
  drift, 114
  stake, 107, 114
Netting, seine, 107
New England, 262
Newfoundland, 115
New Hampshire, 173, 266
Newhouse, Sewell, 63, 64
New Mexico, 263
New York, 49, 59, 64, 70
Nieu Amsterdam, 49
Nixon, President, 266
Noctuae, 95
Noose, 14, 17, 18, 24, 42, 161
  spring, 28, 30
North America, 18, 39, 50, 53, 58, 62, 106, 112, 115, 161, 162, 163, 164, 174, 178, 191, 192, 215, 251, 252, 260
North West Co of Canada, 191
Noyes, J. H., 64
National Research Development Corp, 212
Nutria, 59, 225, 242

Oklahoma State laws, 263
Oncorhynchus spp, 112
Oneida Community, 63, 64
Opossum, 162, 163, 174, 194, 242, 263, 265
Ostrich, 17
Otter, 37, 57, 59, 68, 260, 263, 265
Owl, 122, 240, 245
  decoy, 122
Ox, giant, 27
  wild, 29

Palaeolithic period, 15, 26, 169
Partridge, 124, 125, 129, 131, 219, 245, 257
Penn, William, 261
Pennsylvania, 261–5

Pesticides, 23
Pests, 20, 30, 89, 249, 250, 251, 256, 259, 263
Pest control, 121, 132
Pfizenmayer, E. W., 128, 175
Pheasants, 124, 127, 128, 129, 131, 171, 219, 245, 257
Philopotamus, 84
Pigeon, 124, 125, 129, 135, 136, **141**, 142, 240, 242, 245
Pike, 118, 119
Pileta, Malaga, 28
Pitcher Plant, 12, 75, 76
Plants, insectivorous, 12
Plaquemines, 263
Plectronemia, 84
Pliny, 41
Poachers, 22, 43, 127, 131, 161, 170, 178, 188, 256, 257
Poland, 38, 39
Polecat, 204, 220, 247, 249
Pollen analysis, 39
Poona, 48
Pots, **109**
    American lobster, 110
    crab, 109, 110, 111
    French, 110
    inkwell, 109
    lobster, 111
    osier, 110
    steel lobster, 110
Prawns, 108
Predator, 20
    control, 22
Presnell, Clifford C., 69
Pullinger, Colin, 66
Putchers, **34**, 108, 113 ff, 119, 120
Putts, **34**, 113 ff, 119, 120

Rabbit, 15, 18, 21, 69, 160, 171, 172, 179, 206, 237, 241, 244, 246, 249, 250, 257, 258, 259
Raccoon, 57, 59, 174, 225, 263, 265
Rasmussen, H., 37
Rats, 43, 66, 69, 129, 159, 160, 179, 187, 203, 206, 216, 239, 246, 258, 260

Ray, John, 122
Reid, G. O. S., 120
Reid, R. W., 32, 35, 37
Reindeer, 27
Research, scientific, 19, 20, 132, 222, 248, 252, 253
Revillon Frères, 54
Rhinoceros, 24, 25
Ringing (banding), 129, 132, 143, 144
Ritchie, J., 249
River Authority, Severn, 114
    Usk, 114
Robidoux, Antoine, 55
Robinson, H. S. & P. J. M., 90, 91, 94, 95
Rocky Mountains, 53, 54, 55, 58, 178
Rogers, 55
Romans, 40, 42, 121, 255, 256
Rook, 135, **136**, **139**, **140**, 151
Roth, C., 43, 46, 166, 216
Royal Society for Protection of Birds, 251
    Prevention of Cruelty to Animals, 251
Russell, Carl P., 50, 191
Russia, 18, 60, 192

Sable, 18, 57
Sage, Rufus, 53
Sahula, Isaac ibn, 43
Salmon, 11, 63, 111, 112, 113, 114, 115, 117, 124, 164
Salmo salar, 112
Sarcophaga sarracenia, 76
Sargasso Sea, 115
Sarracenia minor, 75
    pupurea, 76
Savory, Theodore H., 81
Schenkel, R., 243
Scotland, 109, 146, 194, 195, 249, 259, 260
Scott, Peter, 132
Sedges, 84
Set, bait, 200
    box, 202
    cubby (coop), 202

Set—*continued*
  dirt hole, 201
  trail, 199
Severn, River, 108, 113, 115, 146, 147
Sheep, 29, 263
Sheeting, 92
Shellfish, 108
Shrew, 16, 222, 224
Shrimps, 108, 111, 113, 114, 115
Siberia, 25, 30, 60, 128, 151, 176, 200, 233
Sidebotham, W. & G., 68, 196
Sieves, 69
Silverhorns, 84
Simmonds, P. C., 109
Skins, 18
Skunk, 57, 162, 164, 244, 247, 263, 265
Slagysters, 188
Slugs, 71
Snakes, 245
Snares, 12, 15, 30, 40, 43, 44, 60, 70, 127, 128, 154, 169 ff
  Aldrich, 171, 172, **174**
  Burmese, **86**
  cluster, **117**
  double box, 117, 179, **180**
  hanging, 28
  North Carolina, 174, **175**
  pole, **176**
  portable, 178, **179**
  squirrel, **86**, 171
Sotheby's, auctioneers, 61
South America, 17, 66, 152
South Dakota State laws, 262
Spade (trowel), 196
Sparrow, 135, 151, 245
Sparrowhawk, 127
Spider, 11, 71, 76, 77 ff
  garden, 80
  money, 80
  trap-door, 11, 77, 78
Sprats, 115
Spring, 14, 15, 26, 35, 44, 50, 63
  coil, 14
  flat, 14
  helical, 14

Squirrel, 15, 21, 68, 69, 194, 217, 218, 219, 241, 244
  flying, 242
  grey, 179, 206, 218, 219, 241, 259
  red, 218, 219
Stag, 27
Starling, 130, 151, 242, 245
Steinbok, 227
Stoat, 15, 22, 69, 162, 164, 165, 172, 179, 194, 200, 204, 206, 217, 225, 247
Sugaring, 98
Sundew, 74

Tarantula, 78
Taylor, 106
Taylor, Capt Daniel, 191
Taylor, Garth, 30
Teale, Edwin Way, 77
Tegenaria domestica, 80
Teltow, 39
Tetra Engineering Co, 209
Tetragnathidae, 80
Thomand weir, 117
Thompson, Ernest E., 65
Thrush, 127, 130
Tiger, 17, 66, 241
Training, survival, 12
Traps
  American parlour, 111
  antelope, **173**, 232, **235**, 236
  approval order, 206, 209
  aviary-type, 135 ff
    collecting box for, **142**
  badger, **208**, 227, 228
  balance, 67
  bamboo, 222, **223**
  barrel, **103**, 109, 111, 158, 160, 182
  basket, 111
  bear, 64, 65, **138**, **174**, 195, 196, 253
  beaver, **193**, 213, **215**
  bird, 12
  board flap, 168, **169**
  box, 14, 16, 58, **85**, 92, 93, 97, 118, **119**, 129, **131**, 154, 212, 216–31, 252

Traps—*continued*
  box, insect, **92**
  breakback, 15, 60, 70, 180, 185, **186**, 206, 244, 260
  bug, **33**, 47, 99
  cage, 11, 16, 17, 28, 44, **45**, 47, **51**, 68, 69, 101, 124, 154, 164, 205, 216, 231, 243, 252
Chardonneret, **130**
  circuit, 55
  clap-net, 132, **133**
  Clausius tunnel, **207**, 224
  cleaning, 187, 197, 198, 213
  Conibear, **215**
  construction, 12
  crab, Star, 120
  crow, 125
    carrion, **136**, **139**, 140
    'hoodie', 125
  deadfall, 13, 28, 43, 45, **46**, 49, 60, 122, 123, **124**, 154, 161 ff, 243, 264
    box, **168**
    English brick, 122, **123**
    log, 123
    pole, **163**
    trail-set, **165**
  deer, 37
  Dorset, 195
  Dunlin, **144**
  eel, 115, **116**
    Suffolk, **34**, 119
  elaborate, 16
  Fenn, 69, **155**, 206, 209, 213
  figure-4, 65, 161, **162**
  fish, 12, 36, 40, 107 ff, 126
    boom, 16
    portable, 119
  floodlit, 150
  foot, 15, 17
  formalin fly, **105**
  fox, **138**, 213, 226
    Arctic, 157, **158**
  Fuller, **189**, 206, 212, 213
  Gin, 14, 15, 16, 22, 36, 44, 50, 53, 68, 127, 131, **138**, 180, 188 ff, 212, 213, 216, 249, 252, 259, 260

giraffe, **208**, 232
gopher, 15, 213, **214**
goshawk, **52**, 126
guillotine, mole, **86**, 184
  mouse, **104**, 184–5
hangman's, 127
Havahart, 70, **85**, 120, 217, 225–7
  'Ketch-All', 230, **231**
Heligoland, **143**
home-made, 12, 222
Hungerford, **97**
Idstone, 200, **201**
Imbra, 68, **156**, 206, 209, **210**, 211
Insect, 17, 89 ff, **92**, **93**, **94**, **96**, **97**, **100**, **101**, **105**
iron, 49, 50
Juby, 68, **156**, 206, 211
jump, 50, **53**, **193**, 194
light, **92**, **93**, **94**, **96**, **97**
live, 60, 63, 70, 107, **190**, 228, 264, 266
lizard, 231, **233**
Lloyd, **189**, 206, 211, 212, 213
Longworth, 20, 220, **221**, 222, 226
Malaise, **101**
mammal, 121
man, 22, **137**, 181, 191, 256–7
marten, 220
Mascall, **50**, 192
mink, 226
minnow, Gee's improved, 120
mirror, 42
mole, **frontis**, 15, 42, 63, 67, 68, 70, **86**, **103**, 118, 181, 182, 184, 229
  Arouze, **183**
  Monmouthshire, **85**, 160
  tongs-type, **183**
'Mortis', 166, **167**
moth, 93
mouse, 15, 21, 30, 43, 44, **45**, **46**, **47**, 48, 63, 66, 67, 70, **104**, 166, 184–7, **186**, 190, **208**, 230, 231
  pottery, **190**, 218